John Reeves

**A History of the Law of Shipping and Navigation**

John Reeves

**A History of the Law of Shipping and Navigation**

ISBN/EAN: 9783742819475

Manufactured in Europe, USA, Canada, Australia, Japa

Cover: Foto ©ninafisch / pixelio.de

Manufactured and distributed by brebook publishing software (www.brebook.com)

John Reeves

**A History of the Law of Shipping and Navigation**

# A HISTORY

### OF THE

# LAW

### OF

## Shipping and Navigation.

By JOHN REEVES, Esq.

AUTHOR OF

" THE HISTORY OF THE ENGLISH LAW."

LONDON:
PRINTED FOR C. AND R. BROOKE, BELL-YARD,
TEMPLE-BAR; AND J. SEWELL, CORNHILL.

M,DCC,XCII.

TO THE RIGHT HONOURABLE

# LORD HAWKESBURY,

PRESIDENT

OF THE

## COMMITTEE OF PRIVY COUNCIL

APPOINTED FOR THE

CONSIDERATION OF ALL MATTERS

RELATING TO

TRADE AND FOREIGN PLANTATIONS;

THIS BOOK,

COMPOSED FOR THE USE OF THE COMMITTEE,

IS RESPECTFULLY INSCRIBED

BY HIS LORDSHIP'S MOST OBEDIENT

AND FAITHFUL SERVANT,

*June* 1792.   JOHN REEVES.

## CONTENTS.

tions—Plantation Bonds—Acts of Navigation enforced—Relaxed and difpenfed with—Stat. 7. & 8. Will. 3.—Navigation Act relaxed—Irifh Linens—Rice—Sugar—American Acts Stat. 4. Geo. 3. Stat. 5. Geo. 3. and Stat. 6. Geo. 3.—Free Ports eftablifhed—The Export Trade from Ireland—Import and Export Trade granted more fully—The Reftraining and Prohibitory Acts—Newfoundland.—Honduras—Surat,     —     —     —     58

### CHAPTER II.

#### THE TRADE WITH ASIA, AFRICA, AND AMERICA.

To be carried on in Englifh Shipping—and directly with thofe Countries—Exceptions thereto—Perfian Goods through Ruffia—Coarfe Calicoes—The Eaft India Company—South Sea Company—Hudfon's Bay Company—African Company—Fourth Section of the Navigation Act—What is a Manufacturing—Of direct Importation—Of the ufual Ports for firft Shipping—Of returned Goods,     —     139

### CHAPTER III.

#### THE EUROPEAN TRADE.

The Eighth Section—Complaints againft the Act—Prohibition of Goods from the Netherlands and Germany—Provifion in the Treaty of Breda

## CONTENTS.

Breda—The Prohibition relaxed—The Eastland Company—The Russia Company—The Turkey Company—Usages contrary to the Prohibition—Of Shipping in the European Trade—Foreign Prize Ships—Of English Ships sold to Foreigners—Of the Country where foreign Ships built—Stat. 22. Geo. 3. c. 78.—Of the Country of the Master and Mariners—Of Prize Goods—What is an Importation—Act of Navigation dispensed with in War-Time, 196

### CHAPTER IV.

THE COASTING TRADE, 278

### CHAPTER V.

THE FISHERIES.

Certain Sorts of Fish foreign-caught to pay double Aliens' Duty—The Herring, North-Sea, and Westmony Fisheries encouraged—The Greenland and Newfoundland Fisheries free of Duty—Importation of Fish foreign-caught in foreign Ships prohibited—The Newfoundland Fishery—All Fish bought of Foreigners prohibited—Allowances on salted Fish British-caught and cured—Bounties in the Greenland Fishery—Bounties in the Newfoundland Fishery—and in that of the Gulf of St. Laurence and Labrador—Bounties in the Southern Whale Fishery—The Society of the Free British Fishery instituted, — — — 280

# CONTENTS

## CHAPTER VI.

### OF BRITISH SHIPS.

How English-built Shipping to be understood—Foreign Ships, English-owned, to be registered—English Ships to be English-built—The Plantation Register Act, Stat. 7. & 8. Will. 3. c. 22.—Of Registers lost or mislaid—When foreign Seamen employed—Ships made free by Letters Patent—By Private Acts—By the Commissioners of the Customs—Of Prize Ships—Of Master and Mariners naturalized,  302

# PART III.

INTRODUCTION,  341

## CHAPTER I.

### THE PLANTATION TRADE.

The American Intercourse Bill, Stat. 23. Geo. 3. c. 39.—The Newfoundland Supply Bill—Stat. 28. Geo. 3. c. 6.—Intercourse with the West-Indies—With the American Colonies—The American Orders in Council—Doubt thereupon removed by an Explanatory Order—Free Port Act.  —  —  344

# CONTENTS.

## CHAPTER II.

TRADE WITH ASIA, AFRICA, AND AMERICA, 378

## CHAPTER III.

THE EUROPEAN TRADE, 380

## CHAPTER IV.

THE COASTING TRADE, 385

## CHAPTER V.

### THE FISHERIES.

The Newfoundland Fishery—The Greenland Fishery—The Southern Whale Fishery—The British Fisheries—The Herring Fishery—The Deep-Sea Fishery, — 386

## CHAPTER VI.

### OF BRITISH SHIPS.

Frauds in Regiſtering—Smuggling—Defects in the Regiſtering Laws—Intended Amendments therein—Points ſubmitted to the Commiſſioners of the Cuſtoms—Their Report thereupon—Propoſals

## CONTENTS.

Proposals for amending the Laws—The Opinion of the Committee of Trade thereupon—Stat. 26. Geo. 3. c. 60.—Of British-built Ships—Of Registering—The Bond—Indorsement on the Certificate—Bill of Sale—Change of Name—Certificate lost or mislaid—Prize Ships—Amendments made in Stat. 26. Geo. 3. c. 60.—Of Shipping in the Eastland Trade—Remedies proposed in Aid of British Shipping—Easement in Duties for British Ships—The Case of a Bill of Sale—Macneal's Case, — 410

CONCLUSION, 515

APPENDIX, 549

# A HISTORY

### OF THE

# L A W

### OF

# Shipping and Navigation.

## INTRODUCTION.

IT is propofed to take an hiftorical view of the law of England with regard to Shipping and Navigation. The increafe of fhipping, and the improvement of navigation, are objects that have frequently engaged the attention of the Legiflature; and various provifions have been made from time to time, by which it was endeavoured to confine, as much as poffible, the trade to and from this country, the employment of the fifheries, and the conveyance coaftwife, to the fhipping and mariners of this country

country alone. The History, therefore, of Shipping and Navigation includes in it the history of the different branches of foreign and domestic trade, and of the fisheries carried on either upon our coasts or abroad; and we shall accordingly, in pursuing this enquiry, be led to consider the laws that have been made for better regulating those various objects of commercial policy.

BUT this, understood in its largest extent, opens to us a field of more space and greater variety than is necessary for our present purpose; some limit must therefore be set to our research: in so doing it is meant to confine ourselves merely to such matters as belong to *shipping* and *navigation* in the stricter sense of those words, or at least in the parliamentary sense which they have acquired from the use and application of them in different acts of parliament. Thus, whatever relates to a *ship*, and its qualifications of *ownership*, or *built*, the master who commands, and the seamen who *navigate* it, the *goods* and *commodities*, and the *places* from which it may import by virtue of such qualifications; all these are peculiarly subjects of the present History, and will of themselves bring before us the trade and commerce of the whole

INTRODUCTION.

whole world. But any incidents and circumstances relating to that trade and commerce, and not originating from, or belonging to, the precise nature of such qualifications of the *ship* and its *navigation*, are extraneous and foreign. Thus the whole concern of customs and duties being merely regulations of revenue; the detail for collecting and securing such revenue, including the numerous provisions about smuggling; with an infinitude of other matters lying within the department of the customhouse, are all excluded, as no part of this work. In short, it is intended to touch upon those topics, and those only, which compose the famous *Act of Navigation* made in the 12th year of king Charles the Second, and which has in its title the same words in the same sense in which they are here to be understood : *An Act for the Encouraging and Increasing of* SHIPPING *and* NAVIGATION.

Such is the nature and extent of the proposed design; which will comprize a history of what are usually termed *The Acts of Navigation*. This history may properly be divided into Three Periods: the First containing the laws made from the earliest appearance of any such, down to and including

INTRODUCTION.

the Act of Navigation made in 1651, during the time of the Commonwealth. The Second will commence with the famous Act of Navigation paſſed in the 12th year of Charles II. and will contain all the laws paſſed down to the time of making the peace in 1783. The Third will commence after the peace, and contain all the laws which have been made down to the preſent year 1792.

AFTER we poſſeſs the text of the law, we become curious to learn what conſtruction it has received, and what practice has been founded upon it. It is intended, therefore, to interſperſe ſuch information relative to the conſtruction and uſage, that has obtained in conſequence of the paſſing of the different Acts of Navigation, as the beſt ſearch has been able to diſcover. The place where a lawyer would naturally look for materials of this ſort, is the books of reports, containing deciſions and opinions of the courts. This ſearch has been made, but it has not anſwered the expectations that might be entertained either from the importance of the ſubject or the lapſe of time, which promiſed many occaſions for judicial diſcuſſion on theſe laws. All the caſes to be

INTRODUCTION.

be found in the printed books, from the time of passing the Act of Navigation to the present moment, do not exceed ten; nor has repeated inquiry been able to draw forth any information of this kind from manuscripts. One great source therefore of illustration, and that which principally commands the attention of the professors of the law, is extremely deficient in this branch of jurisprudence.

THIS dearth of recorded judgments must surely be ascribed to no other cause than that there were very few worth recording: for it is not to be believed that, among the variety of matter collected from term to term in Westminster-hall, *that* furnished by the laws of navigation should have escaped without receiving its due portion of attention: and this appears the less likely, when it is considered that such causes belong to the jurisdiction of a particular court, that they are instituted by a board of revenue, and are advised and conducted by the law-officers of the crown. The circumstances attending these suits give them a very special appearance. There are officers of an established board, promoting and watching the progress of them in every stage,

INTRODUCTION.

stage, whose situation makes it their interest to pick up every suggestion that can be added to the stock of official information; and it is not very likely, that any decision worth remembering should have escaped both the general reporters and those who collect for the use of the custom-house: if the latter will not supply the deficiency of the former, we may rest satisfied that it can be supplied from no other source.

It is in the memory of many persons, who are officially bound to know it, that for twenty or thirty years back, very few points of law have been argued in the court of exchequer upon any of the Acts of Navigation. From the experience of this period we are enabled to form some judgment of the preceding; and we may readily believe, that in former times, as we know it is in our own, the generality of suits grounded upon these statutes, turned upon some point of fact, without any dispute about the meaning of the law; and from such suits no legal materials were to be derived for the information of posterity.

It might be inferred from this, that the laws of navigation are penned with great clearness,

### INTRODUCTION.

clearness, and are happily exempt from those ambiguities, which have been seen to cloud the construction of other laws, framed by persons of the best learning and experience. But in truth a want of clearness is not the only nor the most common cause of doubt and difficulty in the interpretation of laws: they originate from other defects than those in the laws themselves; from the conceit of the parties interested, and the weak judgments of their first advisers. Such dispositions and such intellects will easily persuade themselves, that the law speaks the language they wish it should speak; and at any rate they will think it worth trying, whether they cannot prevail with a court to confirm their opinion. These considerations have generally had their full effect to plunge the parties into a suit, before the matter comes into the hands of those, who are best able to distinguish, but who are then obliged to exercise their ingenuity instead of their judgement, and to torture and confound every thing, in order to support what in their closets they would pronounce untenable. Yet it is to such occasions as this, that we are indebted for two-thirds of the legal argument to be found in the Report-books; and out of such attempts to
mis-

INTRODUCTION.

mislead and misrepresent, grow the true exposition and the real learning of the law.

BUT the king's suits are brought into court in a different manner: they are, in the first instance, well considered by the solicitor of the board of customs, who is qualified by his daily practice to form a sufficient opinion upon the point of law; they are usually submitted to the opinion of the attorney and solicitor general, whose judgement and discretion are looked to for advice and direction. These officers feel themselves responsible in their professional character for that which they advise and promote; and they will always have in view, that the opinion given in their chambers is such as they need not scruple to support in public argument. In addition to their own reputation, they consult likewise the honour of the crown, whose rights should never be brought judicially in question without a reasonable confidence of success. While such considerations have their influence, no points of law will be hazarded, that do not appear really and substantially to contain doubt and difficulty.

### INTRODUCTION.

IF few determinations of courts are to be found on this subject of Shipping and Navigation, there is not wanting information of another kind. This is from the opinions of law-officers, which have been taken from time to time ever since the reign of Charles the Second, by the board of customs, for the direction of themselves and their officers in points of practice as they arose. Wherever this can be obtained, I shall endeavour to make it supply the deficiency of judicial matter, in expounding and illustrating the laws made by the Legislature.

I AM aware that the scrupulous dignity of the law of England has not been accustomed to receive, as authorities, any thing less than the opinions delivered by judges upon the bench; the arguments of counsel in court, and their opinions at chambers, are placed among those extrajudicial and private matters that are wanting in the essential quality which should constitute a juridical authority. But it may be said, with due deference to the oracles which speak in our courts, that the opinions of lawyers have an advantage which *those* have not; they come down to us in the writing of the author,

author—his own meaning conveyed in his own words; the opinions of courts, on the other hand, are usually conveyed by standers-by; and the clearest judgement may, in after-time, be brought in question from the inaccuracy of contradictory reports. Indeed I can entertain no doubt but an opinion ascertained to be really given by a person filling the office of king's attorney or solicitor upon points of revenue and rights of the crown, will be received by lawyers as a very high authority; and I shall think myself very fortunate in having had an opportunity to bring together a considerable degree of information from materials of that sort.

With these helps from the decisions of courts, and the opinions of law-officers of the crown, it is hoped some light may be thrown on the acts of parliament, which are the object of this History.

# PART I.

*First Act of Navigation—Petition of the Commons on the Carrying Trade—An Easement in Duty for English Ships—Stat. 5. Eliz.—The Fisheries encouraged—The Coasting Trade—The Plantation Trade—Act of Navigation 1651.*

THE first provision made by parliament that can be classed under the denomination of a *Navigation-Act*, is stat. 42. Ed. 3. c. 8. which enacted, that all ships of England and Gascoigne which came into Gascoigne, should be first freighted to bring wines into England before all other. But this preference (such as it is) being enjoyed in common with the people of Gascony, who were then the king's subjects equally with the English; and the English being actually restrained by another part of the act from going to Gascony to buy wines, which were to be brought only by the Gascons and

other

PART I.
41 ED. III. TO
A. D. 1651.

other Aliens, this has not been considered sufficiently favourable to English shipping to be ranked among the Acts of Navigation.

First Act of Navigation.

THAT which has usually been deemed the first Act of Navigation, is stat. 5. *Rich.* 2. st. 1. c. 3. which is expressed in the beginning of it to be made *for the increase of the navy of England, which was then greatly diminished.*

IT was thereby ordained, that none of the king's liege people should from thenceforth ship any merchandize in going out, or coming within the realm of England in any port, but only in ships of the king's liegeance, under the penalty of forfeiting all the merchandize shipped in other vessels, or the value thereof; a third part to go to the informer, or, as it is expressed, " the " person who *duly espieth and duly proveth* " any offence against that statute."

BUT this attempt to encourage English shipping seems to have been made before the actual state of our navigation would quite warrant it; for in the very next session of parliament it was enacted, by stat. 6. *Rich.*

6. *Rich.* 2. c. 8. that the said law should only take place "as long as ships of the said "liegeance were to be found *able and suf-* "*ficient* in the parts where the merchants "happened to dwell." Again, in the 14th year of that king, the same regulation was repeated by parliament; but it was on that occasion accompanied with a qualification which suggests an important observation upon these laws of navigation; for when it was enacted by stat. 14. *Rich.* 2. c. 6. "that "merchants of the realm of England should "freight in the said realm the ships of the "said realm, and not strange ships," this proviso was added, *so that the owners of the said ships take reasonable gains for the freight of the same.* If, therefore, English ships could not be got, or if the owners demanded an unreasonable freight, foreign ships might still by law be employed.

From these concessions and qualifications it is seen how early our ancestors felt, that these beneficial regulations, with all their advantages, contained in them the inconveniences and mischiefs of a monopoly; and that the navigation and shipping of the country could not be favoured without exposing its trade to some degree of burden and

PART 1.  and reftraint. Indeed it will be found,
42. ED. III. TO  from the wording and tenor of various fta-
A. D. 1651.  tutes made on this fubject, that the Acts of
Navigation were regulations more of a political than commercial nature; and that the
whole advantage to be derived therefrom
was intended to center in the navy of England. We fhall find, in all fubfequent regulations, that the object in view is the increafe of fhips and not of commerce, and that
the intereft of the latter is made frequently
to give way to that of the former.

THERE appears to have been no ftatute on
this fubject from the reign of Richard II. till
the reign of Edward IV. when it was enacted
by ftat. 3. *Edw.* 4. c. 1. among other regulations refpecting the trade of wool, that
no perfon inhabiting within the realm of
England, other than merchant ftrangers,
fhould freight nor charge within the realm
any fhip or other veffel of any alien or
ftranger with merchandize to be carried
out of the realm, nor fhould bring any
into it, if he could have fufficient freight
in the fhips or veffels of denizens, on pain
of forfeiting the merchandize, half to the
king and half to the perfon feizing. But
this provifion in favour of Englifh fhipping

was

was to laſt no more than three years; and we find no other ſtatute on this ſubject till the reign of Henry VII.

BUT in the mean time a petition made by the commons in parliament in the 18th year of *Henry* 6. is well worthy of notice. It was there prayed, that thenceforward no Italian, or other merchant of the countries beyond the Straits of Morocco, ſhould ſell in this realm any other merchandize than that of the countries beyond the Straits, on pain of forfeiture thereof. And the reaſon there alledged for ſuch a regulation is, that ſince the Italian merchants had become carriers of the commodities of Spain, Portugal, and other countries without the Straits, in addition to the productions of the countries within the Straits, thoſe articles were not brought in ſuch abundance, nor were they ſold ſo cheap as when they were brought by the merchants of thoſe countries reſpectively, or were fetched by the merchants of this country in their own ſhips; the conſequence of which was, not only the decreaſe of the king's cuſtoms, and the depreciation of the merchandize of this realm, but alſo a great hurt to all the navy of the realm.

SUCH

*Petition of the Commons on the Carrying Trade.*

PART I.
48. ED. III. TO
A. D. 1651.

Such are the mischiefs which were meant to be remedied; and the benefits the commons proposed by the regulation thus prayed were stated to be, that the countries without the Straits would be more desirous of peace and friendship with England, in order that their merchants might have safe-conduct to bring their goods hither; and that our merchants carrying the goods of this country themselves might sell them at the first hand, and so make greater profits. They prayed this might pass into a law for ten years; but the king did not assent to it *(a)*. In this parliamentary document we discover a branch of the navigation-system begin to disclose itself; namely, the confining of foreign ships to carrying the productions of the country to which they belong.

It is another branch of the navigation-system to give some favour or preference to articles of merchandize, if imported in ships of this kingdom. An experiment of this sort likewise made its appearance in the be-

*(a)* Rolls Parl. 18. *Hen.* 6. 59. The great increase of Italian merchants at this time led to stat. 1. *Rich.* 3. c. 9. for restraining them and their trade.

ginning

ginning of the reign of Henry VII.; and the
liament, in adopting this principle, carried
it at once to the extremeſt length by prohibiting all commodities of a certain deſcription, that were not ſo imported; for it was
enacted by ſtat. 1. *Hen.* 7. c. 9. that no one
ſhould buy or ſell within this realm, Ireland,
Wales, Calais, or the Marches thereof, or
Berwick, any manner of wine of the growth
of the Duchy of Guienne or Gaſcony, but
ſuch as ſhould be adventured and brought
in an Engliſh, Iriſh, or Welſhman's ſhip,
the mariners of which were Engliſh, Iriſh,
or Welſhmen, for the moſt part, or men
of Calais, or of the Marches of the ſame,
on forfeiture of ſuch wine; half to the
finder of the forfeiture, the other half to
the king.

THIS ſtatute is introduced by a preamble
expreſſing the decay of the navy and *the
idleneſs of the mariners*, and that if the ſame
were not reformed, the realm would not be
of ability and power to defend itſelf. Conformably with the ſolicitude there expreſſed
concerning the employment of mariners,
this act required, for the firſt time, that *the
mariners*, as well as the ſhip, *ſhould be of this
country*.

This statute, which deserves remembrance for having brought forward two principles of our navigation-system that have been applied, with some variation, on numberless occasions in later times, was an experimental regulation, and to endure only to the next parliament. In the next parliament it was revived by stat. 4. *Hen.* 7. c. 10. with some alterations; namely, it was extended to the article of *woad* called *Thoulouse woad*. The forfeiture was laid not only on the article when bought and sold, but when conveyed or brought in. The ship was to belong to the king, or some of his subjects of England, Ireland, Wales, *Calais*, or Berwick, as owners, possessors, or proprietaries; and instead of requiring the *mariners* for the most part, it requires the *master (a)* and mariners, for the most part, to be men of those places.

This statute contains a provision of the same nature with the statutes of Richard II. and the temporary act stat. 3. *Edw.* 4. c. 1. " No person inhabiting within this realm,

* (a) The expression in the statute is, " The master " *under God*, and the mariners," &c. Bills of lading usually begin, " *Shipped by the grace of God.*"

" other

"other than merchant strangers, shall
"freight or charge within this realm, or
"Wales, any ship or other vessel of any
"alien or stranger with merchandize, to
"be carried out of, or brought into, this
"realm or Wales, if he may have sufficient
"freight in ships of denizens at the port
"where he makes his freight, on forfeiture
"of the merchandize, half to the king,
"and half to the person seizing the same."
There was a *proviso* that merchandize
brought in contrary to this act, in cases of
stress of weather, or enemies, should not
be liable to forfeiture, so as the owners
made no sale thereof, otherwise than
for victuals and necessary repairs of the
ship.

THE stat. 1. *Hen.* 7. had, at the close of
it, a saving of the king's prerogative. No
such reservation was made in stat. 4. *Hen.* 7.
But, notwithstanding, we find that many
licences were obtained, both by aliens and
denizens, in the reign of Henry VIII. for
bringing in wine of Gascony and Guienne,
and Thouloufe woad, contrary to statute;
and these licences were expressly declared
void by stat. 7. *Hen.* 8. c. 2.; with a saving,
however, in favour of such as should be

executed

PART I.
45. ED. III. TO
A. D. 1651.

executed before a certain short day then to come.

THE decrease of shipping and mariners was again made a subject of complaint by parliament in stat. 23. *Hen*. 8. c. 7.; by which statute the parliament made no new regulation, but contented themselves with reciting stat. 5. *Rich*. 2. stat 6. *Rich*. 2. and stat. 4. *Hen*. 7. which they declared should stand in full force and effect. This act being made to continue only to the last day of the next parliament, it was thought proper by stat. 32. *Hen*. 8. c. 14. intituled, *An Act for the Maintenance of the Navy of England, and for certain Rates of Freight*," again to confirm the said statutes, in the same manner as had been done by stat. 23. *Hen*. 8. c. 7. In order better to insure the employment of English shipping, this act further ordains a certain price of freight between London and the principal trading towns of Europe; which price was not to be exceeded, except in times of war.

An easement in duty for English ships.

IT seems, a proclamation had been obtained from the Crown, granting to merchant strangers, for a certain time, the privilege of importing

porting and exporting merchandize, on paying the same custom and subsidy as natural-born subjects. This liberality of the Crown was qualified by the present statute, which confined it to such articles as were imported or exported in any *ship, bottom, or vessel of this realm of England, commonly called an English ship, bottom, or vessel;* which is the first instance of an easement in duty made in favour of English ships. But to this was subjoined a proviso, That should no such English ship be at the port, and the merchant gave notice thereof to the Lord Admiral, or his deputy, or if none such were resident at the port, then to the customer or comptroller, and obtained from him a certificate, under his seal, of such lack of English ships, he might then freight any foreign ship in the port, and have the benefit of the proclamation.

To facilitate the execution of this act, owners of English ships were directed to affix a notice in some public place in Lombard-street, for the space of seven days, of their intention to sail, and the voyage they meant to make. Provisions were made for the speedy departure of ships, safe custody of goods committed to their care, and the due performance of their engagement, by a complaint and hearing, in a summary way, before the admiral, his lieutenant, or deputy.

Such were the endeavours used by this parliament to recommend, and gain a preference for English shipping. But the competition between commerce and navigation had various success; and we shall see in the next reign that a turn was given to the former in prejudice of the latter. In stat. 5. & 6. *Edw.* 6. c. 18. we are told, that stat. 4. *Hen.* 7. was supposed to be made for the maintenance of the navy, and in good hope that the articles there mentioned would be obtained cheaper; but, on the contrary, those articles daily sold dearer, " and the " navy was thereby never the better main- " tained." The present statute accordingly provides, that in future, between the first day of *February* and the first day of *October*, any person, being of the parts or countries in amity with our sovereign, might bring in those wines, or *wines of any other parts of France*, or *Thoulouse woad*, in whatsoever ships, crayers, or boats, whoever might be owner (being of parts in amity with our
sove-

SHIPPING AND NAVIGATION.

(fovereign), and whoever might be the master or mariners *(a)*.

PART I.
42. ED. III. TO
A. D. 1651.

THE expectation expreffed in this ftatute to obtain foreign goods cheaper when the carrying of them was granted as a monopoly in favour of Englifh fhipping, was rather fuch as would be held out by interefted perfons who feek a privilege, than entertained by wife men who look on, unlefs in times when the nature of commerce is very little underftood.

THE caufe of commerce was backed by the jealoufy of foreign ftates, who retaliated our prohibitions to freight foreign fhips, by making penal laws againft fuch as fhould fhip goods out of their countries in any other than the veffels of the country. This point was taken into confideration by the parliament at the beginning of the reign of

---

*(a)* By ftat. 23. *Hen.* 8. c. 7. fect. 2: no wines of *Gafcony* or *Guienne*, or any manner of *French* wines, were to be landed between the Feaft of St. *Michael* the Archangel and the Purification of Our Lady. This act was expired when the ftat. 5. & 6. *Edw.* 6. was paffed, otherwife the time here limited for importing would in effect have been no limitation at all, but an entire permiffion. *Quære*, If that prohibition of ftat. 23. *Hen.* 8. was continued by any other ftatute?

C 4                                     queen

queen Elizabeth, and by ſtat. 1. *Eliz.* c. 13.
a formal repeal was made of ſtat. 5. *Rich.* 2.
and ſtat. 4. *Hen.* 7.; and thereby it was
hoped to conciliate the friendſhip of our
neighbours, who were running the ſame
race with us in navigation and commerce.
But that the intereſt of navigation might
not be wholly abandoned, another mode
was attempted, by which it was intended,
with leſs envy and more appearance of
equity, to accompliſh a like end. To prevent a fraudulent practice, which then had
obtained, of ſubjects entering the goods of
ſtrangers in their own names, and ſo de-
frauding the Crown of the aliens' duties,
the following regulation was made; which,
under the maſk of revenue, ſeems to have
nothing in view but re-eſtabliſhing the
ſpirit of the Navigation-Acts repealed in
the foregoing clauſe. It was enacted, that
all owners of merchandize, who in time of
peace, and when there was no reſtraint
made of Engliſh ſhips, ſhould embark, ſhip,
lade, or diſcharge, by way of merchandize,
any wares or merchandize (maſt, raffe,
pitch, tar, and corn only excepted) out of,
or into any ſhip, bark, hoy, veſſel, or bottom, whereof the queen, or ſome of her
ſubjects of this realm, were not poſſeſſors and
pro-

proprietors, and the masters and the mariners for the most part subjects of the queen, should pay the subsidy and custom for the same, as strangers and aliens born.

Thus, by the laws repealed, all subjects were required to import and export in English ships; by the present law, all subjects, who imported or exported in foreign ships, were liable to pay the aliens' duties. It is true, the former acts were enforced by forfeiture; but the aliens' duties, though a less sanction, were motives sufficient with men, whose occupation in commerce habituated them to the comparison of every rise or fall in their profits. The design and expectation of the parliament was fairly discovered in the title they gave to this act, *An Act for the Shipping in English Bottoms.*

The act goes on to ordain, that no hoy or plate owned by an English subject should carry merchandize from this kingdom to parts beyond the seas, on pain of forfeiting such hoy or plate, with all the munition, tackling, and other necessaries pertaining thereto; a provision, that probably was designed to promote the building of larger ships.

An

AN exception, similar to what we have before seen, was made to the regulation in favour of English ships; namely, that the merchants adventurers, and merchants of the staple, might, at the time of their shipping cloth and wool, twice in one year at the most, from and out of the river Thames, ship merchandize in a ship belonging to a stranger, or alien, at such times as ships belonging to subjects were not to be had, sufficient in number and goodness for the safe conveyance of goods to Flanders, Holland, Zealand, or Brabant. The merchants of Bristol also, who had suffered greatly in their shipping by enemies at sea, were allowed to ship, within forty miles of their city, merchandize on board strangers' bottoms, without paying other customs than for merchandize in English bottoms.

THE whole of this act was only of temporary duration, namely, for five years; and so to the end of the parliament next following. But, before it expired, the regulation about hoys was repealed by the Navigation-Act passed in 5. *Eliz.* which ordained, that English hoys and plates might cross the seas as far as Caen in Normandy, and eastward as far as Norway. This partial

tial indulgence was taken away by ſtat. 13. *Eliz.* c. 15.; but this laſt act being to continue only to the end of the next parliament, when that period arrived, the proviſion of ſtat. 5. *Eliz.* again revived.

THE ſtat. 5. *Eliz.* c. 5. is intitled *An Act touching politic Conſtitutions for the Maintenance of the Navy.* In this act were brought forward two principles of our ſyſtem of navigation, that have been ſteadily adhered to, under different modifications, ever ſince. One was the encouraging of the fiſheries, as the means of increaſing our ſhipping and navigation; the other was, the confining the coaſting-trade to Engliſh ſhipping.

MANY proviſions had, before this ſtatute, been made reſpecting the fiſheries; but in none of them had this ſubject been taken up with a view to ſhipping and navigation. The laws made till towards the latter end of Edward III. related to the inland fiſheries of ſalmon and other river-fiſh; as ſtat. Weſtm. 2. 13. *Edw.* 1. c. 47. But in 31. *Edw.* 3. proviſions were made about the ſale in market of herrings, of which Great Yarmouth was then, as now, the principal market *(a)*. Theſe

*(a)* Stat. 31. *Ed.* 3. ſt. 2. c. 1. Stat. 31. *Ed.* 3. ſt. 3.

were

were followed by several others in the subsequent reigns; in all of which fish was considered in the light of victual merely; was often joined with corn, butter, cheese, and the like; and the great anxiety seemed to be, to obtain a regular supply, to prevent forestalling or regrating, either by buying it at sea, or taking any undue advantage of the fishermen when they came to shore, so as to prevent a fair and open sale in market, for the supply of the public on the best terms; such are stat. 31. *Ed.* 3. st. 2. c. 2. stat. 31. *Ed.* 3. st. 3. stat. 35. *Ed.* 3. st. 1. stat. 6. *Rich.* 2. c. 11. stat. 25. *Hen.* 8. c. 4. among many others. To attain this object, encouragement was given by stat. 6. *Rich.* 2. c. 10. (which was enforced by several statutes passed in after-times, as stat. 1. *Hen.* 4. c. 17. stat. 14. *Hen.* 4. c. 6.) to aliens, being friends, to bring in fish and sell it in market, notwithstanding any privileges or charters granted to others.

In the time of Henry VIII. the parliament, for the first time, expressed an opinion, that the fisheries had a connection with the state of our navigation and maritime force. In stat. 33. *Hen.* 8. c. 2. which was made for preventing the old practice of buy-

buying fish on the high sea, it is stated in
the preamble, that many towns on the
coast of Kent and Sussex had, in former
times, possessed wealth and great population, owing to their fisheries; that there
was in consequence a building of boats and
ships in those parts, and mariners always to
be found for the navy; lastly, that the markets were well supplied with fish, many
grew rich, and the poor were employed.
It then complains, that the fishermen of
those parts had of late thought it more advantageous to go over to the coasts of
Picardy and Flanders, or to meet the fishermen of those countries at sea and buy of
them with the coin of the realm their fish;
whereas if they did not so regrate these supplies (which seems to have been the principal grievance), these Picards and Flemings
would bring their own caught fish, and sell
it here at a *cheaper rate*. A penalty was,
by this act, imposed on those who bought
such fish, and brought it here to market.

ANOTHER statute may be mentioned as
bearing a semblance of encouraging the
fisheries. By stat. 2. & 3. *Edw.* 6. c. 6.
no toll was any longer to be taken by the
officers of the admiralty from any merchant

or

or fisherman for a licence to pass out on voyages to Iceland, Newfoundland, Ireland, or other places commodious for fishing upon the seas.

It remained for the reign of queen Elizabeth to make some regulations that would plainly and materially contribute to render the fisheries subservient to the end of shipping and navigation. This was done by the abovementioned stat. 5. *Eliz.* c. 5.

By this statute it was enacted, that, for four years to come, the queen's subjects might export, in ships and vessels of subjects, herrings and other sea fish taken upon the seas by subjects to any place out of the queen's dominions, without paying any custom, subsidy, or poundage-money for the same. In ports, cities, markets, and other places, none were to set a price on, or make any restraint, or take a toll or tax of sea fish taken by subjects in ships or vessels of the same subjects; nor was any purveyor to take the same but on agreement with the owner or seller *(a)*. None were to buy of any stranger, or out of a stranger's bottom, any herring not being sufficiently salted, packed, and casked,

*(a)* Sect. 1, 2. 4.

on pain of forfeiture, except such herrings came in by shipwreck *(a)*. To promote the confumption of fish, various regulations were made concerning the due keeping of fish-days *(b)*, with other matters conducing to encourage and recommend the great object of the fishery.

In the course of this reign several other regulations were made upon this head. In stat. 13. *Eliz.* c. 11. which also is intituled, *An Act for the Maintenance of Navigation*, it was enacted, that no fish taken or brought into the realm by a stranger, nor fish commonly called Scottish fish, or Flemish fish, should be dried within England, to be sold, on pain of forfeiture thereof *(c)*. Again, in stat. 23. *Eliz.* c. 7. intituled, *An Act for the Increase of Mariners, and for Maintenance of the Navigation*, provision was made against the merchants and fishmongers sending into foreign parts, and ingrossing salted fish, and salted herrings, instead of employing our own fishermen; owing to which, the preamble of the act says, two hundred sail and more of good and serviceable ships, which used to trade yearly to

*(a)* Sect. 6, 7.   *(b)* Sect. 14, 15, 16, to 23.
*(c)* Sect. 4.

Iceland,

Iceland, had now decayed; and also a great number of mariners and seamen fit for her majesty's service: however, salted fish might, by this act, be brought by aliens, being the real owners thereof. This provision was relaxed by stat. 27. *Eliz.* c. 15. so as to allow such salted fish to be imported by English subjects, for the use of some of the northern ports of England, which, it seems from the preamble of the act, used to be supplied with herrings and other fish from the coast towns of Norfolk and Suffolk, till the exportation of them had been encouraged by taking off the export duty by stat. 5. *Eliz.*; since which, so much of that article was sent to Zealand, France, and Portugal, and up the Streights for Italy, that the northern parts of this kingdom suffered greatly from scarcity. The act of 23. *Eliz.* was afterwards wholly repealed by stat. 39. *Eliz.* c. 10.; and the reason given is, that the navigation of this kingdom was not bettered, nor the number of mariners increased by the prohibition on the importation of foreign salt fish by our own merchants, and that the natural subjects were not able to furnish a tenth part of the realm with salted fish of their own taking; while, in the mean time, the foreign merchants only

only enhanced their prices since the late act
of parliament. Further, it alledged, that
considering the subjects of this country
might carry out salted fish, it was unequal
not to allow them also to bring it in, but
rather to entrust this branch of trade wholly
to foreigners.

BY stat. 1. *Jac.* 1. c. 23. and stat. 3. *Jac.* 1.
c. 12. provision was made for encouraging the
fishery of pilchards and sea fish on the coasts
of Somerset, Devon, and Cornwall. And
this may be considered as the whole of what
was done by parliament, till the Act of Navigation, for promoting this branch of employment for ships and mariners, which has
been deemed in later times so necessary for
increasing and advancing both.

WITH regard to the second principle
of the navigation-system brought forward
by stat. 5. *Eliz.* It was enacted, that no person should cause to be loaden or carried in
any bottom whereof a stranger born was
owner, ship-master, or part owner, any
kind of fish, victual, wares, or things of
what kind or nature soever, from one port
or creek of this realm to another port or
creek of the same, on pain of forfeiting the
goods so laden or carried (*a*).

(*a*) Sect. 8.

In addition to this, the antient regulation concerning French wines and Thoulouse woad, that had lately been repealed, was revived. No wine coming out of the dominions of France, nor Thoulouse woad, was to come into this realm of England, but in vessels of which some subject of the queen was only owner, or part owner, on pain of forfeiting such wine or woad (a); with an exception in favour of Wales, the county of Monmouth, and the Isle of Man, where strangers might bring, in ships owned by strangers, any quantity of Rochelle wine, and not exceeding a certain quantity of other French wines, in one year (b). A permission was given to all persons, being subjects, to export wheat, rye, barley, malt, peas, or beans, when they did not exceed certain prices, into any parts beyond sea in ships, crayers, or other vessels, whereof English subjects should be the only owners.

This act was temporary: the part of it that allowed the exportation of herrings and other fish free of duty, was continued by stat. 13. *Eliz.* c. 11. for six years, but was at length left to expire: the other provisions above-mentioned were kept on foot by the

(a) Sect. 11.  (b) Sect. 11. 46, 47, 48.

continuing acts, stat. 39. *Eliz.* c. 18.
stat. 1. *Jac.* 1. c. 25. stat. 21. *Jac.* 1. c. 28.
stat. 3. *Car.* 1. c. 4. stat. 16. *Car.* 1. c. 4.

BEFORE we leave this stat. 5. *Eliz.* c. 5. it should be remarked, that the description which prevailed in the former statutes of the ownership of the vessel, whether English or foreign, was varied by this act, which introduced the alternative of *only owner*, or *part owner*, as well with regard to one as the other; and in both cases it had the effect of rendering the regulation in favour of English ships more strict.

IN another act *(a)* made in the same sessions of parliament, for regulating the exportation of corn, the encouragement of shipping was still kept in view. The act is intituled, *For the Increase of Tillage, and Maintenance of the Navy*. The exportation of corn is required to be in English ships; and this is done in the same words as had been before used in stat. 5. *Eliz.* c. 5. before noticed.

IT was upon the regulations of stat. 5. *Eliz.* c. 5. that the shipping and navigation of this country depended for support

*(a)* C. 13.

and encouragement till the middle of the last century; when a set of men who had violated all scruples and rights to possess themselves of the government, manifested a more laudable courage in despising the delicacy hitherto observed towards the rival maritime powers, and resolved, by one legislative act, to advance the interest of English navigation, in opposition to all competition from foreigners of every description.

THE first law made at this time for the advancement of navigation, was one for promoting the interest of our foreign plantations, which we shall from this time perceive to be intimately connected with the interests of navigation and of shipping.

THE plan of colonization, which had been begun in the reign of James I. had, all along, been conducted under the immediate administration of the crown. The adventurers engaged in the enterprize under the sanction of royal charters; and every thing relating to their settlement and trade had been ordered by the king and the privy council, without any participation of the Legislature. In these regulations we discover

ver some traces of the policy then conceived, and since more particularly pursued, with regard to the trade of these distant possessions; the striking features of which were, to give encouragement to their productions, in preference to the like articles from other countries; and in return for that preference to require of them, that they should send all their productions to this country, and employ only English shipping.

JAMES I. had unfortunately conceived a capricious dislike of tobacco, the only production of Virginia, which he himself was so proud of having settled. This novel plant was prohibited by proclamation, and the Virginia Company were driven to establish houses in Holland and Zealand, for the import and sale of their consignments. But the customs which used to be received upon tobacco in this kingdom failing, the king was willing to come to an understanding with the Company; and after this question had been agitated between them and the crown for some time, a compromise was at length agreed upon in 1623, by which James consented to receive a duty of 9d. *per* pound in lieu of all charges, and the Company were to have the sole importation,

upon

upon the exprefs condition, that the whole production of the colony fhould be brought to England (a). Again, in 1624 the king prohibited by proclamation the importation of tobacco into England or Ireland, except from Virginia or the Somer Iflands, and except in fhips belonging to his fubjects. He prohibited alfo the planting of it in England or Ireland, or in the ifles to the fame belonging. As a compenfation for the lofs of duties on Spanifh and other foreign tobacco, the merchandize was to be received by royal agents, at a ftipulated price, and to be fold by them for the benefit of the king (b).

In the following reign a like policy was maintained under the authority of royal proclamations. In 1639, in the inftructions given to fir William Berkeley, then appointed governor of Virginia, we find it alledged, that many fhips laden with tobacco and other merchandize had carried the fame from thence directly to foreign countries, whereby the king loft the duties due thereon, as nothing was anfwered upon the exportation in Virginia; the governor is therefore directed to be very careful that no veffel depart thence, loaded with thofe commodities,

(a) Chalmers Pol. Ann. pa. 52 to 57.   (b) Ibid. 67.

before

before bond, with sufficient sureties, should be taken to his majesty's use, to bring the same into his majesty's dominions, and to carry a lading from thence, in order that the staple of these commodities might be made here; whereby his majesty, after so great an expence upon that plantation, and so many of his subjects transported thither, might not be defrauded of what was justly due for customs on the goods. The bonds were to be transmitted, so that delinquents might be proceeded against. It was at the same time given in charge to the governor, to forbid all trade with any foreign vessels, except upon necessity. The governor was also to take bonds of the owners of tobacco, that it should be brought to the port of London, there to pay such duties as were due (a). A custom-house regulation that we shall see was afterwards adopted by parliament, and carried into full execution.

Thus far had the king proceeded, with the advice of his privy council, to settle and arrange the trade between the mother-country and the plantations. Some few years after, the parliament, which had then assumed the sovereign power, took up this subject;

(a) Chalm. Pol. Ann. pa. 132.

subject; and on 23 January 1646 they passed an ordinance, intituled, *Privileges granted to several foreign Plantations.*

THIS ordinance begins by reciting, *that the plantations in Virginia, Bermuda, Barbadoes, and other places of America, had been much beneficial to this kingdom, by the increase of navigation, and the customs arising from the commodities of the growth of those plantations imported into this kingdom;* and it recites, that persons trading there had been permitted, for their better encouragement, to transport thither merchandizes and necessaries for carrying on such plantations, without paying any custom for them: for continuing this encouragement it was now enacted, that all goods exported to such plantations, for their use and support, should be exported free of all custom or duty whatsoever, except that they were, for the next three years, to be subject to the excise *(a)*. This privilege, however, was not to apply to exports made to the plantations *in new-found lands.*

(*a*) There is an ambiguity in the wording of the ordinance in this place; it might be read, "that they were to be exempt from the excise for the three years."

A CUSTOM-HOUSE

A CUSTOM-HOUSE regulation was subjoined, of a sort that will frequently be met with in other laws relating to the plantations. Security was to be given to the commissioners of the customs for really exporting such merchandize to the plantations, there to be used; and a certificate was to be returned from thence, within one year after the lading, of the ship's arrival and discharge in the plantations. Permission was given to entertain and transport to the plantations, persons, subjects of this kingdom, who were willing to serve and be employed in them, provided the names of such persons were registered in the custom-house, and no force were used to take up such servants, nor any apprentices were enticed to desert their masters, or children under age admitted without express consent of their parents; and provided a certificate, within one year of the arrival, should be returned from the governor, or other chief officer, that no fraud was used to carry such person to any other place.

AFTER these provisions another was added, which more particularly belongs to our subject, and which is added in the form of a *proviso*, and was meant as a condition to be
performed

performed on the part of the plantations, to intitle them to the benefits intended them by this ordinance. "Provided, That none
" of the said plantations do suffer or permit
" any ship, bark, or vessel, to take in any
" goods of the growth of the said planta-
" tions, from any of their ports, and carry
" them to any foreign parts and places,
" except in English bottoms. And in case
" any of the said plantations shall offend
" herein, then the plantation so offending
" shall be excluded from the benefit of the
" ordinance, and shall pay custom, as other
" merchants do to France, Spain, Holland,
" and other foreign parts."

IN this manner was brought forward another principle of our system of navigation, that of confining to the mother-country the trade of its colonies and plantations; which we shall see adopted and completely secured in the more permanent and extensive policy that was soon to be established.

BEFORE we come to that, we find some of the foreign plantations, having attached themselves to the cause of the exiled family, had incurred the displeasure of the ruling authority in this kingdom; and an ordinance

nance was passed by the parliament, 3d October 1650, for discontinuing any further intercourse with them, and for declaring them in a state of rebellion. This ordinance is intituled, *Trade with the* BARBADA, VIRGINIA, BERMUDA'S, *and* ANTEGO, *prohibited*. This ordinance declares those colonies and plantations to have been planted at the cost, and settled by the people and the authority, of this nation; and that they were, and ought to be, subordinate to, and dependent upon, England; and had ever since the planting thereof been, and ought to be, subject to such laws, orders, and regulations, as were and should be made by the parliament of England. It then alledges, that divers persons inhabiting therein had usurped a power of government, seized the estates of many, banished others, and set themselves up in opposition to, and distinct from, this state and commonwealth; they were therefore declared robbers, rebels, and traitors; and the parliament forbade to all manner of persons, foreigners and others, all manner of commerce, traffic, and correspondence, whatsoever, to be held with those rebels. Power was accordingly thereby given to seize and take all ships and goods of persons trading, or going to trade,

or

or coming from trading, with them, or holding correspondence with, or yielding them any assistance. Ships and goods were not to be embezzled, but to be proceeded against in the court of admiralty.

At the same time the parliament laid a restriction upon all the plantations in general; which has continued, in some degree, to the present time. " To prevent for the
" time to come, and to hinder the carrying
" over of any such persons as are enemies
" to this commonwealth, or that may prove
" dangerous to any of the English planta-
" tions in America, the parliament doth
" forbid and prohibit all ships of any foreign
" nation whatsoever to come to, or trade
" in, or traffic with, any of the English
" plantations in America, or any islands,
" ports, or places thereof, which are planted
" by, and in possession of, the people of
" this commonwealth, without licence first
" had and obtained from the parliament or
" council of state." And power was given to seize all foreign ships so circumstanced, and not having such licence; and they, with their goods, were declared to be prize.

WITH

WITH respect to the plantations in actual rebellion, power was delegated to the council of state to grant licence and leave to any ship of this nation to trade thither, notwithstanding this act. The council of state were also authorised to send a naval force thither, and to grant commissions to enforce obedience; and also to grant pardons, and appoint governors, and to do and use all lawful means to settle and preserve them in peace, till the parliament took further order therein.

SUCH was the nature of the prohibitory law passed on that occasion; and so early in the parliamentary history of our colonies was a model afforded to be followed in aftertimes, when it was judged that the like remedy should be applied for correcting diforders of a similar sort.

BUT the grand scheme for establishing English shipping and navigation on a footing of distinction that had never been before attempted, was brought forward in the following year.

THIS was the famous Act of Navigation passed by the parliament 9th October 1651.

In

In this act we shall see the principles, which had been gradually developing in former laws, and which had been enforced, repealed, or qualified, according as different opinions prevailed, and circumstances allowed, now adopted, and expanded to their full extent, in one system of regulation, that has subsisted, without any very material change in its substance, to the present day.

The great object of jealousy at the time of passing this act was the immense carrying trade possessed by the Dutch; and the title of the act is suited to this leading idea, *Goods from foreign parts by whom to be imported* (a). The portion of the carrying-trade with our colonies, which the Dutch had obtained, was the most serious grievance, and that which the nation bore with least patience. Notwithstanding the engagements, stipulations, and regulations, made for confining that branch of navigation to the mother-country, it is said, that in the West-India Islands there used, at this time, out of forty ships to be thirty-eight ships Dutch bottoms. The ordinance sets out with a regulation that was to strike at this abuse; it enacts, That no goods or commodities whatsoever, of

(a) Vide Scob. Acts, ann. 1651. cap. 22.

the growth, production, or manufacture, of *Asia, Africa,* or *America,* or of any part thereof, or of any islands belonging to them, or any of them, or which are described or laid down in the usual charts or maps of those places, as well of the English plantations as others, shall be imported or brought into this commonwealth of England, or into Ireland, or any other lands, islands, plantations, or territories, to this commonwealth belonging, or in their possession, in any other ship or vessel whatsoever, but only in such as do truly, and without fraud, belong only to the people of this commonwealth, or the plantations thereof, as the proprietors or right owners thereof, and whereof the master and mariners are also, for the most part of them, of the people of this commonwealth, under the penalty of the forfeiture of the goods, as also of the ship (with all her tackle, guns, and apparel) in which the goods shall be so brought in and imported, half to the commonwealth, and half to the person seizing the goods and prosecuting them.

HAVING thus secured the whole import of the productions of three quarters of the globe

globe to English ships, it goes on to enact, That no goods, the growth, production, or manufacture, of *Europe*, or of any part thereof, shall be imported or brought into this commonwealth of England, or into Ireland, or any other lands, islands, plantations, or territories, to this commonwealth belonging, or in their possession, in any ship or vessel whatsoever, but in such as do truly, and without fraud, belong only to the people of this commonwealth, as the true owners and proprietors thereof, and in no other, except only such foreign ships and vessels as do truly and properly belong to the people of that country or place of which the said goods are the growth, production, or manufacture, or to such ports where such goods can only be, or most usually are, first shipped for transportation, under the same penalty as in the former case; and no goods or commodities that are of foreign growth, production, or manufacture, and which are to be brought into this commonwealth, in shipping belonging to the people thereof, shall be by them shipped or brought from any other place or country, but only those of their growth, production, or manufacture,

or

or from those ports where the said goods
and commodities can only, or are, or
usually have been, first shipped for transportation, and from none other place or
country, under the like penalty of forfeiture. By these two prohibitions the
Dutch were cut off from the carrying-trade
of Europe, and our merchants were obliged
to fetch the productions of the rest of the
world from the place of their growth, instead
of buying them in Holland. In the second
of these three provisions we see that idea
carried into execution which had been
pressed on the parliament by the commons
in 18. *Hen.* 6. (*a*), and which was afterwards
actually followed in the case of Thoulouse
woad, and French wines.

To these great lines of this act were added
the following provisos:

FIRST, This was not to restrain the importation of the commodities of the Straits,
or Levant seas, laden in the shipping of
this nation, at the usual ports, or places for
lading them theretofore, within the Straits
or Levant seas; nor East-India commodities laden in the shipping of this nation,
at the usual place for lading in any
part of those seas, to the southward and

(*a*) Vid. ant. pa. 16.

eastward

eastward of the Cape of Good Hope, although they were not of the growth of those places.

SECONDLY, The people of this commonwealth might bring, in vessels or ships to them belonging, and whereof the master and mariners were of this nation, from any of the ports of Spain, or Portugal, goods or commodities that came from, or anyway belonged to, the plantations or dominions of either of them respectively.

THIRDLY, It was not to apply to silk, or silk wares brought by land from Italy, and there bought with the proceeds of English commodities sold for money, or in barter; but the people of this commonwealth might ship them in English vessels from Ostend, Nieuport, Rotterdam, Middleburgh, Amsterdam, or any ports thereabouts, the owner making oath before the comptrollers of the customs, or one of the barons of the exchequer, that the goods were so bought for his account in Italy.

FOURTHLY, It was not to extend to bullion, nor to goods taken by way of reprisals, by ships having commission from the commonwealth.

Thus far of foreign trade. The next object was the *fisheries*, in which the rivalship and success of the Dutch had been long regarded as a national loss and disgrace. It was now resolved to give an advantage and preference to the exertions of our own fishermen; and it was enacted, that no sort of cod-fish, ling, herring, pilchard, or any other kind of salted fish usually fished for and caught by the people of this nation, nor any oil made of any kind of fish whatsoever, nor any whale-fins or whale-bones, should be imported into this commonwealth, or into Ireland, or any other lands, islands, plantations, or territories, thereto belonging, or in their possession, but only such as should be caught in vessels that truly and properly belonged to the people of this nation, as proprietors and right owners. And the fish was to be cured, and the oil made, by the people of this commonwealth, under the penalty before-mentioned. Nor was such fish, when caught and cured by the people of this commonwealth, to be exported from any place belonging to this commonwealth in any other ship or vessel than such as truly and properly appertained to the people of this commonwealth, as right owners, and whereof the master and mariners were, for the most part of them, English, under the like forfeiture.

The last object was *the coasting trade*, in which the act follows the very words of stat. 5. *Eliz.* It enacts, that no person whatever should load, or cause to be loaded, and carried, in any bottom, ship, or vessel, whereof any stranger born (unless such as were denizen or naturalized) were owner, part owner, or master, any fish, victual, wares, or things, of what kind or nature soever, from one port or creek of this commonwealth to another, under pain of forfeiting the goods and ship.

Such was the scheme of navigation, which the bold reformers of that day designed for increasing the naval strength and consideration of this country. It may be said to have originated in jealousy, and to have caused the decline and diminution of a neighbouring nation; but it was founded in a policy, which the necessities and the advantages of an insular situation suggested; and the nation having, from supineness or ignorance, permitted an active neighbour so long to take a share in the fisheries and foreign trade which belonged to us, thought itself justified

in

in asserting, at length, its rights, and carrying them into full effect by this legislative act. And although this measure brought upon the country an obstinate and bloody war; and though the authority on which it was founded was unconstitutional and usurped, yet a plan so wise and solid was strenuously maintained by those who formed it; and it was not suffered to pass away with the transient government from which it derived its origin: the great features of it were adopted, by the lawful government, at the restoration of Charles II. when a new Act of Navigation rose out of the ashes of this, and became the basis of all those laws that have since been made for the increase of shipping and navigation.

# PART II.

## INTRODUCTION.

*PART II.*
*12. CAR. II. TO*
*A. D. 1783.*

THE second period in the history of shipping and navigation begins with the restoration of Charles II. In the statute for laying new duties of tonnage and poundage on the import and export of merchandize, provision was made, in certain cases, to give an abatement in the duty, where shipping of English-built was employed (a). But the great regulation in favour of English shipping was, THE *Act of Navigation*, as it is usually called, to distinguish it from others of the same policy and nature. This is stat. 12. *Car.* 2. c. 18. intituled, *An Act for the Encouraging and Increasing of Shipping and Navigation.*

This act pursues the policy and detail of the one made in 1651, using sometimes its

---

(a) Stat. 12. Car. 2. c. 4.

very

very words. It has made however some
alterations, and has added considerably to
the scope of the former act. In order to
present the regulations of this law in a clear
view, it will be proper to class them under
heads. The obvious way to promote the
increase of shipping is to facilitate its employment.
The laws of shipping become
therefore the laws of trade; and the heads
under which they most naturally arrange
themselves, are the *trades* in which ships are
employed between the different quarters of
the globe. The late act begun by defining
what ships should be employed in carrying
the productions of Asia, Africa, and America;
which might very properly be called
*the Plantation trade*. It then proceeded to
*the European trade*. Then it regulated ships
as far as regarded *the Fisheries*; and concluded
with the carrying from port to port in this
kingdom, which might be called *the Coasting
trade*.

THE new act has considered shipping and
navigation as they relate to these same
branches of employment. But it has made
two divisions that are important. *The Plantation
trade*, as I have ventured to call it,
is considered somewhat differently, when
carried

PART VI.
12. CAR II TO
A. D. 1783.

carried on with our own plantations, and when with thofe parts of Afia, Africa, or America, that belong to other fovereigns. Again, in *the European trade* a great diftinction is made as to the productions of Ruffia and Turkey, and certain enumerated articles, and as to articles of trade in the reft of Europe. Thefe are the principal alterations made in the heads of regulation contained in the old act. The new act contains a head of regulation that had not been entered into by the old act; namely, for preventing foreign fhips paffing as Englifh, and for afcertaining the ownerfhip and built of Englifh fhips. Other differences in the detail and execution of this fcheme will be difcovered on a clofer comparifon of thefe two acts; but the leading ones juft mentioned are as much as need be noticed at prefent.

This Act of Navigation paffed after the Reftoration being looked back to as the origin and great charter of our navigation-fyftem, upon which all fubfequent laws may be confidered as comments, it feems moft natural to purfue our further enquiries in the courfe directed by this act, and to clafs the matter of our work under the heads
into

into which this act is divided. These are, *the Plantation trade—the trade with Asia, Africa, and America—the European trade—the Coasting trade—the Fisheries—*and, lastly, *of British ships.*

MAKING these divisions of the enquiry, I shall begin each with stating the groundwork laid by the Act of Navigation, and then follow the changes and improvements made by subsequent laws *(a).*

*(a)* An act was passed in the Scotch parliament for a similar purpose in 1661, intituled, *An Act for Encouraging Shipping and Navigation.* By this act goods and commodities are to be imported by Scotch ships, or ships of the countries where the commodities are produced, with an exception of the commodities of *Asia, Africa,* and *America,* and those of *Musco* and *Italy,* until Scots merchants had actual trade to those places. A double custom was laid on goods imported in foreign ships, except ships of England or Ireland; but that exception was to endure no longer than while Scotch vessels enjoyed the like benefit of trade within England and Ireland. A scheme of regist'y and certificate for Scots ships is also sketched out in the act \*. The policy and wording of this act plainly shew, that the parliament had our statute in view.

\* C. 44.

CHAPTER

## CHAPTER I.

*Import and Export in English Ships—Enumerated Goods—European Goods sent to the Plantations—Plantation Bonds—Acts of Navigation enforced—Relaxed and dispensed with—Stat. 7. & 8. Will. 3.—Navigation Act relaxed—Irish Linens—Rice—Sugar—American Acts Stat. 4. Geo. 3. and Stat. 5. Geo. 3. Stat. 6. Geo. 3.—Free Ports established—The Export Trade from Ireland—Import and Export Trade granted more fully;—The Restraining and Prohibitory Acts—Newfoundland—Honduras—Surat.*

PART II.
12. CAR. II. TO
A.D. 1783.
PLANTATION
TRADE.

THE first and grand object in the Act of Navigation seems to have been *the Plantation trade.* For securing this to the Mother-country, it was ordained, that no goods or commodities shall be imported into, or exported out of any lands, islands, plantations, or territories, to his majesty belonging, or in his possession, or which may hereafter belong unto, or be in the possession of his majesty, his heirs, and successors,

successors, in Asia, Africa, or America, in any other ship or vessel but in such ships or vessels as do truly, and without fraud, belong only to the people of England or Ireland, the dominion of Wales, or town of Berwick-upon-Tweed, or are of the built of, and belonging to, any of the said lands, islands, plantations, or territories, as proprietors and right owners thereof, and whereof the master, and three-fourths of the mariners, at least, are English, under pain of forfeiting the goods, and also the ship or vessel, with all its guns, furniture, tackle, ammunition, and apparel, one third to the king, one third to the governor of the land, island, plantation, or territory, where the default was committed, in case the ship be there seized, or otherwise such third part to the king, and the other third part to the person seizing, informing, or suing for the same. Further, all admirals and commanders of king's ships are authorised to seize, and bring in as prize, ships so offending, and to deliver them to the court of admiralty. And in case of condemnation, one moiety of such forfeiture is to go to such admiral or commander, and his company, to be divided as prizes are; the other moiety to the king *(a)*.

*(a)* Sect. 1.

IN pursuance of the like policy, it was moreover ordained, that no alien, or person not born within the king's allegiance, or naturalized, or made a free denizen, shall exercise the trade or occupation of a merchant or factor in any of the said places, on pain of forfeiting all his goods and chattels; one third to the king, another third to the governor, and the other to the person informing and suing for the same. And to secure, as much as possible, the execution of these laws, it is required, that all governors, before they enter into their government, shall take a solemn oath to do their utmost, that the before-mentioned regulations should be punctually and *bona fide* observed; and a governor wittingly or willingly negligent in doing this duty is to be removed from his government (*a*).

Enumerated Goods.

HAVING provided that none but English ships should carry the plantation-commodities, it was thought proper, that the principal articles of them, which are named in the act, and are therefore called *enumerated*, should be carried only to the mother-country, that so the profit of bringing them home, and that of carrying them to other parts of

(*a*) Sect. 2.

Europe,

Europe, if they were to be carried, should center in the mother-country.

THUS no sugar, tobacco, cotton, wool, indigoes, ginger, fustick, or other dyeing wood, of the growth, production, or manufacture of any English plantations in America, Asia, or Africa, shall be shipped, carried, conveyed, or transported, from any of the said plantations, to any land, island, territory, dominion, port, or place, whatsoever, other than to such other English plantations as belong to his majesty, or to the kingdom of England or Ireland, or principality of Wales, or town of Berwick-upon-Tweed, there to be laid on shore, under pain of forfeiting the goods, or the value thereof, and also the ship, with all her guns, tackle, apparel, ammunition, and furniture; one moiety to the king, the other to the person seizing and suing for the same *(a)*.

AND to secure the execution of this restriction, for every ship or vessel sailing from England, Ireland, Wales, or town of Berwick-upon-Tweed, for any English plantation in America, Asia, or Africa, sufficient bond shall be given, with one surety, to the

*(a)* Sect. 18.

chief

chief officer of the customs at the port from whence the ship shall sail, in a certain penalty, for bringing such commodities to some port of England, Ireland, Wales, or to the port of Berwick-upon-Tweed, and there unload and put on shore the same, the danger of the seas excepted. And in the case of all ships permitted to come to the plantations from any other place, the governor is, in like manner, to take a bond, that the ship shall carry her goods to some other of his majesty's English plantations, or to England, Ireland, Wales, or the town of Berwick-upon-Tweed. And if any of the enumerated goods are taken on board before such bond in the latter case is made to the governor, or before a certificate in the former case is produced from the officers of the customs that such bond has been duly given here, the ship is forfeited, with all her guns, tackle, apparel, and furniture, to be recovered as before-mentioned. The governors are twice a-year to return copies of such bonds to the chief officers of the customs in London (a).

THE parliament shewed how much they considered the trade of the nation as interested in preserving this policy with regard

(a) Sect. 19.

to the plantations, by soon after passing an act which still more confined their trade to the mother-country.

By stat. 15. *Car.* 2. c. 7. which is intitled *An Act for the Encouraging of Trade*, the supplying the plantations with European goods was meant wholly to be confined to the mother-country. In the preamble to this regulation, it is stated to be with a view of maintaining a greater correspondence and kindness between them and the mother-country, and keeping the former in a firmer dependence upon the latter; for increasing shipping and seamen, promoting the vent of English woollen manufactures, making this kingdom the staple both of the commodities of the plantations and of other countries, in order to supply them; and, lastly, that it was the usage of other nations to keep their plantation-trade to themselves. After alledging these motives, it ordains, that no commodity of the growth, production, or manufacture, of Europe shall be imported into any land, island, plantation, colony, territory, or place, to his majesty belonging, or in his possession in Asia, Africa, or America (Tangier only excepted), but what shall be, *bonâ fide*, and without

out fraud, laden and shipped in England, Wales, or the town of Berwick-upon-Tweed, and in English-built shipping, or which were, *bona fide*, bought before a certain day then past, and had such certificate thereof as is required by stat. 13. & 14. *Car.* 2. c. 11. (an act that will be noticed hereafter), and whereof the master and three-fourths of the mariners at least are English; and which shall be carried directly to the said lands, islands, plantations, colonies, territories, or places, and from no other place whatever, under pain of forfeiting such commodities, as shall be imported from any other place whatever, by land *(a)* or water; and if by water, of the ship importing them; one third to the king, another to the governor where seized, and another to the informer *(b)*.

There is a proviso allowing salt to be carried from any part of Europe for the fisheries of New England, and Newfoundland; and wines from the Madeiras, being the growth thereof; and from the western islands of Azores, wines of the growth

*(a)* Importing by land, is an expression to be found in other acts of parliament.
*(b)* Sect. 6.

thereof;

SHIPPING AND NAVIGATION.      65

thereof; and servants or horses from Scotland or Ireland; and from Scotland and Ireland all sorts of victual of the growth or production of those countries respectively (a).

PART II.
12. CAR. II. TO A. D. 1783. PLANTATION TRADE.

To secure the due execution of this act, strict rules are laid down to be carried into execution by the governors in the plantations, both with regard to importations by land and by water. They are to take a solemn oath for the special performance of this duty, and if they offend therein, they are to be deprived of their government, and be incapable of that or any other, and moreover forfeit 1000l.; a moiety to the king, the other to the informer (b).

AGAIN, by the same act, a penalty of losing his place, and forfeiting the value of the goods in question, is imposed on any officer of the customs, who suffers any sugar, tobacco, ginger, cotton, wool, indigo, speckle wood, or Jamaica wood, fustic or other dyeing wood (being in effect the articles enumerated in stat. 12. *Car.* 2. c. 18.), of the growth of any of the said lands, islands,

(a) Sect. 7.    '(b) Sect. 8.

F                    colonies,

PART II.
12. CAR. II. TO
A. D. 1783.
PLANTATION
TRADE.

colonies, plantations, territories, or places, to be carried into any other country or place whatsoever, until they have been first unladen, *bona fide*, and put on shore in some port or haven in England, Wales, or Berwick; a regulation which at once cut off the direct trade with Ireland, and indeed any intercourse between the colonies themselves in those articles *(a)*: though, as to the latter, that does not seem to have been the construction the act received, as will be seen presently.

But this indirect way of depriving Ireland of the benefit given her by stat. 12. *Car.* 2. c. 18. without expressly repealing the provision respecting bonds therein made, seems not to have been regarded as an express law would have been. Persons had refused to give bond for landing goods only in England; or had, notwithstanding such bonds, carried the goods to Ireland. This practice went on till stat. 22. & 23. *Car.* 2. c. 26. was made to set things right, by an express declaration of the law. This act directs, that the word *Ireland* shall be left out of all bonds taken for any ship sailing

*(a)* Sect. 9.

SHIPPING AND NAVIGATION. 67

from England, Ireland, Wales, or Berwick upon Tweed, for any English plantation in Asia, Africa, or America; and in case such ship shall load any of those commodities, they are to be brought to some port in England or Wales, or to the town of Berwick, and be there unloaded and put on shore: and so of all other ships coming from any other port or place, and permitted by the Act of Navigation to trade thither; namely, ships of the plantations themselves. The reason given in the act for thus excluding Ireland, is, that it was England which suffered by numbers transporting themselves from hence to people the plantations.

*PART II.*
*12. CAR. II. TO A. D. 1763. PLANTATION TRADE.*

THE governors of the plantations are directed, before any such goods are permitted to be loaden on board, to take bond to the value mentioned in the Act of Navigation, that the ship shall carry the goods to some other of his majesty's English plantations, or to England, Wales, or the town of Berwick upon Tweed; and the penalty of forfeiture of the ship is inflicted, if the goods are loaded without such bond, or without a certificate from England of such bond

*Plantation Bonds.*

F 2        having

having there been given, or if the bond is not complied with *(a)*.

BECAUSE many ships belonging to the plantations used to carry goods to several parts of Europe, and there unload them, the act directs all governors to make a return once a-year at least to the officers of the customs in London, or to some person that shall be appointed to receive the same, of a list of all ships lading such commodities, and also of all bonds so taken. And in case any ship belonging to his majesty's plantations having on board any sugars, tobacco, cotton, wool, indigo, ginger, fustic, or other dyeing-wood, shall be found to have unladen in any port, or place of Europe, other than England, Wales, or town of Berwick, it is to be forfeited *(b)*.

THE territory of *Tangier*, which came to his majesty by marriage with a daughter of Portugal, was declared not to be a plantation belonging to his majesty in Asia, Africa, or America, within the meaning of this and the former acts *(c)*.

*(a)* Sect. 11.    *(b)* Sect. 12.    *(c)* Sect. 14.

THE contraband trade carried on by plantation-ships in defiance of the Act of Navigation, was a subject of repeated complaint: it seems, they not only carried goods to Europe, but vended them at sea to the shipping of other nations, which brought them to Europe. The act states this to be a great grievance, considering the free trade they enjoyed at home from one plantation to another, lading and unlading these commodities without paying any custom; while in this kingdom those articles could not be consumed, but after paying heavy customs and impositions: it was alledged, that the ease of supplying themselves, and the great increase of their trade and navigation, ought to content them without engaging in this illicit traffick with Europe.

To prevent this in future, it was ordained, by stat. 25. *Car.* 2. c. 7. that if any ship should come to take on board those commodities, and bond was not first given with one sufficient surety for bringing them to England, Wales, or the town of Berwick, and to no other place, those commodities should, before the lading of them, be subject to certain duties of custom therein mentioned; and if the party had not ready money, the officer

officer might take a portion of the commodities in lieu thereof *(a)*. Thus was the parliament of England induced to lay duties on the export-trade from one plantation to another, in order to prevent an unlawful export to Europe of the enumerated articles.

As the plantations were combined with the interests of shipping and navigation, so was that grand article of produce, tobacco; and in the same manner as they had been coupled in the proclamations of king James, and king Charles, they were now united in several provisions made by the Legislature *(b)*. In the same sessions in which the Act of Navigation was passed, it was enacted by stat. 12. *Car.* 2. c. 34. that no one should plant tobacco in England, Wales, Guernsey, Jersey, Berwick, or in Ireland, on pain of forfeiting it, or 40s. for every rod of ground so planted. This penalty was increased to 10l. by stat. 15. *Car.* 2. c. 7. f. 18. And because this was not found sufficient to restrain the cultivation, it was

*(a)* Sect. 2.
*(b)* For the many proclamations about tobacco, whether importing or planting it, see Chalm. Pol. Ann. p. 129.

further

further provided by ſtat. 22. & 23. *Car.* 2.
c. 26. ſect. 2. that conſtables ſhould ſearch
out and make preſentment at the ſeſſions,
of all perſons who had planted tobacco, or
were the immediate tenants of lands ſo planted: ſuch preſentment was, after filing, to
be conſidered as a conviction, unleſs upon
notice thereof the party traverſed it at the
next ſeſſions. Conſtables are authoriſed, by
warrant from a juſtice, to pluck up and deſtroy all tobacco; and there is a penalty on
conſtables neglecting to do this duty (*a*).
This act is continued by ſtat. 5. *Geo.* 1.
c. 11. during ſuch time as the act of tonnage
and poundage, ſtat. 12. *Car.* 2. c. 4. is
continued, and no longer.

PART II.

12 CAR II. TO
A. D. 1783.
PLANTATION
TRADE.

IN ſuch manner was the trade to and
from the plantations tied up, almoſt for the
ſole and excluſive benefit of the mothercountry. But laws which made the intereſt of a whole people ſubordinate to that
of another reſiding at the diſtance of three
thouſand miles, were not likely to execute
themſelves very readily; nor was it eaſy to
find many upon the ſpot, who could be depended upon for carrying them into execution.

(*a*) Sect. 3. 4.

THE government was not slack in employing those whose service they could readily command.

IMMEDIATELY after passing the Act of Navigation, the lord admiral was ordered to give in charge to all the commanders of the king's ships specially to attend to the execution of this act. As occasions called for it, similar orders were made upon the rest of the king's officers. It having been suggested, that divers ships laden at Barbadoes were gone to Holland, and that it was common for the ships of Holland to bring to the port of London, and other ports, goods *prohibited by the act in Holland vessels*, it was ordered, the 15th of August 1662 (*a*), by the privy council, that the lord treasurer should direct the commissioners and farmers of the customs to take care to see the execution of that part of the act which is to prevent ships loading in the plantations going to foreign parts without first touching in England.

WE find the lords of the committee of council for the plantations wrote a circular letter on the 24th of June 1663 to the governors of the plantations, calling upon them

(*a*) Counc. Regist.

in very strong terms to do their part in enforcing the regulations of this law. It is there alledged, that persons traded from *Virginia, Maryland,* and other plantations, both by sea and land, as well into the *Monadoes* (so *New-York* was then called) and other plantations of the Hollanders, as into *Spain, Venice,* and *Holland*; which was occasioned by the neglects of governors, in not taking a view of foreign-built ships coming in, to see if they had a certificate of their being made free; as also in not duly taking bond for carrying goods to England or Ireland, or to another English plantation. These bonds had not been regularly taken and transmitted; and the governors were now commanded to transmit twice a-year a perfect account of all ships that loaded, and copies of all such bonds, on pain of the penalties inflicted by the act being enforced against them; " it being," as the letter concludes, " his majesty's pleasure, that this said law be very strictly observed, in regard it much concerneth the trade of his kingdom (*a*)."

But the laws of navigation were nowhere disobeyed and contemned so openly

(*a*) Chalm. Pol. An. 260.

as in New England. The people of Massachusetts Bay were from the first disposed to act, as if independent of the mother-country; and having a governor and magistrates of their own choice, it was very difficult to enforce any regulations which came from the English parliament, and were adverse to their colonial interests. Their agents however, who were sent over to negociate their affairs with king Charles's ministers, knew too well the necessity of temporising, not to submit themselves in every thing to the order of the privy council. When the Bostoners were charged with refusing to publish the statute of frauds of the stat. 13. & 14. *Car.* 2. and stat. 25. *Car.* 2. and the king's different proclamations for better observing the acts of trade; and with imprisoning the officers of the king's customs, and not suffering them to plead the general issue in actions brought against them for what was done in the execution of their duty; they denied the charges, and maintained the disposition of their principals to obey the laws, in the same manner as the rest of his majesty's subjects. They alledged as an instance, an act passed by the general court of Boston in the year 1676, in pursuance of one of his majesty's proclamations for enforcing

forcing these very Acts of Navigation; in the preamble of which act it was declared, that they had not before been advertised of his majesty's pleasure. But to this it was replied, that they had long before been advertised of his majesty's pleasure herein from the circular letter of 1663, the receipt of which circular letter was acknowledged in an act passed by the general court in 1663, and printed in 1672, and publicly known, and in every one's hands at the time of the declaration made in the act of 1676. In minds so tempered, obedience and disobedience were much the same thing, as to the interests of the mother-country (a).

But the regulations of these laws were received even by those colonists who were attached to the sovereignty of the mother-country, with grudging and discontent. The complaint made by Sir William Berkeley, the governor of Virginia, in a letter of the 20th of June 1671, is conveyed in words very expressive, and significant: " Mighty and destructive have been the ob-
" structions to our trade and navigation by
" that severe act of parliament, which ex-
" cludes us from having any commerce

(a) Journ. Comm. for Trade.

" with

"with any nation in Europe but our own, so that we cannot add to our plantation any commodity that grows out of it, as olive-trees, cotton, or vines: besides this, we cannot procure any skilful men for our own hopeful commodity of silk; and it is not lawful for us to carry a pipe stave, or a bushel of corn, to any place in Europe out of the king's dominions. If this were for his majesty's service, or the good of the subject, we should not repine, whatever were our sufferings; but, on my soul, it is the contrary for both; and this is the cause, why no small or great vessels are built here. For *we* are most obedient to all laws, whilst the New-England-men break through them, and trade to any place that their interest leads them to. I know of no improvement that can be made in trade, unless we had liberty to transport our pipe staves, timber, and corn, to other places besides the king's dominions (*a*)."

Again, in 1676 the island of Barbadoes complained to the committee of plantations of the acts of trade as grievances, inas-

(*a*) Chalm. Pol. An. 327.

much

much "as a free trade is neceſſary for ſettling new colonies." But this was deemed a dangerous notion with regard to the mother-country. A relaxation of thoſe laws having been urged by the agents for that iſland, the propoſal was debated at the committee on a ſubſequent day, but rejected: the reaſon given was, "that they ought to be ſupported, as being the ſettled laws of the land (*a*)."

In ſome inſtances, however, the crown was prevailed upon to diſpenſe with the execution of theſe laws. In the year immediately after paſſing the Act of Navigation, a repreſentation was made by the merchants trading to New-England, complaining that bond was required of them at the cuſtom-houſe, for bringing to England or Ireland *all* commodities laden in New-England; that the commodities of that plantation were uſually boards, pipe ſtaves, and other timber, fiſh, and the like groſs articles; all which ſold better elſewhere, and enabled them to bring home the proceeds of ſuch ſales, which were of great value, from Spain and other parts; they therefore requeſted they might be permitted

*Acts of Navigation relaxed and diſpenſed with.*

(*a*) Chalm. Pol. An. 324.

mitted to continue this traffic. This request seemed so reasonable to the committee of privy council for the affairs of the plantations, that they ordered, on the 13th of Feb. 1661(*a*), the lord treasurer to authorize the commissioners and officers of the customs to take bond only for returning the proceeds of commodities laden in New-England, and not to bind them up to return the goods in specie, notwithstanding the clause in the Act of Navigation; and letters were to be written to the governors of that plantation to the like effect.

In this proceeding we may remark two instances of impropriety: in the first place, the custom-house officers seem to have had no right to require such a bond, as is here complained of; the clause in the Act of Navigation about plantation bonds applying only to the articles *enumerated* in the preceding section: in the next place, by permitting, as was here done, the bond to be taken for bringing the proceeds only of *all* goods there laden, instead of confining it to boards and the articles particularly mentioned by the merchants, the whole colony-system was at once broken; for after this, not only the New-Englanders might send

(*a*) Connc. Regist.

the

the enumerated commodities (if they produced any) to any part of Europe, but the other plantations might by law fend them to New-England, and the New-Englanders might, by virtue of this order, fend them to any part of Europe. In point of fact, it became a great caufe of complaint, that the Weft-India iflands did carry on, through New-England, this fort of traffic; either tempted to it by this fpecial licence, or trufting to the fuperior courage and fkill of the New-Englanders in the contraband trade. It does not appear how long the abovementioned order continued in force.

The articles meant by the Act of Navigation to be confined to the market of England, were all productions of the fouthern colonies; but the lumber trade was left open, and fo it continued till it was confined by a ftatute of *Geo.* 1. as will be fhewn hereafter. We have juft feen, that the lumber trade of Virginia continued to be hampered with the fame bonds as low down as 1671. Perhaps the principal produce of that colony being the enumerated article of tobacco (which, too, was fo great an object of revenue), was a reafon for not imparting to that plantation a fimilar indulgence even in the

article

article of lumber, left it might be made a cover to a contraband trade in the other article; but we are still at a loss to account for such bonds being insisted upon, without any authority from the act on which they were supposed to be founded.

THE advantages of a lucrative trade were judged sufficient reasons for relaxing the colony-system. On the 2d April 1685 (*a*), a circular letter was sent to the governors in the plantations, enjoining them not to permit foreign vessels belonging to strangers, or not made free, to trade there; but out of this proscription were excepted ships employed by Spaniards, and coming to Jamaica or Barbadoes to buy negroes; and these were to be treated civilly, and encouraged: such ships were also to be permitted to bring money, or goods the produce of the Spanish dominions in America.

BUT where such commercial advantages did not offer, the system was preserved with jealous attention. In the year 1686 the Irish government applied to obtain a dispensation from stat. 22. & 23. *Car.* 2. in

(*a*) Counc. Regist.

order

order that the Irish might once more be let
into the plantation-trade. This was discussed
at the committee of council for trade, and
the commissioners of the customs were heard
upon it; but it was resolved, that it would
be highly disadvantageous to this country,
to consent to any such measure. The customs
paid here on the import of tobacco, and on its
export to Ireland, and the dependence and
correspondence which was kept up between
the commissioners of the customs here, and
the governors abroad, which would be broken and incomplete, if this alteration were
to be made, were prevailing reasons with
the committee in coming to this determination (a).

The plantation-trade was again brought
under consideration of parliament in the
reign of king William; when, having in
view the Act of Navigation, and the acts
just mentioned, namely, stat. 15. Car. 2.
c. 7. stat. 22. & 23. Car. 2. c. 26. and stat.
25. Car. 2. c. 7. they thought proper to
make further improvement in the mode of
carrying it on. This was by stat. 7. & 8.
Will. 3. c. 22. intituled, *An Act for Preventing Frauds, and Regulating Abuses in the*

(a) Journ. Comm. for Trade.

*Plantation Trade*; the greater part of which act relates to the plantation-trade, the remainder to the regiſtering of ſhips.

This act ſets out by confining that privilege to ſhips of the *built* of England or Ireland, which before was allowed to ſhips *owned* in England or Ireland, or *built and owned* in the plantations. No goods or merchandize are to be imported into or exported out of any colony or plantation to his majeſty in Aſia, Africa, or America, belonging, or in his poſſeſſion, or laden in or carried from any port or place in the ſaid colonies or plantations, to any other port or place in the ſame, the kingdom of England, Wales, or town of Berwick, in any ſhip or bottom but what is the built of England, Ireland, or the ſaid colonies or plantations, and wholly owned by the people thereof, or any of them, and navigated with the maſter and three fourths of the mariners of the ſaid places only, under pain of forfeiting the ſhip and goods, one third to the king, another third to the governor of ſuch colony or plantation, and the other to the informer. An exception is made in favour of prize ſhips condemned in England, Ireland, or the colonies or plantations, which muſt be navigated

navigated by the master and three fourths of the mariners English, or of the plantations, and whereof the property doth belong to Englishmen. There was another exception, which was to last only for three years, in favour of foreign-built ships' employed by the commissioners of the navy, or upon contract with them, in bringing only masts, timber, and other naval stores, for the king's service, from the colonies to this kingdom, to be navigated in the manner before mentioned: and for such purposes prize and foreign-built ships might be respectively employed (*a*).

FURTHER, it begun to be noticed, that the oath required in the Act of Navigation to be taken by governors, was only for the due execution and observance *of the clauses therein before mentioned*; so that they were not strictly obliged by that oath to see the subsequent clauses of that act carried into execution, much less the different regulations that had been made by subsequent acts: this act therefore requires, that all governors shall, before their entrance into their government, take a solemn oath to do their utmost, that all the clauses, matters, and

(*a*) Sect. 1, 2, 3.

things contained in the before-mentioned acts, and then in force relating to the colonies, and all the clauses in the present act, should be punctually and *bona fide* observed. This oath is to be taken before such persons as the king shall appoint to administer it; and on complaint and proof before the king, or such as shall be by him appointed, on the oath of two or more credible witnesses, that a governor has neglected to take such oath, or has been wittingly or willingly negligent in doing his duty accordingly, he is to be removed from his government, and forfeit £1000. (*a*)

VARIOUS other regulations were made for better guarding against fraud in the detail of import and export to and from the colonies, which we may content ourselves with stating shortly.

THE officer appointed by the governors in the colonies, under the authority of stat. 15. *Car.* 2. c. 7. (*b*) was commonly known there by the name of *the naval officer*. By the connivance of persons in this situation many frauds were committed. These persons are now required to give security to the

(*a*) Sect. 4.   (*b*) Sect. 5.

commissioners

### SHIPPING AND NAVIGATION.

commissioners of the customs for the true
and faithful performance of their duty; and
until they so did, the governor is to be an-
swerable for any of their neglects or misde-
meanors (*a*). All the rules with respect to
entering, lading, and discharging, laid
down by stat. 13. & 14. *Car.* 2. c. 11. for this
kingdom, are to take place in the plantations. Officers are to have the same powers for visiting and searching ships, taking
entries, seizing and securing; and all
wharfingers, owners of keys and wharfs,
lightermen, bargemen, watermen, porters,
and other persons assisting in conveying,
concealing, or rescuing goods, are made
liable to the same penalties. Officers are to
have the like assistance, and to be liable to
the same penalties for corruption, connivance,
or concealment (*b*).

To explain a misconception of the meaning of the duty laid by stat. 25. *Car.* 2. c. 7.
on commodities carried from one plantation
to another, which the colonists (ever ea-
ger to catch a pretence for freeing themselves from the restraint of the Navigation
Act) had construed to amount to a permission to carry such goods to any foreign

(*a*) Sect. 5.   (*b*) Sect. 6.

market

market in Europe, it was declared, that such commodities should not be laid on board, till such security was given, as is required by stat. 12. *Car.* 2. c. 18. and stat. 22. & 23. *Car.* 2. c. 26. to carry them to England, or some of his majesty's plantations; and so *toties quoties*, under the penalty mentioned in those acts (*a*): which was in effect no more than a declaration of that, which the law-officers had pronounced to be the construction of the act (*b*).

It further declares, that all laws, byelaws, usages, or customs, in practice in the plantations, contrary or in anywise repugnant to any law made, or to be made, relating to, and mentioning the plantations, shall be null and void (*c*).

To prevent obtruding false and counterfeit certificates, whether of having given security to bring home ladings of plantation goods, or of having discharged such ladings in this kingdom, and also cocquets and certificates of having taken in ladings of European goods in England; the governors and custom-house officers, having reasonable suspicion, may require sufficient security for

(*a*) Sect. 8.      (*b*) Sir Wm. Jones's Opinion.
(*c*) Sect. 9.

discharging

discharging the plantation lading in England, and may suspend the vacating of the security there given, till they are informed from England, that the matter of the certificate is true: and a penalty of £500. is imposed on any person counterfeiting, rasing, or falsifying any cocquet, certificate, return, or permit (*a*). Bonds taken in the plantations according to the directions of stat. 22. & 23. *Car.* 2. c. 26. are to have sufficient sureties named therein of known residence and ability in the plantations; and the condition is to be, for producing within eighteen months the certificate of having landed the goods (*b*).

THE commissioners of the treasury are authorised to appoint officers of the customs in the plantations, as often as to them shall seem needful. Upon juries in causes of unlawful importation or exportation, there shall be none but natives of England or Ireland, or persons born in the plantations; a corrective of so little force, that they were at length obliged to institute courts of admiralty (*c*). All places of trust in the courts of law, or in what relates to the treasury of the islands, are to be in the hands of na-

(*a*) Sect. 10.  (*b*) Sect. 13.  (*c*) Sect. 11.

tive-

tive-born subjects of England, or Ireland, or of the said islands (*a*). Persons having right to property in any islands, or tracts of land in America, by charter, or letters patent, shall not alien, or dispose of the same, other than to natural-born subjects of England, Wales, or the town of Berwick, without the licence of his majesty, signified by an order in council, first had. And better to secure the execution of the Acts of Navigation, which had been particularly lax in the proprietary governments, all governors nominated by persons having a right to make such nominations are to be approved by his majesty, and shall take the oaths enjoined by this and any other act to be taken by governors or commanders in chief in the plantations, before entering upon their governments, under the penalties in such case provided (*b*).

Thus far with respect to the plantations, and the regulating of the trade while in those parts. When it arrived in Europe, it was left on the provisions of former laws; except only, that the enumerated commodities having, sometimes, been landed in Scotland and Ireland, in consequence of real or

(*a*) Sect. 12.  (*b*) Sect. 16.

pretended

SHIPPING AND NAVIGATION. 89

pretended ſtreſs of weather, it was thought
proper to declare, that ſuch commodities
ſhould, on no pretence whatſoever, be
landed in Scotland or Ireland (a); but that
in caſes where a ſhip was ſtranded by ſtreſs
of weather, or ſhould be driven by reaſon of
leakineſs, or other diſability, into any port
of Ireland, and not be able to proceed on
her voyage, in ſuch caſes only the merchandize might be permitted to be put on
ſhore, but ſhould be delivered into the cuſ-
tody of the collector of the cuſtoms, to remain there till they ſhould, at the charge
of the owner, be put on board ſome other
ſhip, to be carried to ſome port in England
or Wales, or to the town of Berwick; the
officer firſt taking good and ſufficient ſecu-
rity for the delivery of them according to
the directions of this act (b). No proviſion
of the like ſort was made as to Scotland.

PART II.
12. CAR. II. TO
A.D. 1783.
PLANTATION
TRADE.

Such are the regulations made by this
act; and upon the footing of this and the
preceding acts, the plantation-trade may be
ſaid to ſtand at this day; the variations that
were made therein by ſubſequent acts being
exceptions in a few caſes, and reſpecting cer-

(a) Sect. 14. (b) Sect. 15.

tain

tain articles of commerce that were particularly circumstanced, and not any substantial alteration of the system.

This act was followed up by an address from the house of lords to the throne, recommending a special instruction to be given to the governors, to attend more strictly to the observance of the plantation-laws; that where there was no governor of the king's appointment, the proprietors should enter into security for their deputy-governors duly obeying the king's instructions; and because in the colonies of Connecticut, Rhode Island, and in Providence Plantations, they annually chose their own governors, and those places had become receptacles for pirates, and for persons carrying on several illegal trades, recommending, that the king should take special care that the governors in those plantations should give security for observing such instructions as they should receive from the king. This address was taken into consideration at the board of trade, and measures were pursued for carrying it into effect (a).

(a) May 26, 1697.

WITH

WITH the same view of securing the execution of this and the other Acts of Trade and Navigation, the Government soon after proceeded to institute courts of admiralty, and to appoint persons to the office of attorney-general in those plantations, where such courts and such officers had never before been known; and from this time there seems to have been a more general obedience to the Acts of Trade and Navigation.

SOON after this a grand event took place in the plantation-trade: this was the letting-in the kingdom of Scotland to a participation in this, as well as in every other branch of English trade. By the fourth article of the Act of Union, stat. 5. *Ann.* c. 8. all the subjects of the united kingdom of Great Britain are to have full freedom and intercourse of trade and navigation to and from any port or place within the united kingdom, and the dominions and plantations thereunto belonging.

THE following are the small alterations which, from time to time, were made in the colony-system. By stat. 3. & 4. *Ann.* c. 5. rice and molasses, that had grown to be a considerable article of export to Europe, were

were put on the same footing as the articles enumerated in the Act of Navigation, and in stat. 25. *Car.* 2. c. 7. and were thenceforward to be brought to this kingdom under the like securities as in such case are required by the former acts (*a*). The same was done with copper ore by stat. 8. *Geo.* 1. c. 18. sect. 22.

*Navigation Act relaxed.*

On the other hand, in stat. 3. & 4. *Ann.* c. 8. the plantation-law was relaxed in favour of linens the manufacture of Ireland. These, as an European manufacture, could not since stat. 15. *Car.* 2. c. 7. be carried to the plantations but from England, Wales, or the town of Berwick; but by this act any native of England or Ireland may lade them in any port of Ireland, in English-built shipping, whereof the master and three-fourths of the mariners at least are English or Irish, and transport them to the plantations, and there freely traffic with them (*b*). But if any goods of woollen manufacture not laden in England (the necessary wearing-apparel of the commander and mariners excepted), or linen goods not laden in England, nor of the manufacture of Ireland,

*Irish Linen.*

(*a*) Sect. 12. (*b*) Sect. 1.

are found in the ship, the goods and ship are forfeited. Such ship is liable to be visited in the plantations in the same manner as ships from England *(a)*.

Again, the article of rice having become a great object of export in the province of Carolina, it was enacted, by stat. 3. *Geo.* 2. c. 28. that any subject of his majesty, in a ship built in Great Britain, or belonging to any of his majesty's subjects residing in Great Britain, and navigated according to law, clearing outwards in any port in Great Britain for the province of Carolina, might load rice in that province, and carry it directly to any port of Europe southward of *Cape Finisterre*; the master, before he cleared out from Great Britain, first taking a licence under the hands of the commissioners of the customs for that purpose, on the collector and comptroller certifying that bond was given not to carry certain other articles the growth, production, or manufacture of any British plantation, and that the ship should proceed directly with the rice to some port of Europe southward of *Cape Finisterre*, and there land the same *(b)*.

(*a*) Sect. 2, 3.   (*b*) Sect. 2.

THE liberty which had been given to export salt directly from Europe to New England and Newfoundland by stat. 15. *Car.* 2. c. 7. s. 7. was extended to Pennsylvania by stat. 13. *Geo.* 1. c. 5. and to New York by stat. 3. *Geo.* 2. c. 12. These importations were to be in British ships manned and navigated according to law. All the northern parts of America had originally been comprehended under the name of New England; but since new provinces and colonies had been formed with distinct names, these acts had become necessary. Again, by stat. 2. *Geo.* 3. c. 24. the same privilege was extended to the colony of Nova Scotia.

IN the next session of parliament, an opening was given to communicate to Ireland part of the *import* trade from the colonies. This was done by stat. 4. *Geo.* 2. c. 15. which recites, that certain enumerated goods could not by law be carried but to some other plantation, or to Great Britain; and that by stat. 7. & 8. *Will.* 3. c. 22. no goods of the produce of the plantations could be put on shore in Ireland, unless they had been first landed in England, Wales, or Berwick; which law had been construed to prohibit the import into that kingdom of goods *not* enu-

enumerated, to the great prejudice of the plantation-trade: and then it enacts, that goods of the plantations not enumerated may be landed in Ireland, notwithstanding the said act. By stat. 5. *Geo.* 2. c. 9. it was declared, this should give no permission to import hops from the plantations.

PART II.
12. CAR. II. TO
A. D 1783.
PLANTATION
TRADE.

As the lower part of South Carolina had been formed into a separate province by the name of Georgia, it was doubted, Whether the inhabitants thereof continued to enjoy the benefits of the statute permitting the carrying of rice directly to any part of Europe? To remove this doubt it was declared, by stat. 8. *Geo.* 2. c. 19. that they should have that privilege. By stat. 4. *Geo.* 3. c. 27. it was permitted also to carry rice from these colonies to any part of America southward of these colonies *(a)*. And by stat. 5. *Geo.* 3. c. 45. sect. 19. this privilege of carrying rice from any place in America to the southward of South Carolina and Georgia, was extended to the colony of North Carolina.

THE privilege which had been granted to these provinces in the article of rice, was thought

Sugar.

*(a)* Sect. 1.

thought to be merited by the West India islands with regard to sugars, their grand article of culture and of commerce. Accordingly, by stat. 12. *Geo.* 2. c. 30. a similar relaxation of the plantation-laws was made in their favour, in a reasonable expectation, says the preamble of the act, that the produce and exportation of this article would be thereby greatly increased, for the mutual benefit of this kingdom and the colonies. It is enacted, that any subject of his majesty, in any ship or vessel built in Great Britain, and navigated according to law, and belonging to any of his majesty's subjects, of which the major part shall be residing in Great Britain, and the residue either in Great Britain or in some of his majesty's sugar colonies in America (which property is to be verified on oath), that shall clear outwards in any port of Great Britain for any of the said colonies, may load there any sugar of the growth, produce, or manufacture of those colonies, and carry it from thence to any foreign part in Europe, provided a licence be first taken out for that purpose under the hands of the commissioners of the customs at London or Edinburgh.

THE act contains a long detail of regulations for preventing this liberty of trading being converted to any illicit purpose. The master is to enter into bond, conditioned, among other things, that the ship shall proceed from Great Britain to the sugar colonies, there deliver the licence to the collector, comptroller, and naval officer; and that, if he makes use of the liberty granted, no tobacco, molasses, ginger, cotton, wool, indigo, fustic, or other dyeing-wood, tar, pitch, turpentine, hemp, masts, yards, bowsprits, copper ore, beaver skins, or other furs, of the growth, production, or manufacture of any British plantation in America, be taken on board, unless for the necessary provisions of the voyage; and that when the ship has delivered her lading in Europe, she shall return to Great Britain within eight months after such delivery, and before she returns to any of the plantations (a). Ships so licensed are to touch at some port in Great Britain, or their licence becomes void; unless the master declares in writing in the colony, that the sugars he intends to load are to be carried to some port or place to the southward of *Cape Finisterre*; in which case

(a) Sect. 23.

he may proceed thither directly. These are the parts of the act that are sufficient to answer our present purpose, the rest being a series of custom-house detail for securing the execution of the act against fraud.

THIS permission was by stat. 15. *Geo.* 2. c. 33. sect. 5. extended to all ships *belonging* to Great Britain, and navigated according to law. But this privilege, which was represented at the time as promising great advantage to the colonies, and was sought by them with great earnestness, ended in disappointment. It appears that only one licence has been granted at the custom-house for this purpose, and that cargo, it is believed, was carried to Hamburgh. The merchants found that the mother-country was the best market for sugar, and they no longer desired any other.

BY stat. 7. & 8. *Will.* 3. c. 22. the time of eighteen months was limited in the condition of plantation bonds for producing a certificate of having landed and discharged the goods therein mentioned. This regarded only such bonds as were taken in the

### SHIPPING AND NAVIGATION.

the plantations. It was enacted, by stat. 15. *Geo.* 2. c. 31. that in plantation bonds taken in England, with respect to goods to be landed in Great Britain, there shall be a condition to produce a certificate within eighteen months from the date thereof. This was not to extend to bonds given for ships lading rice at Carolina or Georgia, to be carried to Europe to the south of *Cape Finisterre,* pursuant to stat. 3. *Geo.* 2. c. 28.; nor for ships lading sugars in his majesty's sugar colonies, to be carried directly to any foreign part of Europe, except Ireland, pursuant to stat. 12. *Geo.* 2. c. 30 *(a).*

PART II.
12. CAR. II. TO A. D. 1783.
PLANTATION TRADE.

AFTER the peace of 1763, the plantations in America, which had been the cause and the great stake in the war, naturally drew the attention of parliament. By stat. 4. *Geo.* 3. c. 15. many regulations were made for better ordering the plantation-trade, as well with regard to duties as to the import and export, which comes within the scope of our enquiry.

ONE of the grievances in the American trade was, that great quantities of foreign

American Act. Stat. 4. Geo. 3. and 5. Geo. 3.

*(a)* Sect. 4.

molasses and syrups were clandestinely run on shore in the British colonies. To prevent this, it was ordained, that bond should be given in the like penalty as that respecting enumerated goods required by stat. 12. *Car.* 2. c. 18. at any port of the British American colonies or plantations, with one surety, besides the master of the ship taking on board goods not particularly enumerated in any of the foregoing acts, being the product or manufacture of the said colonies or plantations; with condition, that if any molasses or syrups, the produce of any plantations not under the dominion of his majesty, shall be laden on board, the same shall be brought without fraud or wilful diminution by that ship to some of his majesty's colonies or plantations in America, or to some port in Great Britain, and that the master on his arrival shall make a just and true report of all the goods laden on board. All goods laden on board before such bond given, are to be forfeited, together with the ship (*a*). The master is also to take from the officer of the customs a certificate

(*a*) Sect. 23.

of

of having given such bond, to be delivered
by him at the port where he discharges his
lading *(a)*.

THE next regulation was to add certain articles to those enumerated by former acts, and required to be brought only to the mother-country. Thus coffee, pimento, cocoa-nuts, whale-fins, raw silk, hides and skins, pot and pearl ashes, of the growth, production, or manufacture of any British colony or plantation in America, are to be imported directly from thence into this kingdom, or some other British colony or plantation, under the like securities and penalties as those provided by stat. 12. *Car.* 2. c. 18. and stat. 25. *Car.* 2. c. 7. *(b)*.

AGAIN, no iron, nor any sort of wood, commonly called lumber, as specified in stat. 8. *Geo.* 1. c. 12. *(c)* the growth, production, or manufacture of any British colony or plantation in America, shall be loaden before bond given, with one surety, in double the value of the goods, that such goods shall not be landed in any other part of Europe except Great Britain *(d)*.

(*a*) Sect. 24.   (*b*) Sect. 27.   (*c*) *Vide* Sect. 2.
(*d*) Sect. 28.

PART II.
12 CAR. II. TO
A. D. 1783.
PLANTATION
TRADE.

It was found that British vessels, arriving from foreign parts at the out-ports of this kingdom, fully or in part laden abroad with goods that were pretended to be destined to some foreign plantation, frequently took on board some small parcels of goods which were entered outwards, and a cocquet and clearance were thereupon granted for such goods; but under cover of such clearance the whole cargoes were landed in the British American dominions, contrary to the laws in force. To prevent this practice it was enacted, that no vessel should clear outwards for any of the dominions belonging to his majesty in America, unless the whole and entire cargo was, *bonâ fide*, and without fraud, laden and shipped in this kingdom *(a)*.

An exception was made in favour of such articles as were permitted by former acts to be carried without landing in Great Britain; namely, salt laden in Europe for the fisheries in New England, Newfoundland, Pennsylvania, New York, and Nova Scotia, or any other place to which salt was al-

*(a)* Sect. 30.

lowed

lowed by law to be carried; wines laden in
the Madeiras of the growth thereof; and
wines of the growth of the western isles, or
Azores, and laden there; and horses, victuals, or linen cloth, of and from Ireland *(a)*.

MANY provisions were made in this act to prevent illicit trade with the American colonies. Amongst others, it was thought adviseable, for better securing the due execution of stat. 12. *Car.* 2. c. 18. and stat. 7. & 8. *Will.* 3. to subject vessels to seizure that were found hovering within two leagues of the shore, in a similar manner as had been ordained by stat. 9. *Geo.* 2. c. 35. and other acts respecting the coasts of this kingdom, and of Ireland *(b)*.

THE provision made respecting iron and lumber in this act, was altered in the next sessions. By stat. 5. *Geo.* 3. c. 45. such iron may be carried to Ireland, and such lumber may be carried to the Madeiras, or the western isles, called the Azores, or to any part of Europe southward of *Cape Finisterre*, upon bond being given that they shall be

(*a*) Sect. 31.    (*b*) Sect. 33.

landed there, and not in any other part of Europe, except Great Britain, to be discharged, on producing certificates of their being so landed (*a*).

In order to stop the illicit trade carried on through the Isle of Man, it was provided by stat. 5. *Geo.* 3. c. 39. that no rum or other spirits should be shipped in any British plantation in America, but on condition that they should not be landed in the Isle of Man, under the like securities and penalties as those provided in stat. 12. *Car.* 2. c. 18. and stat. 25. *Car.* 2. c. 7 (*b*).

Another regulation about plantation bonds was made by stat. 6. *Geo.* 3. c. 52. in order more effectually to prevent the enumerated goods being privately carried from the colonies into foreign parts of Europe, in vessels that clear out with non-enumerated goods, as well as to prevent the clandestine importation of foreign European goods into the colonies. Bond is to be given in the colonies, with one surety besides the master of the ship that shall take on board non-enumerated goods, with condition, that such

(*a*) Sect. 12.   (*b*) Sect. 5.

goods shall not be landed at any part of
Europe to the northward of *Cape Finisterre*,
except in Great Britain, and to produce a
certificate of landing goods in Great Britain
within eighteen months, and in any British
colony in America within six months, under
the hands and seals of the collector and
comptroller, or other principal officer of the
customs; and in any other place where the
same may be legally landed, the like certificate, within twelve months, under the common seal of the chief magistrate, or under
the hands and seals of two known British
merchants residing there. The bond may
also be discharged on proof, upon oath,
that the goods were taken by enemies, or
perished in the sea. If any non-enumerated
goods are laden on board without such bond
first given, the goods and ship are forfeited.
These provisions are not to extend to vessels
*bona fide* bound to some of the ports of Spain
within the Bay of Biscay *(a)*.

IT was soon found, that the condition of
this bond not to land such non-enumerated
goods in any part of Europe to the north of
Cape Finisterre, except in Great Britain,
would throw Ireland out of the import trade

(*a*) Sect. 30, 31.

that

PART II.
12. CAR. II TO
A. D. 1753.
PLANTATION
TRADE.

that had been given by stat. 4. *Geo.* 2. c. 15. It was therefore enacted by stat. 7. *Geo.* 3. c. 2. that such bonds might be discharged by the certificate of the principal officer of the customs at any port in Ireland, testifying the landing of such goods there, in the same manner as if they had been landed in Great Britain.

A CONTRABAND trade of a very lucrative kind had always been carried on in the West-Indies between the Spanish and English colonists. This was contrary to the laws of both nations; but, as far as it related to ourselves, it had been connived at; and we have seen, in Charles II.'s reign, that the governors were, by an order in council, expressly directed to permit Spanish ships to come with particular articles of commerce (*a*).

IT was now resolved to legitimate this clandestine traffic, and to put it upon a footing of law, under certain regulations. The best way of carrying this into execution seemed to be, by opening particular ports for the free importation and exportation of certain specified articles; and this led to the *Free-Port Act*, stat. 6. *Geo.* 3. c. 49. By this act live cattle, and all manner of goods and

Free Ports established.

(*a*) Vid. ant. p. 80.

commodities

commodities whatfoever (except tobacco), the growth or produce of any colony or plantation in America, not under the dominion of his majefty, might be imported into the ports of Prince Rupert's Bay, and Rofeau in the ifland of *Dominica*, and (except fugars, coffee, pimento, ginger, molaffes, and tobacco) into the ports of Kingfton, Savannah la Mar, Montego Bay, and Santa Lucia, in the ifland of *Jamaica*, from any foreign colony or plantation in America, in any foreign floop, fchooner, or other veffel, not having more than one deck *(a)*. The act contained feveral provifions concerning the import and export of various articles, all calculated to guard this anomalous trade from being made a means of infringing the reft of the plantation-fyftem, and injuring the revenue. This act was temporary, but was continued by ftat. 14. *Geo.* 3. c. 41. and afterwards, by ftat. 21. *Geo.* 3. c. 29. it was continued fo far only as related to the free ports in Jamaica, thofe of Dominica being intended to be fhut. Upon this footing remained the free ports till the ftat. 27. *Geo.* 3. was paffed, which repealed this act, and made other regulations that contain

*(a)* Sect. 1, 2.

the

the whole of the present law on that subject.

THE fishery carried on from Guernsey and Jersey to Newfoundland contributed to make a sort of direct commerce between those islands and the American plantations, which was contrary to stat. 15. *Car.* 2. but which it was thought proper now to authorize in certain particulars. For this purpose it was enacted by stat. 9. *Geo.* 3. c. 28. that any sort of craft, cloathing, or other goods, the growth or manufacture of Great Britain, or of those islands, and food or victuals being the growth or produce of Great Britain, Ireland, or those islands, may be transported from those islands to Newfoundland, or any other British colony where the fishery is carried on, the same being necessary for the fishery, or the mariners, or persons employed therein, notwithstanding stat. 15. *Car.* 2. c. 7. Such articles are to be properly certificated *(a)*.

AGAIN, it was enacted, that any non-enumerated goods (except rum) may be

(*a*) Sect. 1, 2.

landed

landed in Guernsey or Jersey; which with regard to rum is a new law, but with regard to the other non-enumerated articles is only declaratory. It provides, that stat. 6. *Geo.* 3. c. 52. as far as it relates to the bond and security for landing goods, shall extend to Guernsey and Jersey, and that such bonds may be discharged by certificate under the hands and seals of the magistrates of the royal courts of Jersey or Guernsey, and the principal officer of the customs *(a)*.

THE last alteration made in the plantation-trade during this period was the measure of opening it, in a very extensive manner, to the people of Ireland, by allowing, contrary to stat. 15. *Car.* 2. the export of certain goods from thence directly to the British plantations in America, and the settlements belonging to Great Britain on the coast of Africa. This was by stat. 18. *Geo.* 3. c. 55. which ordains, that it shall be lawful to export from the kingdom of Ireland, directly, into any of the British plantations in America or the West-Indies, or into any of the settlements belonging to Great Britain on the coast of Africa, in ships or vessels that

*The export trade from Ireland.*

*(a)* Sect. 3.

may lawfully trade to and from those places, any goods, wares, and merchandize, being the produce or manufacture of Ireland (wool and woollen manufacture, in all its branches, mixed or unmixed, cotton manufactures of all sorts, mixed or unmixed, hats, glass, hops, gunpowder, and coals, only excepted), and also all goods and commodities of the growth, produce, or manufacture of Great Britain, which have been, or which may be, legally imported from thence into the kingdom of Ireland, woollen manufacture in all its branches and glass excepted *(a)*. Proper custom-house provisions are made, by requiring certificates and invoices to ascertain the exportation to be conformable to the act *(b)*.

This permission was not to allow the export from Ireland of foreign linens, whether they were white or brown, or painted, stained, or dyed, in Ireland *(c)*; nor to allow the export of bar-iron, slit-iron, rolled, plated, or tinned, nor of any sort of manufactured iron-wares, until a duty of 2l. 10s. *per* ton on such bar-iron, of 3l. 3s. 11d. Irish *per* ton on such slit, rolled,

(*a*) Sect. 1.   (*b*) Sect. 2.   (*c*) Sect. 3.

plated,

### SHIPPING AND NAVIGATION.

plated, or tinned iron, and manufactured iron-wares exported from Ireland to such colonies or plantations and settlements, should be imposed by some act of parliament to be made in Ireland *(a)*; nor to allow the export of such iron, or iron-wares, during the continuance of any bounty or premium granted in Ireland on such exportation *(b)*. No cotton manufactures, mixed or unmixed, are to be exported from Ireland to the plantations or settlements, unless the exporter produce a certificate from the custom-house of some port in Great Britain, particularizing the quantities, kinds, and marks thereof, and specifying that they have been legally exported from Great Britain, under pain of forfeiting the same *(c)*.

In addition to the restriction on iron and iron-wares, another of a general nature was made, to guard all British manufactures from being undersold, and to preserve the competition between the two countries with some sort of equality. The liberty given by this act to export goods and merchandize the manufacture of Ireland is not to take place, but in cases where they stand charge-

*(a)* Sect. 4.    *(b)* Sect. 5.    *(c)* Sect. 6.

able,

## HISTORY OF THE LAW OF

*PART II. CAR. II. TO A. D. 1783. PLANTATION TRADE.*

able, and pay duties and taxes to as great an amount, as goods and merchandize of the same denomination and quality exported from Great Britain to the same places *now* (that is, at the time of passing the act) stand chargeable with; whether such charges be on the importation of the materials of which the goods and merchandize are made, or by duties on their exportation, or by inland excise not drawn back, or compensated for by bounties (*a*).

*Import and export trade granted more fully.*

But the share of export in the colony trade given by this, in addition to former acts, did not satisfy the Irish; they pressed for still further privileges, and claimed a right to enjoy the like unlimited intercourse as Great Britain, both in import and export. This was accordingly granted them by stat. 20. *Geo.* 3. c. 10. By this act, any goods, wares, or merchandize, of the growth, product, or manufacture, of the British colonies or plantations in America or the West Indies, or of any of the settlements belonging to Great Britain on the coast of Africa, and which by any act of parliament are required to be imported from thence into

(*a*) Sect. 7.

Great

Great Britain; and also all other goods which, having been in any way legally imported into such colonies, plantations, or settlements, may be legally exported from thence to Great Britain; may be laden in, and exported from, such colonies, plantations, or settlements, and imported from thence into Ireland.

So far the *import* trade was granted; the act then goes on to grant the *export* trade. Any goods or commodities of the growth, product, or manufacture, of the East Indies, or other places beyond the Cape of Good Hope, which are now required by any act of parliament to be shipped or laden in Great Britain, to be carried directly from thence to any British colony or plantation in Africa or America, as also any other goods, wares, or merchandize, which now, or hereafter, may be legally shipped or laden in Great Britain, to be carried directly from thence, and imported into any colony or plantation in America or the West Indies, or any British settlement on the coast of Africa, may be exported directly from Ireland, and imported into such colonies, plantations, or settlements; and the regulations of the following statutes were not to stand in the

PART II.
12. CAR. II TO
A. D. 1783.
PLANTATION
TRADE.

way of this new arrangement, namely, stat. 12. *Car.* 2. c. 18.; stat. 22. & 23. *Car.* 2. c. 26.; stat. 15. *Car.* 2. c. 7.; stat. 4. *Geo.* 3. c. 15.; stat. 7. *Geo.* 1. c. 21.; all which, directly or indirectly, prevented the Irish participating in this trade (a).

BUT this general privilege to import and export was still granted upon certain terms; which were, to preserve an equality in the colony trade of the two countries. It was to commence and to have continuance only in such cases, where the goods imported and exported were liable, by some act or acts to be passed in Ireland, to equal duties and draw-backs, and were made subject to the same securities, regulations, and restrictions, as in Great Britain; and in the consideration of such equal duties and draw-backs due attention is to be given to, and allowance made for, any duty or imposition, or the part of it which shall be retained in Great Britain, or not drawn back, or not compensated by bounty in Great Britain, upon the export of any such goods, wares, or merchandize, from thence to Ireland; as also for any duty paid on the importation

(a) Sect. 1.

of

of them into Ireland, so as they be not exported from Ireland with less incumbrance of duties or impositions, than shall remain on them when legally exported from Great Britain (*a*); and, with a view to changes that might hereafter be made, if any alteration is made in Great Britain in such duties or draw backs, when the Irish parliament is not sitting, the import and export is to continue in the old state for four calendar months after the meeting of the next session of the Irish parliament. If the Irish parliament shall be sitting at the time, then it is to continue for four calendar months from the time the alteration shall be made, in case the Irish parliament shall so long sit; and in case it shall be prorogued or dissolved, then for four calendar months after the meeting of the next following session (*b*).

However, the restrictions of this act were to have no influence to restrain any liberty given to import from, or export to, the colonies, by stat. 18. *Geo.* 3. c. 55. or any other act of parliament (*c*).

The scheme of trade thus offered to Ireland was carried into execution by the parliament

(*a*) Sect. 2.  (*b*) Sect. 5.  (*c*) Sect. 6.

parliament of that kingdom, which paffed an act impofing duties on the import, conformably with thofe in Great Britain. But the equalizing the duties with reference to the draw-backs allowed in Great Britain, in order to the export of European goods, was an affair of nice calculation, which the parliament thought it neceffary to delegate to the officers of the cuftoms. The parliament was content with laying down this general rule for the government of the officers in completing their calculations, namely, That European goods fhould draw back fo much of the duties paid on importation as fhould leave the remainder equal to the duties retained in Great Britain on goods of the like quality and quantity ; and if the duties were equal, then that no draw-back fhould be allowed ; and if not equal, they fhould pay on export as much as would make them equal. Having laid down the principle of trade, as held out by the Britifh act, they directed the commiffioners of the revenue to form fchedules of the drawbacks and duties conformably thereto, which were to be figned by four of them at leaft ; and from that day fuch drawbacks and duties were to become the law of export to the colonies (a).

(a) Annual Irifh Act for Duties.

THE

THE performance of this agreement on the part of Ireland was left in this state; which, for a national transaction, seems to be somewhat uncertain. For where is the jurisdiction, or what is the mode, for trying the question, Whether the Irish have entitled themselves, under this or the preceding statute, to the import or export trade with the colonies in any particular article? Can a seizure be made, and can a court examine and compare, and calculate the duties and drawbacks in the British and Irish statute-books?

ON the occasion of the corn act, stat. 31. *Geo.* 3. where an offer of an advantageous corn trade was held out to the Irish, on the condition of their passing a law with certain provisions, a better mode was prescribed for securing the exact performance of the condition on their part. For the trade there offered was not to take place, till it was notified in the London Gazette, that such a law, with all proper provisions, was passed by the Irish parliament. So that the executive government had an opportunity first to satisfy itself, whether the act passed in Ireland was such as the British parliament required; and if it was not, no notification would

PART II.
12. CAR II. TO
A D. 1783.
PLANTATION
TRADE.

would be made, and the trade would not commence till a proper act was passed. It does not seem, that such negotiations and treaties between the parliaments of the two kingdoms can well be conducted to a prosperous issue, without the intervention of such a mediating authority, which is always upon the watch for the common protection of both. It has happened, that, on similar occasions, the contracting party, which makes the grant, has recognized the performance of the condition by the grantee, and ratified it by a public acceptance, signified in an act of the Legislature. Thus, the proposal in stat. 26. *Geo.* 3. c. 60. to allow to Irish ships the privileges of British ships, as soon as similar regulations were made on that head by the Irish parliament, was plainly carried into effect by the parliament declaring next session, in stat. 27. *Geo.* 3. c. 19. that such regulations had passed into a law in Ireland, and that Irish ships were accordingly entitled to the privileges proposed; but, surely, as long as conditional regulations, like the present, are left as these are, there is something unfinished and uncertain in the transaction; and it is not easy to say, what is actually the state of the law between the two kingdoms.

WE

WE cannot close this period of our planta-
tion-history without noticing the measures
taken by parliament for chastising the rebellious colonies, by first *restraining* their trade,
and then wholly *prohibiting* it.

14. CAR. II. TO
A. D. 1783.
PLANTATION
TRADE.

THE first of these measures was stat. 14.
*Geo.* 3. c. 19. which discontinued the landing and shipping of goods at the town and
harbour of Boston. A power was thereby
lodged in his majesty, upon the restoration
of peace, and obedience to the laws, and
upon satisfaction being made to the East-
India Company for the teas that had been
destroyed, to open the port of Boston, and
limit the extent of it, as he should judge
expedient.

The Restrain-
ing and Pro-
hibitory Acts.

BUT that time did not arrive; for, instead
of peace, and obedience to the laws, the
combinations and disorders there increased,
and the parliament thought it necessary to
pass stat. 15. *Geo.* 3. c. 10. for *restraining* the
trade and commerce of the provinces of
Massachusetts Bay, and New-Hampshire;
and the colonies of Connecticut and Rhode-
Island, and Providence Plantation; by which
act no goods enumerated in stat. 12. *Car.* 2.
c. 18. or any other act, being the growth,
product,

product, or manufacture of those places, which were to be brought to some other British colony, or Great-Britain, nor any such enumerated goods as should have been brought into those places, nor any other goods whatsoever, the growth, product, or manufacture of those places, should be transported or carried from thence to any land, island, territory, dominion, port, or place whatsoever, other than to Great-Britain, or some of the British islands in the West-Indies (*a*); and no wine, salt, or any goods whatsoever (except horses, victual, and linen cloth, the produce and manufacture of Ireland imported directly from thence), were to be imported into those places, unless such goods were *bona fide* shipped in Great-Britain, and carried directly from thence (*b*). But this was not to hinder the importation into those places from the British islands in the West Indies of such goods, the produce or manufacture thereof, as might by law be imported from thence (*c*). The act also *prohibited* absolutely ships belonging to those places from going to the fisheries in those parts, as we shall see in its proper place.

(*a*) Sect. 1.   (*b*) Sect. 4.   (*c*) Sect. 5.

By

By stat. 15. *Geo.* 3. c. 18. the same restraint was put on the trade of the colonies of New-Jersey, Pennsylvania, Maryland, Virginia, and South-Carolina. There was the same prohibition of goods to be carried to those colonies, and the same proviso respecting imports from the West-Indies. No goods were to be carried from the counties of Newcastle, Sussex, and Kent on Delaware, to any other place, but to Great-Britain or Ireland, or the British West-Indies, till oath was made that the goods were the product or manufacture of those counties (*a*); which was intended for preventing the trade of New-Jersey, Pennsylvania, and Virginia, being carried on through those counties.

The following year was passed stat. 16. *Geo.* 3. c. 5. for *prohibiting* all trade and intercourse with the provinces and colonies that had been put under *restraint* by the two former acts, and adding to them the three lower counties on Delaware, and the colonies of North-Carolina and Georgia, which were all pronounced to be in a state of rebellion. The act ordains, that all trade and

(*a*) Sect. 7.

commerce with those places should be prohibited, and all ships and vessels belonging to the inhabitants thereof, together with their cargoes, and all other ships and vessels whatsoever, together with their cargoes, which should be found trading, or going to trade, or coming from trading in any port or place of those colonies, should be forfeited, as if they were ships and effects of open enemies (*a*). In all these acts powers were given to the king to suspend their execution, as soon as any of the colonies should return to obedience. By this act the three former acts, namely, stat. 14. *Geo.* 3. c. 29. stat. 15. *Geo.* 3. c. 10. & c. 18. were repealed, as become unnecessary after the passing of this act.

For carrying on the war against the colonies the lords of the admiralty were empowered by stat. 17. *Geo.* 3. c. 7. to grant commissions to private ships, to make prize of all vessels trading contrary to the provisions of stat. 16. *Geo.* 3. before mentioned, so that the whole of the laws now subsisting against the American trade and intercourse were stat. 16. *Geo.* 3. c. 5. and stat. 17. *Geo.* 3. c. 7.

(*a*) Sect. 1.

HAVING

SHIPPING AND NAVIGATION.

PART II.
15. CAR. II. TO
A. D 1783.
PLANTATION
TRADE.

HAVING gone through the statutes made within this period for regulating the plantation-trade, we come now, according to the plan before laid down, to consider such matter as has been furnished by the decisions of courts, or the opinions of lawyers, for ascertaining the meaning of these laws, or enforcing their execution. But the materials of this sort are very scanty. There are no decisions of courts, and the opinions that are preserved go only to one single point, namely, What is, or what is not such a *foreign possession*, as is properly an object of the different regulations made by these laws?

*What a Colony or Plantation?*

THUS it became a question, Whether Newfoundland was a colony or plantation? A ship, being a French prize, but not legally condemned, was owned and manned by English, and had imported fish and oil from Newfoundland; but by stat. 7. & 8. *Will.* 3. no importation can be made from any colony or plantation except in an English-*built* ship. This importation was thought by *Sir Thomas Trevor* to be against that statute, inasmuch as the ship was not condemned in some court of admiralty; but *Sir John Hawles*, in an opinion he gave on the same point, was

*Newfoundland.*

more

more explicit. He says, he should have thought Newfoundland was neither a colony nor a plantation belonging to his majesty, having no settled governor there, nor the king pretending to any dominion therein, as he could be informed of; but since stat. 15. *Car.* 2. c. 7. and 25. *Car.* 2. c. 7. reckoned Newfoundland among his majesty's plantations, he thought this ship being a prize, tho' not legally condemned, and having been trading between England and Newfoundland, was forfeited by stat. 7. & 8. *Will.* 3. c. 22 *(a).* Whatever doubt there might then have been of the king's sovereignty in that island, there could be none after the treaty of Utrecht, by which the king of Great-Britain was acknowledged to have the dominion and sovereignty of that island. From that time it unquestionably *belonged* to his majesty, and there could be no doubt but respecting the description of possessions under which it should be classed; and a notion long prevailed, that this island, being used merely for the fishery, was not a colony or plantation. Yet this question was never raised but it was answered, that this island was to all intents a colony and plantation.

*(a)* 24th of January, 1698.

THUS when beaver-skins, which are required by stat. 8. *Geo.* 1. c. 15. s. 24. if the produce of a British *plantation*, to be brought directly to this kingdom, were carried from Newfoundland round by Gibraltar, they were held by Mr. *Willes* to be forfeited (a); which could not be, if they had not been the produce of a British *plantation*, as well as carried round by Gibraltar.

AGAIN, when it was in agitation, in 1764, to establish a custom-house in Newfoundland, it was made a question, Whether it was a colony, or plantation, or a mere fishery? But it was held by the board of trade to be a colony, and plantation; and conformably with that opinion the duties of customs were ordered to be received there, under the authority of stat. 4. *Geo.* 3. c. 15. which imposes duties on goods imported into the *colonies* and *plantations* in America. These opinions were certainly right; for although that place has lately been regarded only as a fishery, and the policy of the government has long been to prevent planting and colonization there, yet the original design was to plant that island, as well as Virginia, or any other part

(a) 29th of May 1736.

PART II.
12. CAR. II. TO
A. D. 1783.
PLANTATION
TRADE.

of America: and after that policy was changed, yet the first charters having been granted as well to *planters* as to merchants adventurers, the interest of the planters has been considered more or less, in all the regulations concerning that island; and the term Planter and Plantation is known there, as well as in any part of America, or the West-Indies.

SOME doubts concerning the descriptions of *colony*, or *plantation*, have been coupled with another doubt; namely, Whether the colony, or plantation, if it were one, was a territory which belonged to his majesty? These points were discussed in the cases of *Honduras*, and of *Surat*.

Honduras.

IT was material to ascertain, Whether *Honduras* was a plantation to his majesty *belonging*, or in his possession? for it had become a practice for ships to fit out from Jersey, to fetch logwood from thence, and carry it directly to France, Holland, and other parts of Europe; which, being an enumerated commodity, could not be done from a plantation to his majesty belonging, consistently with the 18th section of the Act of Navigation. This question was put

to

to the law-officers after the treaty of peace in 1763; in the 17th article of which the king had agreed to cause all the fortifications erected there by British subjects to be demolished: but the king of Spain agreed, that the British subjects, or their workmen, should not be disturbed or molested in their occupation of cutting logwood; for which purpose they were permitted to build and occupy houses and magazines necessary for their families and effects. But, notwithstanding these stipulations in favour of British settlers, *Mr. De Grey* (a) was of opinion, that the Bay of Honduras could *not* be considered as a plantation or territory *belonging* to his majesty, within the meaning of the Act of Navigation, but that it was a part of the Spanish territories, subject to such rights and liberties therein as are stipulated for by treaty; and that there is no law subsisting to prevent an English subject, intitled to such rights and liberties, from carrying logwood, cut there, to any part of Europe.

Upon a late question, Whether *Surat* was a plantation or colony within the meaning

(a) 19 November 1768.

of stat. 7. & 8. *Will.* 3. so as to entitle a ship there built to have a plantation-register? it was enquired, what was the nature of the possession which the East-India Company had there. And it being represented, that *Surat* was a port belonging to the Mogul, where several European nations have settlements, and that the English chief, by an instrument from Delhy, is governor of the Mogul's castle, and admiral of his fleet there, but that all merchants indiscriminately build ships there, it appeared to the law-officers, upon this statement of facts, that this ship was not intitled to a register.

But it being apprehended this was not an accurate state of the case, further enquiry was directed; and it appeared, upon information of persons acquainted with the Company's affairs, that they have a settlement at *Surat*, which is governed by a chief and council, who are subordinate to the governor and council of Bombay; and, as the crown by charter has reserved the sovereignty in all settlements acquired, or made by the Company, it was conceived the settlement at Surat is under his majesty's dominion. But whether the king has a sovereignty, depends on the fact of the Company having a territorial

rial property in Surat. And with regard to that point, it appears from their charters, that *Surat*, as to the territorial right of the Company, was always confidered in the fame light with Bombay itfelf, which is denominated *the town and factory of Bombay*. By the charter of juftice, of the 26th year of George II. all civil, criminal, and military power is given to the Company, as well in the fubordinate factories, of which *Surat* is one, as in the ifland of Bombay itfelf. The indenture of 22d July 1702 conveys the *dead ftock* of the Old Company to be held by the New; and, enumerating what fhall be fo confidered, after Bombay, it fays, "Under "the prefidency of the faid ifland of Bom-"bay, the factories of Surat." It was alfo certified, by an officer of the Company whofe knowledge and fituation were judged to intitle him to credit, that the Company deem the territory of all forts and factories, where they have a prefident and council, as their *property*; and this is the cafe at Surat; that the territory round the whole city of Surat is nominally held by the Company as governors for the Mogul, but that this grant was made after the Company had poffeffed themfelves of it by force. Upon this ftatement of facts it was judged by

* K the

the law-officers, that this was such a plantation or colony as entitled the ship built there to a register (*a*).

A very particular question respecting the king's sovereignty and possession arose on the occasion of the island of Guadaloupe being taken from the French in 1759. It was doubted, Whether this island was to be considered as *a plantation or territory to his majesty* BELONGING, *or* IN HIS POSSESSION, within the meaning of the Act of Navigation, and other laws relating to duties on merchandize imported from thence? But the law-officers of the crown at that time gave their opinion that it was; and they alledged such reasons for their opinion as are well deserving our consideration.

The attorney-general (*b*) said, that notwithstanding the advantageous terms granted to the inhabitants, they were disarmed, and in a state of subjection to his majesty's troops. All new commissions were to be taken under his majesty, and all acts of justice were to run in his name. He was in actual possession of all the public revenues; and all the trade of

(*a*) 20 September 1785.   (*b*) Mr. Pratt.

the island had changed its course, passing now in English bottoms only to Great Britain. All this being considered, he thought himself obliged to conclude, that this island was now a plantation belonging to his majesty, and in his possession, in right of the crown of England; and that it was an English and British plantation within the meaning and intent of the Acts of Navigation.

THE great objection to this opinion arose from the condition of the *then* inhabitants, who enjoyed privileges under the articles of capitulation hardly compatible with the state of subjects. But that objection, in his mind, had no great weight, if it was considered, that these were personal privileges, and were confined only to the present inhabitants, who were restrained from alienating to any but the king's subjects; and the capitulation was made not with the French king, but only with the inhabitants.

THE right of sovereignty, therefore, was wholly changed, and the whole island was the king's acquisition by conquest. If any inhabitant should die without heir, his lands would escheat to the king; if any of them should levy war, or plot the king's death, they

they would be guilty of high-treason; and, to illustrate this further, if the inhabitants should agree to sell all their possessions to Englishmen, the island, without any further treaty or capitulation, would become wholly English. The inhabitants plainly understood themselves transferred to his majesty's dominion, and therefore had stipulated for the like privileges in trade as were allowed to the rest of his majesty's subjects; and this was granted, with a proviso, that they complied with the Acts of Trade. In a word, the condition of subjects might be better or worse in different parts, but here the question was about the sovereignty, and it had nothing to do with the privileges which his majesty had been pleased to grant the natives (*a*).

THE solicitor general (*b*) observed, that the Act of Navigation, and the subsequent acts, referred not only to the plantations and territories belonging to, or in the possession of the crown at that time, but to future acquisitions; and he thought the practice that had been observed with regard to St. Christopher's on a former occasion to be in point. That island had been taken possession

(*a*) 7 August 1759.   (*b*) Mr. Yorke.

of by the French and English jointly, in the year 1626. About the year 1688 the French drove the English entirely off the island. In the year 1690, or thereabouts, the English recovered the island, and had entire possession of it, till it was at length ceded to Great Britain by the treaty of Utrecht. It appeared by the custom-house books, that sugars imported from thence into Great Britain, after the year 1690, and before the treaty of Utrecht, had paid the same duty as sugars from the British plantations, without distinguishing between the ancient French and English divisions of the island *(a)*.

THE European goods that were on the island of Guadaloupe at the time it was taken were deemed, by *Sir Fletcher Norton (b)*, not to be such as could be imported from thence into any of the British Islands in the West-Indies, as they had not been shipped and laden in Great Britain; and therefore such importation would have been directly against stat. 15. *Car.* 2. c. 7.

THOUGH these cases throw some light on this subject, there are still difficulties remaining, which deserve consideration.

(*a*) 13 August 1759.   (*b*) 2 February 1764.

THE foreign poffeffions of this country, in Afia, Africa, and America, have not always been denominated in the fame manner in the foregoing acts. Thus, in the Act of Navigation, fect. 1. they are fpoken of as *lands, iflands, plantations,* or *territories*; in fect. 18. the enumerated goods are not to be carried but to fome other Englifh *plantation*. In ftat. 13. & 14. *Car.* 2. c 11. fect. 6. fhips muft be built in the king's *dominions* in Afia, Africa, or America; and perfons of the king's *plantations* are declared to be Englifh, within the meaning of the Act of Navigation. In ftat. 7. & 8. *Will.* 3. c. 22. the terms ufed are moftly *colonies and plantations*; and fometimes *plantation* only. This act recites, that the governors of the *colonies or plantations* were, by ftat. 12. *Car.* 2. c. 18. obliged to take an oath; whereas in the act it is the governors of *lands, iflands, plantations,* or *territories,* without any mention of *colonies.* This act of William III. is intituled, *For Preventing Frauds, and Regulating Abufes in the* Plantation Trade.

WHEN different expreffions are ufed in the fame act of parliament, it cannot be believed but that different things are meant. Thus in that claufe of the Act of Navigation which was

was intended for confining to the mother-country the trade of our foreign poffeffions, the parliament made ufe of the term *plantation* only, and dropped the terms *lands, iflands, and territories*, which had been ufed in other parts of the act. It fhould feem as if the parliament looked upon *plantations*, and upon fuch as were *lands, iflands, and territories*, in a different light; and that the former owing their origin, advancement, and fupport, to the money and men which paffed from this country, it was fair to require, that the benefit which refulted from the application of thofe means fhould return to, and center in, the parent-ftate: but as to other lands, or iflands, or territories, though belonging to the king, if they had not derived from this country that fort of creation, cultivation, and foftering, which would make them *plantations*, there did not exift the fame claim to oblige them to fend their produce to this kingdom. Whatever may have been the reafoning that governed in making the diftinction, the diftinction is certainly made; and, no doubt, made with fome defign, and is not to be afcribed to any inaccuracy in wording.

PART II.
12. CAR. II TO
A.D. 1783.
PLANTATION
TRADE.

But if the king possesses *lands, islands, and territories*, in Asia, Africa, and America, which are not *plantations*, there grows a material difference in what we have all along been calling the plantation-trade; for it will be found, that many restrictions are laid only upon what are called *plantations*; and such dominions as do not come under that denomination are clearly exempted from those restrictions. Thus the whole of stat. 7. & 8. *Will.* 3. is applicable only to *plantations*, or at least to *colonies*; which, as far as concerns the present question, may be considered as the same thing. The prohibition, therefore, in that statute, which forbids any but British-*built* ships trading to the colonies or plantations, does not reach those lands, islands, territories, or whatever other dominions of the king, that, in construction of law, may happen not to be deemed colonies or plantations; all which may still be traded to, by ships British-*owned*, under the first clause of the Act of Navigation.

When we see this result from the foregoing reasoning, we are anxious to discover, how it will operate with regard to the British concerns in Asia, Africa, and America. In glancing over the settlements on the coast

coast of Africa, the settlements of the East-India Company in India, the China trade, Nootka-Sound, and many other places, we see lands and territories under very different circumstances, and dependent upon political considerations of infinite variety; respecting some of which it must be exceedingly difficult to determine, whether they are within stat. 7. & 8. *Will.* 3. as *colonies or plantations*; or indeed, which is a further doubt, whether they are within any part of the Act of Navigation, as lands, islands, or territories, to his majesty *belonging*, or *in his possession*. These are questions of great importance to the navigation-system, and deserve a serious attention.

As to the terms *colony* and *plantation*, whatever distinction may, at one time, have been made between them, there seems now to be none at all. The word *plantation* first came into use. The plantation of Ulster, of Virginia, of Maryland, and other places, all implied the same idea of introducing, instituting, and establishing, where everything was desert before. *Colony* did not come much into use till the reign of Charles II. and it seems to have denoted the
sort

sort of political relation in which such plantations stood to this kingdom. Thus, the different parts of New-England were, in a great measure, voluntary societies, planted without the direction or participation of the English government; so that in the time of Charles II. there were not wanting persons who pretended to doubt of their constitutional dependence upon the crown of England; and it was recommended, in order to put an end to such doubts, that the king should appoint governors, and *so make them colonies.* A colony, therefore, might be considered as a plantation when it had a governor and civil establishment subordinate to the mother-country. All the plantations in America, except those of New-England, had such an establishment; and they were, upon that idea, colonies as well as plantations. Those terms seem, accordingly, to be used without distinction in the statute 7. & 8. *Will.* 3. and in those made afterwards.

CHAPTER

## CHAPTER II.

### THE TRADE WITH ASIA, AFRICA, AND AMERICA.

*To be carried on in English Shipping—and directly with those Countries—Exceptions thereto—Persian Goods through Russia—Coarse Calicoes—The East India Company—South Sea Company—Hudson's Bay Company—African Company—Fourth Section of the Navigation Act—What is a Manufacturing—Of direct Importation—Of the usual Ports for first Shipping—Of returned Goods.*

THE trade with Asia, Africa, and America, was restricted by the Act of Navigation to ships *belonging* to the king's dominions. No goods or commodities whatever of the growth, production, or manufacture of Africa, Asia, or America, or of any part thereof, or which are described or laid down in the usual maps or cards of those places, shall be imported into England, Ireland, or Wales, the islands of Guernsey,

Guernsey, Jersey, or town of Berwick-upon-Tweed, in any other ship or vessel whatsoever, but in such as do truly and without fraud belong to the people of England or Ireland, the dominion of Wales, or town of Berwick-upon-Tweed, or of the lands, islands, plantations, or territories in Asia, Africa, or America, to his majesty belonging, as the proprietors and right owners thereof, and whereof the master and three-fourths at least of the mariners are English, on pain of forfeiting the goods and ship; one moiety to the king, the other to the party seizing and suing for the same (a).

This section is followed by one which is an appendage to the first and third sections, and applies both to the trade of Asia, Africa, and America in general, and also to that which we have called the plantation-trade. It had been provided by those two clauses, that the trade of those places should be carried on in English shipping:— by the following provision it was meant that it should be carried on *directly* with the very countries where the articles of commerce

(a) Sect. 3.

### SHIPPING AND NAVIGATION.

merce were produced. Thus no goods or commodities that are of *foreign* growth, production, or manufacture, and which are to be brought into England, Ireland, Wales, the islands of Guernsey and Jersey, or town of Berwick-upon-Tweed, in English-built shipping, or other shipping belonging to some of the aforesaid places (namely, the trade with the plantations mentioned in sect. 1. and that with Asia, Africa, and America, mentioned in sect. 3.), and navigated by English mariners as aforesaid, shall be shipped or brought from any other place or country, but only from those of the said growth, production, or manufacture, or from those ports where the said goods and commodities can only, or are, or usually have been first shipped for transportation, and from none other places or countries, under penalty of forfeiting the goods and ship, with all her guns, furniture, ammunition, tackle, and apparel; one moiety to the king, the other to the informer (*a*).

To this regulation concerning the usual ports, it was thought necessary to subjoin

(*a*) Sect. 4.

provisoes in favour of certain particular trades, as had been done in the former act. Nothing in this act was to restrain the importation of any commodities of the Streights or Levant seas, loaden in English-built shipping, and whereof the master and three-fourths of the mariners at least were English, from the usual ports *(a)* or places for lading them theretofore within the Streights or Levant seas, though the commodities were not of the very growth of those places *(b)*; nor the importing of East India commodities in English-built shipping, and whereof the master and three-fourths of the mariners at least are English, from the usual places of lading them in any parts of those seas to the southward and eastward of the Cape of Good Hope, although such ports be not the very places of their growth *(c)*. And it is lawful for any of the people of England, Ireland, Wales, the islands of Guernsey or Jersey, or town of Berwick-upon-Tweed, in vessels or ships to them belonging, and whereof the master and three-fourths of the

---

*(a)* Trieste, Venice, Genoa, and Leghorn, are now considered as ports which, by *usage*, are intitled to this privilege for the export of Asiatic goods from the Levant.
*(b)* Sect. 12.   *(c)* Sect. 13.

mariners at least are English, to bring in from any of the ports of Spain or Portugal, or Western Islands commonly called Azores, or Madeira or Canary islands, all sorts of goods or commodities of the growth, production, or manufacture of the plantations or dominions of either of them respectively (a); which permission was, by a subsequent statute (b), extended to cases where the property in the goods imported belonged to aliens.

SUCH are the rules laid down by the Act of Navigation for the government of the trade to Asia, Africa, and America: it was to be carried on in English shipping, and directly with the places where the articles imported were produced or manufactured; so that English shipping could not even bring those articles from any of the commercial countries in Europe, or any of the plantations belonging to these countries. This, like the former part of the act, was principally levelled at the carrying-trade of the Dutch; and it effectually prevented any ports of the United Provinces being the emporium for this kingdom of goods im-

*(a)* Sect. 14.   *(b)* Stat. 17. Geo. 3. c. 36.

ported

PART II.
12. CAR. II. TO
A. D. 1785.
TRADE WITH
ASIA,
AFRICA, AND
AMERICA.

ported from Asia, Africa, or America. It had the same effect upon Denmark, Hamburgh, and other places, where any portion of this circuitous traffic was to be found.

The principle laid down in the Act of Navigation for carrying on the trade with Asia, Africa, and America, has been ever since preserved entire. Occasions have happened, where it was thought wise even to make the restriction closer. The throwing of raw silk being a great employment in this country, and much Asiatic silk being thrown in Italy, and then imported hither as a *manufacture* of that country, instead of a product of Asia imported in English shipping, as it must be if brought hither in a raw state, it was ordained, as the act expresses it, " for better supporting the art " of throwing silk in this realm, and the " poor employed therein, and that useful " and national trade into Turkey," by stat. 2. *Will. & Mary*, st. 1. c. 9. that the throwing of silk should not be construed to be a manufacture within the Act of Navigation; and so thrown silk should not be capable of being imported from Italy, as a manufacture of that country: and further, that

that no thrown filk of the growth or production of Turkey, Perfia, the East Indies, or China, or of any other country or place (except that of the growth or production of Italy, Sicily, or the kingdom of Naples, and which shall be imported in such ships, and fo navigated, as directed by the Act of Navigation, and brought from some of the ports of thofe countries or places whereof it is the growth or production, and shall come directly by fea, and not otherwife), shall be imported into England, Wales, Guernfey, Jerfey, or the town of Berwick, on pain of forfeiting fuch thrown filk *(a)*.

PART II.
12. CAR. II. TO A. D. 1785.
TRADE WITH ASIA, AFRICA, AND AMERICA.

Notwithstanding this difpofition to fupport the principle of the Act of Navigation, exceptions begun to be made in favour of fome articles of commerce which it was thought fhould be procured at any rate, or which were no great objects in the light of navigation. Thus by ftat. 7. *Ann.* c. 8. it was permitted to import from any of the British plantations in America, Jefuits bark, farfaparilla, balfam of Peru and Tolu, and all other drugs of the growth and product of America, in fhips regularly manned and

Exceptions thereto.

*(a)* Sect. 2.

navigated, on paying the same duty, and no more, as if they were imported *directly* from the place of their growth; which operated as a repeal of the clause in the Book of Rates, allowing to drugs (a) imported directly from the place of their growth an easement of two-thirds of the duty; and in that light, though a regulation of duty, it may be considered as assisting the policy of the Act of Navigation. This regulation had the effect of encouraging the trade between our Islands and the Spanish settlements, where such drugs are produced.

AGAIN, by stat. 6. *Geo.* I. c. 14. the proviso in the 12th section of the Act of Navigation was repealed as to the importation of raw silk and mohair yarn of the product or manufacture of Asia, except only as to the ports or places in the Streights or Levant seas which are within the dominions of the Grand Seignior. We are told, that the woollen manufacture in France had greatly increased, and was now a considerable article of export into Turkey; in return for which, raw silk and other com-

(a) Except Jesuits bark, the duty on which was the same, whether it came *directly* or not.

modi-

modities were brought to Marseilles, and other ports of France, and quantities of it thence imported into Italy, and so brought to Great Britain; by which means we were assisting in facilitating the French woollen trade in prejudice to our own: it was therefore meant that raw silk and mohair of Asia should be brought only from the Turkish dominions, and not from Italy, as it might have been under the proviso referred to in the Act of Navigation (*a*). To obtain articles so necessary for our manufactures as cochineal and indigo at a cheap rate, those two commodities were allowed for a certain time to be imported from any port or place, duty free, in British or other ships in amity with this country, by stat. 13. *Geo.* 1. c. 15. and stat. 7. *Geo.* 2. c. 18. which acts have been further continued, and are now in force.

A NEW course of trade had brought the silks and other commodities of Persia through the Russian dominions; and as none of the Russian ports could be said to be the

---

(*a*) Observe the misrecital of *or other shipping*, in the preamble of this statute. Also, place of *the* growth instead of *their* growth; and *parts* instead of *ports*.

*Persian Goods through Russia.*

ports for shipping those articles, in the meaning of the fourth clause of the Act of Navigation, it was thought proper to make a special provision for authorising this sort of importation. This was done by stat. 14. Geo. 2. c. 36. which permits any person being of the Russia Company, exclusive of all others, to import into this kingdom in British-built shipping, navigated according to law, from any port or place belonging to the Czar or emperor of Russia, raw silk, or any other goods or commodities, of the growth, produce, or manufacture of Persia (provided such manufacture be made of articles the growth or produce of Persia), being purchased by barter with woollen or other manufactures, goods, or commodities, exported from Great Britain to Russia, and from thence carried into Persia (gold and silver in coin or bullion excepted), or with the produce arising from the sale of such manufactures, goods, or commodities.

On another occasion, when the price of gum senega had much risen, and the import was not adequate to the great demand made for it in the printing of silks, linens, and callicoes, permission was given by stat. 25. Geo. 2.

25. Geo. 2. c. 32. to all his majesty's subjects to import into this kingdom *gum senega* in British-built ships, navigated according to law, from any port or place in Europe.

PART II.
12 CAR. II. TO A. D. 1783. TRADE WITH ASIA, AFRICA, AND AMERICA.

AGAIN, when the East India Company did not make sufficient importations of coarse printed calicoes, cowries, arangoes, and certain other East India manufactures prohibited to be worn in this kingdom, but which were necessary for the African trade, permission was given by stat. 5. Geo. 3. c. 30. for the Company to import those articles in British ships, navigated according to law, from any part of Europe not within his majesty's dominions, in such quantities as they should think necessary for the African trade (*a*).

Coarse Calicoes.

AGAIN, by stat. 5. Geo. 3. c. 52. f. 20. any sort of cotton-wool may be imported in British-built ships from any country or place, duty free; and in the same manner goat-skins, raw or undressed, by stat. 15. Geo. 3. c. 35. f. 1, 2. which was a temporary act, but has been continued, and is now in force.

(*a*) Sect. 1.

PART II.
11. CAR. II. TO
A. D. 1783.
TRADE WITH
ASIA,
AFRICA, AND
AMERICA.

AMONG the regulations made by parliament in the trade with Asia, Africa, and America, during this period, may be reckoned the sanction given to some chartered Companies, which thereby acquired an exclusive right to trade with certain parts of these three quarters of the world. It is not here meant to give any-thing like a history of *the East-India Company, the South-Sea Company,* or *the African Company,* but merely to state such parliamentary provisions as give and secure to those Companies their trade, and define its limits.

Of the East India Company.

THE first statute in which the rights of the East-India Company were adjusted is stat. 9. & 10. *Will.* 3. c. 44. and the trade is there assigned to be into and from the East-Indies, in the countries and parts of Asia and Africa, and into and from the islands and ports, havens, cities, creeks, towns, and places of Asia, Africa, and America, or any of them beyond the Cape of *Bona Esperanza* to the Streights of Magellan, where any trade or traffic of merchandize is or may be used or had (*a*). These places are not to be visited, frequented, or haunted

(*a*) Sect. 61.

by

by any other of his majesty's subjects, under penalty of forfeiting the ship and cargo, and all the proceeds thereof *(a)*. Persons trading to the East-Indies are first to give security for causing all goods laden on their account in India to be brought, without breaking bulk, to some port of England or Wales, and there to be unladen and put on land *(b)*.

THE penalty herein imposed was found not adequate to prevent the offence. Persons used to go in foreign ships, and bring back goods to foreign ports in Europe; foreign commissions and passes grew very commonly in use for this purpose, and the Company as well as the general trade and shipping of the country suffered much from the interloping traders. It was intended by stat. 5. *Geo.* 1. c. 21. to stop this mischief, by giving stronger powers for restraining it. Thus, the Company may arrest all such persons, being subjects of his majesty, and send them to England *(c)*. Again, a penalty of £.500. is imposed on all persons procuring, soliciting, or acting under any commission, authority, or pass, from

(*a*) Sect. 81.   (*b*) Sect. 69.   (*c*) Sect. 2.

any foreign power, to sail, go or trade in or to the East-Indies (*a*), or within the beforementioned limits.

By a subsequent act, namely, stat. 7. Geo. 1. st. 1. c. 21. no commodity of the growth, product, or manufacture of the East-Indies, or other places beyond the Cape of Good Hope, contained in the patents of the East-India Company, can be imported or carried into the kingdom of Ireland, the islands of Jersey, Guernsey, Alderney, Sark, or Man, or into any lands, islands, plantation, colony, territory, or place to his majesty belonging, in Africa or America, but such only as shall be *bona fide* and without fraud shipped in Great-Britain, in ships navigated according to law, under pain of forfeiting the ship and cargo (*b*). A doubt having arisen, whether ships belonging to the East-India Company could strictly be considered as British ships, considering how many foreigners were proprietors of the Company's stock, this doubt was removed by stat. 21. Geo. 3. c. 65. f. 33.

(*a*) Sect. 3.   (*b*) Sect. 9.

THE trade of great part of America was
exclusively granted to *the South-Sea Company*
by stat. 9. *Ann.* c. 22. in the following manner: They were to have the sole trade and
traffic into, unto, and from all kingdoms,
lands, countries, territories, islands, cities,
towns, ports, havens, creeks, and places,
of America, on the east side thereof, from
the River *Aranoco* to the southernmost part
of *Terra del Fuego*; and on the west side
thereof, from the southernmost part of
*Terra del Fuego* through the South Seas to the
northernmost part of America; and into,
unto, and from all countries, islands, and
places, within the said limits, which were
reputed to belong to the crown of Spain, or
which should thereafter be found out or discovered within those limits, not exceeding
three hundred leagues from the continent of
America, between the southernmost part of
*Terra del Fuego*, and the northernmost part
of America, on the west side thereof, (except the kingdom of Brazil, and such other
places on the east-side of America as were
then in the actual possession of the crown of
Portugal, and the country of Surinam,
in possession of the States-General of the
United Provinces); as it was declared by
the act, not to be the intention to make any
grant

PART II.
13. CAR. II. TO
A. D. 1783.
TRADE WITH
ASIA,
AFRICA, AND
AMERICA.

South Sea
Company.

grant of the trade to the Portuguese or Dutch settlements, which was still to remain open *(a)*; but other persons visiting, frequenting, trading, or trafficking, within the limits granted to the Company, are to forfeit ship and cargo *(b)*.

It was however provided, that the Company should not sail beyond the southernmost part of *Terra del Fuego*, except only through the Streights of Magellan, or round *Terra del Fuego*, nor go from thence into any part of the East-Indies, nor return to Great-Britain, or any other place in Europe, Asia, Africa, or America, by any other way, except through the Streights of Magellan, or by *Terra del Fuego*; nor were the Company to trade, traffick, or adventure in any goods of the growth, product, or manufacture, of the East-Indies, Persia, China, or any other places within the limits granted to the East-India Company; nor to send any ship within the South-Seas, from *Terra del Fuego* to the northernmost part of America, above three hundred leagues to the westward of and distant from the shores of Chili, Peru, Mexico, California, or any other shores of North or

*(a)* Sect. 46.   *(b)* Sect. 49.

South

South America contained between *Terra del Fuego* and the northernmost part of America, on pain of forfeiting the ship and cargo (*a*).

An exclusive trade to another part of America was granted in 1670 by Charles II. *to the Governor and Company of Adventurers of England trading into Hudson's Bay.* They were to have the sole trade and commerce of and to all the seas, bays, streights, creeks, lakes, rivers, and sounds, in whatsoever latitude, that lie within the entrance of the streight commonly called Hudson's Streights, together with all the lands, countries, and territories, upon the coasts of such seas, bays, and streights, which were then possessed by any English subjects, or the subjects of any other Christian State, together with the fishing of all sorts of fish, of whales, sturgeon, and all other royal fish, together with the royalty of the sea. But this extensive Charter has not received any parliamentary confirmation or sanction.

In the ninth year of king William, the trade to a great portion of Africa was in

(*a*) Sect. 58.

PART II.
22. CAR. II. TO
A. D. 1763.
TRADE WITH
ASIA,
AFRICA, AND
AMERICA.

African Company.

the hands of the *Royal African Company*, which, under a Charter from Charles II. enjoyed an exclusive trade from the port of Sallee, in South Barbary, to the Cape of Good Hope, both inclusive, with all the islands near adjoining to those coasts. A new arrangement of this trade was made by stat. 9. & 10. *Will*. 3. c. 26. by which the trade was opened between *Cape Mount* and the *Cape of Good Hope* to all the king's subjects trading from England and the plantations in America, upon paying a duty of ten per cent. *ad valorem* on all goods exported; and between *Cape Blanco* and *Cape Mount*, upon paying the like ten per cent. *ad valorem*, together with an additional ten per cent. *ad valorem* on all goods and merchandize imported into England or the plantations from the Coast between *Cape Blanco* and *Cape Mount*; with this exception, that redwood was to pay five per cent. and negroes nothing at all. This act was to continue in force for thirteen years; and not being renewed, the whole trade reverted again to the exclusive claim of the Company.

THE African trade was put upon a new footing by stat. 23. *Geo*. 2. c. 31. which made it lawful for all the king's subjects freely to trade

trade between the port of Sallee, in South Barbary, and the Cape of Good Hope. Thus was the trade taken out of the hands of the Royal African Company. The act then goes on to provide, that all persons trading to that Coast between *Cape Blanco* and the Cape of Good Hope should be a body corporate, by the name of *the Company of Merchants trading to Africa*; the admission to which Company was made very easy, namely, by the payment only of forty shillings. The trade between the port of Sallee and *Cape Blanco* was left open to all persons whatsoever. By stat. 25. Geo. 2. c. 40. all the forts, castles, and factories, on the Coast, from the port of Sallee to the Cape of Good Hope, belonging to the Old Company, were transferred to and vested in the New Company, for the like purpose of protecting and facilitating the trade. By stat. 4. Geo. 3. c. 20. the fort of *Senegal*, lately ceded by France to Great-Britain, was in like manner vested in the New Company.

In the following year a new policy was attempted. By stat. 5. Geo. 3. c. 44. the stat. 4. Geo. 3. c. 20. concerning the fort of Senegal, was repealed; and the Company were divested of all forts, settlements, and factories,

factories, from the port of Sallee as far south as *Cape Rouge* inclusive, and the same were vested in his majesty. The trade to the territory so vested in his majesty was declared to be open to all the king's subjects, and to be liable to no regulation but such as his majesty should think proper to make for the better government thereof.

The trades carried on by the *Russia* and *Turkey Companies* comprehend some of the products of Asia, and have on that account a connection with the fourth section of the Act of Navigation; but these Companies being, in their primary object, designed for an European trade, will more properly be classed in the following division.

We come now to consider the determinations of courts, and the opinions of lawyers upon this branch of trade: but the former of these two sources of information is as deficient as in the plantation-trade; the latter will afford us some information.

The trade with Asia, Africa, and America, depends upon the third and fourth sections of the Act of Navigation; but since the fourth section applies to the first, as well as the third section, and is therefore an appendage to the plantation-trade, as well as to the present,

SHIPPING AND NAVIGATION. 159

it may be proper, in the first place, to consider that; and then go on to such points as arise on the third section, or on the third and fourth sections equally.

*Part II. 12. Car. II. to A. D. 1783. Trade with Asia, Africa, and America.*

THE wording of the fourth section of the Act of Navigation is so general, that it was supposed by many to include ALL *foreign goods or commodities* whatsoever, and not to be confined, as it is now understood, to the goods and commodities of Asia, Africa, and America. It is true, this misconception does not appear to have prevailed with the courts, at least in any case which has come down to us; but it seems to have been so construed by the law-officers for some time, and still longer by the officers of the customs. The following are examples of the progress made in ascertaining the true meaning of this clause.

*Fourth section of the Navigation Act.*

IN 20. *Car.* 2. an information was filed for importing Malaga wine in a ship not English, nor English-navigated. It was objected, for the defendant, that this section of the act, though general, was yet confined to the products of Asia, Africa, and America; for it related to the sections that went before. The chief baron *Hale* is made by the

PART II.
33. CAR. II. TO
A. D. 1783.
TRADE WITH
ASIA,
AFRICA, AND
AMERICA.

the Reporter to say, that the subsequent sections might include Europe in some particular cases, *but not in the case now before us (a)*; plainly intimating, that this section did not apply to the European trade, and that the clauses which did apply to the European trade did not make this case a cause of forfeiture.

MORE than twelve years after this, we find a case stated for the opinion of the law-officers, which shews, that the officers of the customs still considered this section as affecting the European trade. Some hemp was imported from Holland in an English ship, legally owned and navigated: but Holland was not the place of its growth; nor was it of the growth of Russia or Muscovy, but of Germany; neither was it any of the articles which are prohibited by the Act of Frauds, stat. 13. & 14. *Car.* 2. from being imported from the Netherlands and Germany. It was answered, by *Sir Robert Sawyer*, that this hemp, being none of the particulars prohibited by the Act of Frauds to be brought from Holland, might be brought from thence in English shipping,

(a) Hardres, 487.

and

and was not within the clause in the Act of Navigation, which prohibits goods being imported from any other place than that of their growth ; by which he must have meant the fourth section.

On the same occasion *Mr. Warde* says, that he had considered both the Act of Navigation and Act of Frauds, and also an adjudged case in the exchequer, upon a special verdict in the time of the lord chief baron *Hale* (a) ; and that he conceived hemp of the growth of Europe, but not of Russia, or Muscovy, or the territories of that emperor, might be brought from Holland in English shipping duly navigated, though Holland was not the place of its growth, nor the port where it could only, or usually had been, first shipped for transportation ; for he thought that clause in the Act of Navigation extended not to the goods in question, which were European goods; and hemp is not one of the particulars prohibited in the Act of Frauds from being imported from the Netherlands and Germany (b). Again, where an English ship laden with currants

(a) Probably the case before cited from Hardress.
(b) 13 February 1781.

from *Zante* was taken prize, and carried into France, it was the opinion of *Mr. Somers* (a), that with respect only to the Act of Navigation, they might be brought from France in any English-built ship owned and manned by English.

But the officers of the customs seem still to have entertained doubts upon the extent of this section; for in the year 1702 there were stated for the opinion of *Sir Edward Northey* two instances of Spanish wine imported from Portugal. To both these he answered, that the fourth section of the Act of Navigation was confined to the sections which went before, and applied only to the goods of Asia, Africa, and America; and that the products of Spain might be brought from Portugal.

Some points of difficulty have arisen upon the words *growth, production, or manufacture*, used in the first, third, and fourth sections of the Act of Navigation. It has been made a question, Whether sugar of the French plantations being imported into France, and there refined, the molasses of those sugars could be imported into England as a manufacture

(a) 6 March 1692-3.

manufacture of France? and, as such, Whether they ceased to be subject to the prohibition, which they would be under while merely a production of America? When this point was put to the then attorney and solicitor general, *Mr. Warde* and *Sir T. Powys*, in 1687, it was considered by the former as a new question, well worthy of consideration; yet it seemed to him, that the importing of such molasses from France was against the true intent and meaning of the words of the Act of Navigation; for the separating of the sugars from the molasses in France, did not, in his conception, make the molasses to be such a *manufacture* of France (and no longer a commodity of the *growth* or *production* of America) as might be imported from France; for the molasses still remained, in his opinion, a foreign material, even if the separation had been in England; and so, he said, it had been adjudged in a case of *Bainbrig and Bate*, in the exchequer, upon a special verdict *(a)*.

THE latter observed, that it is a question of fact, rather than of law, what is properly a manufacture. This sugar was originally of the growth and production of America,

(*a*) *Quære*, Where is this case reported?

PART II.
12. CAR. II. TO
A. D. 1783.
TRADE WITH
ASIA,
AFRICA, AND
AMERICA.

and so was restrained, *primâ facie*, from being imported from any other place; and to make it a manufacture of France, the *onus probandi* lay upon the importer by the Act of Frauds, stat. 13. & 14. *Car.* 2. But it did not seem to him, how this could properly be called a manufacture, since the article was no way improved, or altered in its nature by art or labour, but remained the very same it was before, only that it was separated from the part refined.

THE same point being submitted to *Mr. Roger North*, he entered into it more at length, and suggested the following considerations, which he held to be such as would lead to develope and illustrate the present question. First, Goods of the growth of the Indies manufactured in France, might be brought from thence; as wrought silk, cabinets, and other articles. Secondly, If in the working of such manufactures there was a refuse or waste, although the labour of man went to the severing of it, and although it might have also some peculiar uses, yet that refuse or waste was not properly a manufacture, but retained the quality of the original material, and could not be imported, as the manufacture of the place

place where the separation was made. Of this sort was the waste of silk, the chips or shavings of wood, or the like. Thirdly, If a plain separation was made, without any manufacture at all, the case was more clear; as the garble or siftings of spice, though it had a new name, and peculiar uses, and was severed by men's labour, yet it was still, in the sense of the act, the *production* of the spice country, and not the *manufacture* of the place where it was sifted.

In the present case the question was, Whether a mixture of other materials, together with a long process of boiling, curing, and other labour and operations necessary for effecting such a separation, should make the refuse, waste, or dregs, to be a *manufacture* in the sense of this law, and not the goods of the original *production*? And he thought it did not, for the following reasons:

No sugar is refined for the sake of molasses, but the endeavour is, that all should turn into sugar, and no molasses at all be left; and since that cannot be, such are reserved for the uses of which they are capable, but which would be better supplied by clear sugar. Secondly, To clear the sugar from the dregs or molasses, there is a necessity of dissolving in water, boiling, potting, claying, and the like, because no industry can otherwise effect it; all which is done only for the sake of sugar, and as the means to separate that from the dregs or molasses contained in it. Thirdly, If molasses could be separated by hand-sieves, or the like, without all question the dregs or molasses would not be a manufacture of the place where this was performed; and since this could not be, and the process of refining is for the sake of the sugar only, it is to be considered as the manufacturing of *that*, and not of the dregs or refuse.

THE molasses, therefore, themselves were no manufacture, but only the waste, or refuse, or unmanufactured part of sugar, separated by, and consequential from, the operation of refining; and therefore not like the cases of several manufactures out of the same goods, as cordage and linen out of hemp, both which are distinct manufactures, originally designed, and distinctly made.

HE observed, that it was no objection that molasses are not sugars, nor rated as such, but by a distinct name; for merchandize may

may be varied in the denomination several ways, without being manufactured, as appears by the instances of garble, waste of silk, and others; and the word *manufacture* in this act is to be taken strictly, and in such manner as may best support the design of it, because it is a law beneficial to the public.

The discussion contained in this opinion would furnish a principle to guide the judgment, where the distinction turned upon there being or not being an actual and *bonâ fide* manufacturing into a new article. We see in the following case, that the painting and staining of linens was not considered as such a manufacturing. Calicoes imported from the East-Indies were exported to Holland, and the duty drawn back according to the Second Rule in the Book of Rates. During the time they were in Holland, they were painted or stained in imitation of the painted calicoes called chintz, and were then re-imported. *Mr. Trevor* was of opinion, they could not be re-imported by the Act of Navigation, notwithstanding the painting or staining them there.

But where the manufacturing has wholly changed the original articles, it should seem the new commodity so produced may as well be brought from the country where it is so manufactured, as from the place of its growth, or production. It has, at least, been so held in cases of duties; and the reason, as to this point of construction, seems the same upon a question of navigation.

Thus vermillion is a manufacture of quicksilver, made by a chemical process of calcining, levigating, and pulverizing, quicksilver and sulphur. It had been the practice of the custom-house to admit vermillion from Holland, being made there, at the low duty, as coming directly from *the place of its manufacture*, though quicksilver was the growth of the East-Indies, Hungary, Germany, and other places. But the commissioners of the customs thought proper to alter their practice, and, with that view, stated a case for the opinion of the attorney general, Mr. *Wallace (a)*; who was of opinion, that it having been the uninterrupted usage to admit the importation of vermillion from Holland on the low duty,

(a) 21 November 1780.

it was too late to dispute, with any probability of success, the demand of the higher duty. Upon that occasion an opinion of Sir *Dudley Ryder* was considered, who had recommended, that a usage to admit juniper-berries, the growth of Germany, to come from Holland on a low duty, as if that was *the place of their growth*, having been long acquiesced in, ought not to be altered. But although in this case the vermillion was admitted upon the argument of usage, it is probable this usage originated from the consideration beforementioned, of its being a completely manufactured article, retaining no outward trace of the original materials.

BUT such practices obtaining at the custom house with regard to duties, were held on another occasion, by Sir *Dudley Ryder (a)*, not to have any operation to do away the force of the Act of Navigation. And therefore, notwithstanding a practice of the officers receiving duties and passing entries for several sorts of African goods in the same manner as if they had been imported from Africa, though, in fact, they came from America, he held such goods were forfeitable under the Act of Navigation.

(a) 19 November 1751.

THIS

This question concerning the manufacturing in Europe of articles the production of Asia, Africa, or America, was brought to a conclusion by a determination of the court of exchequer, in 18. *Geo*. 3. Some ostrich feathers of African produce were brought to France, and there dressed, and from thence imported into this kingdom. This manufacturing in France appeared to the court to be such as to justify the importation under the Act of Navigation. But to prevent the mischief that might ensue to that and various other manufactures in this kingdom, if this practice was to be sanctioned by law, an act was passed, stat. 19. *Geo.* 3. c. 48. which ordains, that the provision in the fourth section of the Act of Navigation should not be construed to permit any goods or commodities whatsoever, of the growth or production of Africa, Asia, or America, which shall be in any degree manufactured in foreign parts, to be imported or brought into the kingdom of Great-Britain, Ireland, Guernsey, Jersey, or Man, unless they shall be manufactured in the country or place of which they were the growth and production, or in the place where such goods and commodities can be only, or are first shipped (*a*), and

(*a*) Leaving out *usually*, as it stands in stat. 12. *Car.* 2. c. 18.

SHIPPING AND NAVIGATION.

from no other country or place whatsoever *(a)*. But this prohibition is not to prevent the importation of oil of cloves, oil of cinnamon, oil of mace, or oil of nutmegs, or of any of the goods or commodities which are permitted to be imported under particular circumstances and restrictions by any act passed since the Act of Navigation, and in force at the time of passing this act *(b)*.

PART II.
12. CAR. II. TO
A. D. 1783.
TRADE WITH
ASIA,
AFRICA, AND
AMERICA.

THE words of the fourth section, *shall not be shipped or brought from any place, or country, but only those of their growth, production, or manufacture,* have given rise to some discussion.

SOME worm-seed, which is a drug of the Turkish dominions and the growth of Asia, was imported from Leghorn in an English-built ship, and was alledged to have been brought to Leghorn in another English-built ship. This was a case not only upon the above clause of the Act of Navigation, but also, and more strongly, on a clause in the Book of Rates, which gives an easement of two-thirds in the duty, on all drugs imported *directly* from the place of their growth in English-built shipping. On the latter point,

Of direct Importation.

*(a)* Sect. 1.   *(b)* Sect. 2.

it

it was the opinion of Mr. *Warde*, then attorney general *(a)*, that this was not a direct shipping from the place of their growth, within the meaning of the clause in the Book of Rates. That a direct importation would make the place of their growth a *terminus à quo*, and England the *terminus ad quem*; but here there was a *medius terminus*, which was Leghorn; and this was an impediment to the importation, making two voyages of that, which was intended only to be one; the design being to encourage English shipping, by tempting them to bring drugs immediately from the place of their growth. But he agreed, if an English-built ship, fetching these articles from the place of their growth, should at sea, upon some necessity, or some reasonable occasion, put them into another English-built ship, and that ship should bring them to England, this in his opinion should be construed a continuance of the same voyage; which differed from the present, where there was one voyage to Leghorn, and another from Leghorn to England: and the interest perhaps was distinct; one voyage on the account of one person, and one on account of another.

(*a*) 15th of March 1681-2.

THE same case being laid before Mr. *Saunders* (a), he was of a different opinion. He thought a *direct* importation within the meaning, though not within the words of the law, to be an importation from the place of their growth into England by English-built shipping all the way, and not partly by English-built shipping, and partly by foreign ships; but whether by one or more ships was not material, for the law intended to encourage and increase English-built shipping in general, and to restrain foreign ships from such trade; and perhaps it might be difficult to get an English ship to pass, with a small parcel of drugs, quite thorough to England from the place of their growth, though easy enough to get one English ship to Leghorn and another for England. In the case before Mr. *Saunders*, it was stated that the drugs were landed at Leghorn only for transportation, upon which he seemed to lay some stress; but the same statement of facts being laid before Sir *Robert Sawyer*, he does not seem to have considered that circumstance as of any force, but declared, that where clauses of statutes mention *direct* im-

(a) 26th of April 1682.

*portation*

*portation* from the place of growth, whether in prohibiting goods to be brought from other ports, or in giving easement in point of duty, a *direct* importation had always been construed to be such as was made by a *continued* voyage; yet where a deviation was by stress of weather, or other necessity; or when by necessity the goods were taken out, upon the sea, and put into another ship; these should be held not to be deviations from the continued voyage.

Mr. *Warde* and Sir *Robert Sawyer* confined themselves, in this opinion, wholly to the wording of the clause in the Book of Rates; for where a similar question of a discontinued voyage arose upon the Act of Navigation, they both construed this law with the same latitude that *Saunders* had done the other. A parcel of hard soap bought in Turkey, the place of its production and manufacture (such as was usually imported from Smyrna), was carried in English shipping to Hamburgh, and continued there on the account of the importer. They both held in this case, that the importation of this soap into England in an English ship would not be contrary either to the words or meaning of the Act of Navigation; for it was fetched all along in English-built shipping,

shipping duly qualified; and though last brought from Hamburgh, which was not the place of its production or manufacture, nor the usual port where first shipped for transportation, yet it was brought thither from the proper place in English shipping duly navigated, by the same person (or upon his account) who fetched it from Hamburgh, and the property continued all along in him (a).

THESE opinions upon the direct importation, as well with a view to the clause in the Book of Rates as upon the Act of Navigation, have been adhered to on subsequent occasions. Thus drugs of the growth of Barbary were shipped here in an English-built ship bound for London, but which was in her voyage to touch at Lisbon. On her arrival there she was found leaky, and incapable of proceeding on her voyage; the drugs were therefore put directly out of that ship, without landing, on board another ship English-built; and this was held by Sir *Edward Northey* (b) to be a *direct* importation from Barbary, the changing the ships being for

(a) 5th of May 1682.  (b) 8th of May 1706.

necessity;

necessity; and he thought the drugs should be imported on the single duty.

AGAIN, in a case before quoted for another purpose, where bear-skins were brought in a British ship from Newfoundland to Gibraltar, and there re-shipped on board another British ship, and brought to England, it was held by Mr. *Willes (a)*, that the ship and goods were not forfeited by stat. 12. *Car.* 2. c. 18. s. 4. but that they were forfeited by stat. 8. *Geo.* 1. c. 15. s. 25. which requires furs the product of a British plantation to be imported *directly* from thence to Great Britain, and laid on shore there, and not elsewhere, under the penalties contained in the Act of Navigation.

IT had been a practice at the custom-house to admit Barbary copper which had been brought from thence to Gibraltar in English-built ships, and re-shipped there for England. In a case of this sort, where the property had all along continued in the same person, some doubt was entertained, whether upon the re-export of such copper from hence, it should receive a drawback; it

(*a*) 16th of August 1736.

being

being thought such drawback was only payable on such copper when imported *directly* from that place; but *Mr. Willes* was of opinion *(a)*, that though there might be some doubt, whether copper so imported ought to have been entered as Barbary copper, yet he rather thought the entry right, and was clear that, the entry being made, the drawback ought to be paid. In like manner, where train-oil of Newfoundland was imported into Guernsey in a British ship, and there trans-shipped, and imported into this kingdom, and an allegation was made of a practice at the custom-house to admit such oil from Guernsey, *Sir Dudley Ryder (b)* held, that it might be admitted to an entry, and that the importation, under all the circumstances, would not induce a forfeiture. Some instances of navigation of the sort just mentioned, must have been alluded to by *Sir Dudley Ryder* (c), in the case of some rum of our plantations imported from Guernsey; he there says, it was not authorised by stat. 3.*Geo.*1.c. s. 7. and must be forfeited by the Act of Navigation, unless there were other circumstances, as to the manner of importation into Guern-

(*a*) 24. January 1735.  (*b*) 11 January 1743.
(*c*) 7 July 1744.

ley, besides what were stated, that might vary the case.

A SINGULAR case of navigation happened respecting the article of *senna*. It seems, the whole growth of senna in Egypt is farmed and purchased there entirely by the Jews, Dutch, French, and Italians, who send it to their respective countries in Europe. The English, being thus wholly excluded from purchasing it in Turkey, cannot procure it by any other means than through those countries; and all the senna which for several years had been imported into this kingdom, and entered as coming *directly* from Smyrna, and passed at the single duty, had been procured in that manner.

A QUANTITY of *senna* was bought in Holland, carried from thence to Smyrna in a British ship, landed, and afterwards re-shipped in the same ship, and imported at London; the property all along continuing in the same person who made the purchase in Holland. On the side of the importer it was alledged, that the carrying the senna from Europe to Smyrna in a British ship was effectually answering the design of the Navigation Act to encourage shipping, and even did it more

more completely than if there had been the immediate importation only from Smyrna in the first inſtance.

Upon this caſe two queſtions aroſe: Firſt, Whether this article, being carried from Holland, could be imported at all under the Act of Navigation? Secondly, Whether, if it could, this was to be deemed a direct importation from the place of its growth, ſo as to entitle the merchant to enter it on the ſingle duty? To this it was anſwered by *Mr. Thurlow*, that the circumſtance of landing the goods only in order to re-ſhip them, would weigh very little in his judgment, if it was clear that the reſt of the voyage had violated the true meaning of the ſtatute of Charles II. It was ſcarcely a literal truth, that theſe goods were not ſhipped or brought from any other country but that of their growth, or where they were firſt ſhipped for tranſportation; it is only true, that in their laſt voyage, dating that from the fictitious commencement of it by re-ſhipping, they were ſo brought. He doubted much whether the intent of the Act of Navigation was not ſatisfied by the Engliſh ſailor having traverſed all thoſe ſeas which are neceſſary to be paſſed

passed in the course of direct trading in the goods in question.

But he rather thought the true meaning of the Act of Navigation was, to force the English trade, as far as regulation could force it, into the first market, and to give it that very establishment which the merchants alledged to be in the possession of the Dutch, and others; and that to effect this, the very large terms of prohibition, *no goods shall be shipped or brought*, &c. mean to exclude *all* shipping or carriage of such goods whatever, which was not from the place of their growth.

But as there seemed no fraud in the merchants, he recommended to seize only a small quantity for the purpose of trying the question; and as it had been the usage of the custom-house to admit senna the growth of Egypt at the single duty from Smyrna, he thought it would be wrong to change it upon any merchant suddenly, and without some notice; although he thought it too great a stretch to call Smyrna the place of its growth, only because they are, or rather were, both provinces of the Turkish Empire(*a*). It is,

(*a*) 29 November 1772.

in fact, the present practice of the customhouse to admit senna, the produce of Egypt, from Smyrna, and rhubarb, the produce of Tartary, from Russia, as if coming *directly* from the place of their growth.

UPON the whole, it is judged not to be sufficient that the whole of the voyage is performed in a British ship, but it must be in the same ship; for if trans-shipping were allowed, it would be very difficult to prove whether the former voyage was performed in a legal way; and the provision might thus be easily evaded. However, when a ship has suffered such damage as to be unladen at some port, and the goods are put into another British vessel, the importation is always considered as a continuation of the first voyage. But this is a case of necessity, and it must be proved before the importation is allowed.

THE following words of the fourth section of the Act of Navigation, *the ports where goods can only, or are, or usually have been, first shipped for transportation,* have given occasion to some question and debate. Cocoa-nuts of the growth of some foreign plantations in America belonging to Spain or France, from whence the king's subjects cannot fetch

fetch them directly, were, at the time of making the Act of Navigation, and after, to the present time, brought from our plantations; but it was material to know, whether this was a regular importation in point of law; and *Sir Edward Northey* was of opinion, that they now might be so imported, having been *usually* there first shipped for transportation *(a)*. *Sir Constantine Phipps* was of a different opinion; as was also *Mr. Turner*.

But this, after all, is a question of fact; and therefore, when a doubt respecting a like importation from Curassoa was submitted to *Sir Philip Yorke (b)*, he put it upon that circumstance—*if* they were the places where they were usually first shipped: but it may be observed, that Curassoa, or any of the *islands* in the West Indies, could not be the places for the *first* shipping for *transportation* from the Spanish continent, unless that transportation was to signify nothing less than passing the Atlantic Ocean to Europe.

The like reference to fact and usage was made by *Sir Philip Yorke*, when a like ques-

(*a*) 22 November 1717.   (*b*) 17 September 1724.

tion

tion was put to him as to the importation from our plantations of tobacco, the growth of the Spanish colonies.(a). For better clearing up this point, the commissioners of the customs directed the collector, comptroller, and surveyor of the port of London to report their opinion: upon which these officers reported, that it had been the practice for many years to admit drugs of the Spanish West Indies to be imported from our plantations, paying duty as imported from places not of their growth; and afterwards, by stat. 7. *Ann.* c. 8. such importation was approved; and this further privilege was allowed, namely, that such drugs should pay duty *as* coming from the place of their growth. It was also the practice, they said, and still continued, to admit logwood, cocoa, and some other commodities of the Spanish West Indies, to be imported by the way of our plantations; but they could not refer to any other act of parliament that favoured such importation; and there appeared to them no particular reason why Spanish tobacco might not come in the same way. It appeared, that cochineal, logwood, Nicaragua-wood, indigo, Jesuits-bark, and snuff

(a) 11 July 1730.

PART II.
12. CAR. II. TO
A. D. 1783.
TRADE WITH
ASIA,
AFRICA, AND
AMERICA.

of the Havannah, were constantly allowed to be imported from our West India islands; and there were some instances of tobacco of the Brazils; but there had been no instance of bringing Spanish tobacco from any British plantation. Upon these facts *Sir Philip Yorke* was clearly of opinion, that it could not be imported consistently with the Act of Navigation.

But a practice seems since to have obtained, which makes it no longer necessary to enquire for the *usual port* for shipping in America, the whole continent and islands being considered as one place.

In all the regulations that have been made since 1763, for adjusting the intercourse between our colonies and the United States, the principal view was to protect the navigation of this country; the people of the United States were accordingly prohibited from coming by sea to our colonies; but, in the mean time, an intercourse with Canada was kept up by an interior communication through the Lakes, and many articles of the produce of the countries of the United States found their way into the province of Quebec, and were from thence transported

transported to Great Britain. A doubt was
stated, whether this importation was legal;
and the opinion of the law-officers being requested, they desired the practice might be
stated, as to the considering of British and
foreign America one place, or not, in respect to the importation of its produce. Accordingly the collector and comptroller of
the port of London certified, that it was
the established practice to consider the whole
of America in respect to the importation of
its produce into this kingdom as one place;
and in that view that all articles, the growth
of America, have been admitted in British
ships from any part of that country, without regard to the goods being the production of British or foreign America, or to the
port from which they are imported, being
the nearest to the place of their growth, or
the usual port for shipping those goods.

Upon which the law-officers delivered
their opinion, that the importation of the
produce of that part of America which constitutes the territories of the present United
States having been lawful before their separation from Great Britain, must continue
to be so, notwithstanding that separation,
unless

PART II.
13. CAR. II. TO
A. D. 1783.
TRADE WITH
ASIA,
AFRICA, AND
AMERICA.

unless it is prohibited by some law made upon the separation, or afterwards.

INDEED it is stated, so far back as the year 1756, to have been the practice of the custom-house to consider the third and fourth sections of the Act of Navigation geographically, and to give the words *place, or country*, a very extensive construction; for goods of foreign plantations in America had been imported into England from the British colonies; the product of one part of Africa had been imported from another part of Africa, though without the Streights of Gibraltar, and subject to different princes; and such commodities had, notwithstanding, always been deemed to come from the place of their growth.

As to the *shipping* in which the trade of Asia, Africa, and America, might be carried on, upon comparing sect. 3, 4, 8, and 9. of stat. 12. Car. 2. c. 18. and stat. 13. & 14. Car. 2. c. 11. s. 6. *Sir Edward Northey* was of opinion (*a*), that Canary wine might be imported from the Canaries in a foreign-built ship, owned and manned by the peo-

(*a*) 16 April 1706.

ple of England, paying aliens' duty; for the third section, which relates to the goods of Asia, Africa, and America, does not oblige the goods of those places to be imported only in English-built shipping, but allows them to be imported in ships belonging to the people of England; and the fourth section, which refers to the third, makes no alteration; for the words therein, *English-built shipping*, are of no use, the words *or other shipping belonging to England* being in the same clause. None of the subsequent clauses make any alteration in this matter; for the last clause which concerns foreign-built ships owned by the English, does not prohibit the importing in them, but only takes away a privilege belonging to them before, and obliges aliens' duty to be paid for goods imported in them; whereas before, such ships being owned by the English, the duty paid by denizens was the only duty that should be paid for goods imported in them on the account of English subjects.

NOTWITHSTANDING the strict prohibition not to import the commodities of Asia, Africa, and America, but from the place of their growth, production, or manufacture, a practice had been permitted to obtain.

obtain, of allowing such commodities, when once imported and afterwards exported to some European country, to be again imported from thence.

THE first instance of this sort of question was, where goods had been imported and paid the duty, and were exported within the time limited by the second rule of the Book of Rates, having drawn back part of the duty, as there permitted, but not finding a market they were returned; and *Sir Robert Sawyer* held, they were upon such second importation liable to pay the same duties as upon the first importation; for it was entirely a new importation, and the officers of the customs could not take notice that they had been here before, or make any allowance for it. But though he maintained this opinion as to duties, yet he held, that returned goods would not be forfeited within the fourth section of the Act of Navigation, which extends only to the first importation, in order to make England the staple of those commodities; and that having been complied with, the law is executed according to its true intent and meaning. However, he thought the twenty-third clause in the Act of Frauds, stat. 13. & 14. *Car.* 2.

14 *Car.* 2. c. 11. which prohibits certain goods coming from the Netherlands and Germany, extended the Act of Navigation to take away all pretence of returned goods of the kinds enumerated in that act.

BUT this point was considered in a different light by *Mr. Warde* and *Sir John Somers* (*a*), who thought the Act of Frauds applied only to the original importation; and if the goods had been originally imported from the proper place, the end of the law seemed to them to be answered.

INDEED, it became a settled practice to allow the importation of such returned goods: but it was expected, that they should be imported by the same person who exported them. It was submitted to the opinion of *Sir John Somers* (*b*), Whether, if the property passed to another, the goods might be imported as returned goods. Thus, where *A.* a merchant in London, exported opium to Holland, and *B.* another merchant in London, ordered his factor to buy it there, he said, that if the act was taken strictly the

(*a*) 10 & 11 Oct. 1689.    (*b*) May 1692.

exporter

exporter *A.* might not afterwards return the goods to England; but by a reasonable equity in construing the act for the benefit of trade, it had been allowed to the person exporting to return them into England, if he did not find an opportunity to dispose of them in a foreign market. And though it might not seem to be equally reasonable to extend the construction so far as this case (where the exporter had not had the benefit of a foreign market), because if allowed after an alteration of possession and property, it might be made the means to elude the act; yet if the practice at the custom-house, from the making of the act, had been to allow such importation (without making a difference whether the goods were returned by the same person who exported them), upon oath made that the goods were the same, as he had been informed they did, he did not see but the law might be so understood, and pursued accordingly.

Some few years after this practice was laid before *Sir Ed. Northey* (a), who held it proper to be followed, as it had been a constant practice, provided care was taken

(a) 18 February 1703.

that the goods returned were the same goods, and that they were brought back by the same person who exported them.

At the distance of some years, *Sir Phil. Yorke* was consulted upon this point of practice; when he declared, if this question had stood singly on the Act of Navigation, without any practice to influence it, he should have thought it clear, that tea imported into England, and afterwards exported to Holland, could not be returned from thence by virtue of that law; because such returning (as it is called) was a new importation, and the goods are liable to the same duty, and subject to the regulation of the same laws concerning goods imported, in all respects, as they were upon the first importation; and therefore are considered in law as if they never had been brought at all to this kingdom. He thought the practice had arisen without good foundation; and if a seizure should be made of tea so returned, such practice ought not in strictness to alter the construction of the act. But, notwithstanding that, he thought the usage would have an influence with the jury; and the court would probably be tender how they broke in upon that, which had been so long allowed to prevail.

On a subsequent occasion *Sir Phil. Yorke (a)* was again called upon to deliver his opinion, for the government of the officers. He then said, he thought such returned goods were in strictness not liable to the payment of any duty, nor enterable; but they were forfeited for being re-landed after exportation, and the duties drawn back. He said, he did not remember any act of parliament for the indulgence that had been allowed; but he thought it reasonable in some cases (to avoid hardships to merchants), when particularly allowed and directed by the commissioners of the customs. In this case, the goods had been entered on payment of the same duties as on their first importation, although it was a low duty, not payable but on a direct importation from the place of their growth.

The next year the succeeding attorney-general, *Mr. Willes (a)*, was consulted upon this point. It was where sugars had been exported on account of a foreigner, and re-imported by an English merchant; so that the property had evidently been altered. He thought, though the alteration of the

(a) 6 August 1733.    (b) 31 October 1734.

property

property and possession might give greater opportunity to persons to commit frauds, and therefore, in such cases, there ought to be a stricter examination into the identity of the goods returned; yet if there was a full and clear proof that they were the same goods as were exported, he could not see what difference in reason the alteration in the property and possession could make. However, as the practice of admitting entries of returned goods had, ever since the opinion of *Sir Ed. Northey* (a), been confined to such goods only, where there had been no alteration of the property and possession, he thought they might very well proceed to take the opinion of the court upon the case which was then depending. Upon another occasion however, where there was a change of property, he gave his opinion, that if the identity of the goods could be made out, an entry ought not to be refused. And upon the general point of admitting returned goods, he says, he was confirmed in opinion that it was right, by the constant practice, by the opinions of former attorneys-general, and by the judgment of the then *chief justice* EYRE.

(a) In 1703. *Vid. ant.* 190.

This practice however, as far as regards tea, was stopped by stat. 11. *Geo.* 1. c. 30. which complains, that tea imported into Flanders and Holland from the East Indies used to be imported into this kingdom on pretence that it had been formerly exported from hence; and to prevent such abuses in future it enacts, that no tea shall be imported but from the place of its growth, although it may have been formerly exported from hence *(a)*. In other respects the practice seems to have been fully established.

THE following questions arose upon cases peculiarly circumstanced, and were founded on a supposition that the general point was settled. Some sassafras was brought to the port of *Cowes*, but was not landed; it was only reported there for Lisbon, to which place it was carried, and then brought back. *Sir Dudley Ryder (b)*, upon this occasion, was of opinion, that the practice, with regard to goods originally duly imported, on the duties being paid, or secured, was an indulgence justified only by long usage; and as there was no like usage in the present case, and it had not the same equitable reasons attending

---

(*a*) Sect. 8.   (*b*) 25 April 1743.

tending it, he thought the commissioners were not sufficiently warranted to admit these goods to an entry.

ON the other hand, where elephants' teeth had been carried into Ireland as prize, and there condemned, and then shipped for Hamburgh, and brought back from thence, *Sir Dudley Ryder* was of opinion, that as these goods might have been imported here originally from Ireland, they stood upon the same footing as goods returned hither, and therefore might be admitted to an entry as such.

## CHAPTER III.

### THE EUROPEAN TRADE.

*The Eighth Section—Complaints against the Act—Prohibition of Goods from the Netherlands and Germany—Provision in the Treaty of Breda—The Prohibition relaxed—The Eastland Company—The Russia Company—The Turkey Company—Usages contrary to the Prohibition—Of Shipping in the European Trade—Foreign Prize Ships—Of English Ships sold to Foreigners—Of the Country where foreign Ships built—Stat. 22. Geo. 3. c. 78.—Of the Country of the Master and Mariners—Of Prize Goods—What is an Importation—Act of Navigation dispensed with in War-Time.*

PART II: 
12. CAR. II. TO A. D. 1783. EUROPEAN TRADE.

THE *European Trade* is the next object which presents itself in the Act of Navigation. In the act of 1651 the whole of this trade was regulated; and it was, in some respects, subjected to the same restrictions

tions as those imposed on the trade of Asia, Africa, and America, in the fourth section of the new act. But the parliament now thought proper to subject only a portion of it to regulation; the rest was left at large; and in this respect some sacrifice was made to the interests of our commercial neighbours, who had complained so heavily of the partial spirit of the former act.

It was ordained, in the eighth section, that no goods or commodities of the growth, production, or manufacture, of *Muscovy*, or of any of the countries, dominions, or territories, to the Great Duke, or emperor of *Muscovy* or *Russia* belonging; as also no sort of masts, timber, or boards; no foreign salt, pitch, tar, rosin, hemp, or flax, raisins, figs, prunes, olive-oils; no sorts of corn or grain, sugar, pot-ashes, wines, vinegar, or spirits called *aqua vitæ* or brandy wine, shall be imported into England, Ireland, Wales, or the town of Berwick, in any ship or vessel whatsoever, but in such as do truly and without fraud *belong* to the people thereof, or some of them, as the true owners and proprietors, and whereof the master and three-fourths of the mariners

*The Eighth Section.*

mariners at least are English. And that no currants, nor commodities of the growth, production, or manufacture, of any of the countries, islands, dominions, or territories, to the Ottoman or Turkish empire belonging, shall be imported into any of the before-mentioned places, in any ship or vessel but which is of English-*built*, and navigated as aforesaid, and in no other, except only (which exception is construed to apply not only to Turkey, but to Russia, and the enumerated articles before-mentioned) such foreign ships and vessels as are of the built of that country or place of which the said goods are the growth, production, or manufacture respectively, or of such port where the said goods can only be, or most usually are, first shipped for transportation, and whereof the master and three-fourths of the mariners at least are of the said country or place, under pain of forfeiting the ship and goods (*a*).

The prohibition to import, except only in English ships, or ships of the country whence the commodities come, does not, we see, extend by the present act, as it did by the

(*a*) Sect. 8.

old

old one, to all Europe, but is confined to the commodities of Ruſſia and Turkey, and to the articles that are above ſpecially enumerated; ſo that any European merchandize not there enumerated, and not of the growth, production, or manufacture of *Ruſſia* or *Turkey*, may, by this act, be imported in a ſhip not Engliſh-built, nor of the country from whence the merchandize comes.

THE act went a ſtep further with regard to the enumerated articles (except wine and vinegar), and with regard to all goods of the growth, production, or manufacture of Ruſſia and of Turkey; for in order, as the act ſays, to prevent the great frauds practiſed in colouring and concealing aliens' goods, thoſe commodities, if imported in any other than Engliſh-built ſhipping, and navigated as before mentioned, are to be deemed aliens' goods, and pay accordingly to the king, and to the town or port into which they are imported. The ſame was ordained with regard to wines of the growth of France and Germany, or Spain, the iſlands of the Canaries, or Portugal, the Madeira or Weſtern Iſlands *(a)*. So that such arti-

(a) Sect. 9.

cles, even if they came in a ship of the country, as permitted by the preceding clause, were still made liable to a burthen in the payment of the aliens' duty *(a)*.

To these last regulations of the European trade the following provisoes were annexed: That they should not be construed to impose aliens' duties upon corn the growth of Scotland, salt made in Scotland, fish caught, saved, and cured, by the people of Scotland, and imported directly from thence in Scotch-built ships, and whereof the master and three-fourths of the mariners were of his majesty's subjects; nor were they to extend to sea-oil of Russia imported from thence into England, Ireland, Wales, or the town of Berwick, in shipping *bond fide* belonging to some of the said places, and whereof the master and three-fourths of the mariners at least were English *(b)*.

*Complaints against the Act.*

THE restrictions here laid upon the European trade, though less pressing than those in the former act, were yet such as to cause great embarrassment, and were soon

(*a*) But all aliens' duties were abolished by stat. 24. Geo. 3. c. 16.
(*b*) Sect. 16.

complained

complained of, both by the king's own subjects and by foreigners. Among other complaints, a memorial was presented by the agent for the city of Lubec, one of the Hanse Towns, praying for a dispensation from the Act of Navigation, the Lubeckers claiming this indulgence under pretence of usage and custom; and they had actually succeeded in obtaining a licence to come with their own ships and mariners, free from all restriction whatsoever. On the 17th September 1662, this memorial was taken into consideration in the privy council, when the lord chancellor, the lord treasurer, the lord privy seal, and other lords, were appointed a committee to consider the proposal there made, how far it would be beneficial to the trade of this nation, and how far it was merited by the degree of privilege enjoyed by our merchants in the Hanse Towns. The committee were to consult with the commissioners and farmers of the customs, the Eastland merchants, and others. The matter was fully debated and resolved on; and a proclamation was issued, recalling all licences, letters, or warrants, that had been obtained contrary to the Act of Navigation (*a*).

(*a*) Counc. Regist. and Anderson, Vol. ii. 626.

PART IV.
12. CAR. II TO
A. D. 1753.
EUROPEAN
TRADE.

THE representations of our own merchants and of foreigners, at this time, prevailed so far with his majesty, that an order of council was made, on 24th September 1662, directing, that the lord chancellor, lord treasurer, and the chancellor of the exchequer, calling to their assistance the judges, king's counsel, and chief officers and farmers of the customs, should advise about preparing a bill for explaining and invalidating such parts of the Act of Navigation as daily proved destructive to his majesty's trading subjects (*a*). But this was not followed by any project for relaxing, in any manner whatever, the rule of trade already laid down. On the contrary, we see the parliament employed, almost at that very time, in framing the *Act of Frauds*, by which a new restriction, still more embarrassing, was imposed on the European Trade.

Prohibition of Goods from the Netherlands and Germany.

THIS is stat. 13. & 14. *Car.* 2. c. 11. which purports to be for explanation of "doubts and disputes concerning the "Act of Navigation, about some goods "therein prohibited to be brought from "Holland, and the parts and ports there- "abouts." This was declaring plainly the design of that act, but not reciting its words;

(*a*) Counc. Regist.

for

for no such prohibition, in terms, is to be found in the statute: but this was the language of the time; and we have before noticed a public paper, which speaks of *goods prohibited by the act in Holland's ships.* We are told, the doubts and disputes, here alluded to, were those which we know were entertained at one time, Whether the fourth section did not apply to the commodities of Europe, as well as those of Asia, Africa, and America? and that this act was made to settle it, at least in the particular articles here specified. But the occasion of the act may be ascribed to the following considerations:

COMPLAINT had been made, First, that plantation goods used to be carried to Holland and Germany, and were afterwards brought from thence by our own merchants. Secondly, That our own merchants contented themselves with fetching from Holland and Germany many of the commodities enumerated and described in the eighth section of the Act of Navigation. It is true, plantation goods, and the commodities of Asia, Africa, and America, could not lawfully be brought from the Netherlands or Germany, because those were not the usual ports for their first shipping;

PART II.
22. CAR. II. 70
A. D. 1783.
EUROPEAN
TRADE.

shipping; but if they underwent there any manufacturing, we have before seen they might legally be imported from thence. The commodities of the eighth section might also legally be brought from Holland, or any other place, in English shipping. A considerable carrying-trade, therefore, would be lost to us, and would remain with the merchants of Holland, of Hamburgh, and other maritime towns, in spite of the Act of Navigation, if our merchants were permitted to furnish themselves by short voyages to those neighbouring ports, and were not compelled to take upon them the burthen of bringing these articles from the countries where they were produced.

To force the merchants, therefore, upon longer voyages, and so to extend the shipping and navigation of the kingdom, it was by this statute enacted and declared, that no sort of wines (other than Rhenish), no sort of spicery, grocery, tobacco, pot-ashes, pitch, tar, salt, rosin, deal-boards, fir-timber, or olive-oil, shall be imported into England, Wales, or Berwick, from the Netherlands or Germany, upon any pretence whatsoever, in any sort of ships or vessels veffels whatfoever, upon pain of forfeiting the fhip and goods (a).

IT is probable the makers of this prohibitory claufe did not look back to former ftatutes when they penned this provifion. Thofe who had the conftruing of it have taken into their view what had been before done by the Legiflature; and they have conftrued grocery to include fuch articles as are claffed under that title in the Book of Rates, among which is *fpicery*. The articles are thefe; almonds, annifeeds, cloves, currants, dates, ginger, liquorice, mace, nutmegs, pepper, cinnamon, raifins, figs, prunes, and fugar *(b.)*. The Confolidation Act ftat. 27. *Geo.* 3. has followed the fame rule for claffing grocery, with a fmall addition in the articles. They are there ranked thus; almonds, annifeeds, cinnamon, cloves, currants, dates, *figs*, ginger, liquorice, mace, nutmegs, pepper, *pimento*, *plumbs*, *prunes*, raifins, fugar. Moft of the articles,

(a) Sect. 23.
(b) What puts it out of doubt, whether any articles might be confidered as fpicery, though not fpecified among other fpices, under this head of grocery, there is added in the Book of Rates a note for giving an eafement, in point of duty, to *all fpicery* (except pepper, one of the fpecified articles), if imported directly from the place of their growth.

therefore,

therefore, intended by this provision, were the productions of Asia, Africa, or America; and with regard to them the prohibition was no more than a repetition of that provision in the Act of Navigation, which requires such articles to be brought from the place of their growth. If, indeed, they had undergone such a manufacturing in the Netherlands or Germany as would constitute them a manufacture of those places, they might be brought from thence under the Act of Navigation; and in respect to such articles this prohibition was wholly a new law. It was likewise a new law in regard to such articles here mentioned as were European commodities.

THIS prohibition was a severe blow to the shipping of Holland, after what it had suffered from the Navigation Act. Perhaps it was more grating, as it was more marked than the former measure. At the time of settling the articles of navigation and commerce that were signed at Breda, in July 1667, the States-General made a point to stipulate for a repeal of this law. King Charles consented; and the first provision in that treaty is, "that it should be lawful for the States-General, and their subjects, to carry into "England,

"England, in their ships, all such commo-
"dities, as growing, being produced, or
"manufactured, in Lower or Upper Ger-
"many, are not usually carried so fre-
"quently and commodiously unto sea-ports
"(thence to be transported to other coun-
"tries) any other way but through the terri-
"tories and dominions of the United Ne-
"therlands, either by land or by rivers (*a*)."
But no statute was passed for carrying this
stipulation into execution, nor does it appear
that it was at all brought into discussion,
either in the parliament or council.

HOWEVER, after some lapse of time, and
when the advantages and disadvantages of
this prohibition had been weighed and
compared, the parliament consented to
grant a partial relaxation of it with regard
to Germany. First, By stat. 1. *Ann*. st. 1.
c. 12. Hungary wines are permitted to be

(*a*) The description given in this treaty of this Act of
Explanation, and of the Act of Navigation, is worth notice:
"That for the elucidation of that act which the king of
"Great Britain caused to be published in the year 1660,
"for the encouragement of navigation in his own sub-
"jects, whereby strangers are prohibited to import any
"commodities into England, but such as are of their own
"growth and manufacture;" which is by no means a
correct description of the Navigation-Act.

imported

imported from Hamburgh. Secondly, By ſtat. 6. *Geo.* I. c. 15. it was permitted to any of the king's ſubjects to import fir-timber, fir-planks, maſts, and deal-boards, of the growth of Germany, from any port or place of Germany into this kingdom, in Britiſh-built ſhips only, owned by his majeſty's ſubjects, and whereof the maſter and three-fourths of the mariners at leaſt are Britiſh ſubjects, on paying the ſame duty as the ſame articles pay when imported from Norway (*a*). And we ſhall ſoon ſee, that by a ſtatute made in the preſent king's reign certain German wines are permitted to come from the Auſtrian Netherlands.

Such are the principal laws that were made reſpecting the European Trade during this period of our Navigation-Hiſtory. One remains, paſſed in the twenty-ſecond year of his preſent majeſty's reign, and juſt now alluded to (*b*), which was made for amending the Acts of Navigation in ſome particulars where they were thought to be too ſevere. But I ſhall poſtpone the conſideration of this ſtatute till we have firſt ſeen what were the difficulties which occaſioned the parliament to interpoſe, and apply the remedies contained in that ſtatute.

(*a*) Sect. 2.   (*b*) Stat. 22. Geo. 3. c. 78.

A CONSIDERABLE

SHIPPING AND NAVIGATION.   209

A CONSIDERABLE portion of the European trade contained in the eighth section of the Navigation Act, was confined to the exclusive possession of certain Companies; *the Hamburgh Company*, heretofore called *the Merchants Adventurers*, *the Eastland Company*, *the Russia Company*, and *the Turkey Company*.

PART II.
12. CAR. II. TO A. D. 1783.
EUROPEAN TRADE.

THE monopoly enjoyed by these Companies had been great subject of complaint, and this occasioned the interposition of parliament; which, by directing the admission to be made more easy, in a great measure did away the mischiefs of the exclusive privilege. The first instance of this sort of interposition is in stat. 25. *Car.* 2. c. 7. which was made for encouraging the Greenland and Eastland trades: it was thereby ordained, that it should be lawful for all the king's subjects of England, Wales, and Berwick, and for every other person of what nation soever, residing and inhabiting here, freely to trade into and from Greenland and those seas, and there take whales and all other sorts of fish, and to import into this kingdom all sorts of oil, blubber, and fins thereof, and to use and exercise all other trade to and from Greenland and those parts *(a)*.

The Eastland Company.

*(a)* Sect. 1.

P

In the reign of James and Charles I. proclamations had been issued, according to the fashion of those times, prohibiting any, whether natives or foreigners, from importing whale-fins, or whale-oil, except only the Russia Company (*a*). It does not appear that any such prohibitions had been made in the reign of Charles II.; but this parliamentary provision had the effect of removing all doubt or difficulty that might belong to this exercise of prerogative.

The *Eastland Company* subsisted under a charter granted by queen Elizabeth in 1579, for regulating the commerce into the *East country*; a name anciently given, and still continued by mercantile people, to the ports of the Baltic sea, more particularly those of Prussia and Livonia. They were by this charter to enjoy the sole trade through the Sound into Norway, Sweden, Poland, Lithuania (excepting Narva, which was within the charter of the Russia Company), Prussia, and also Pomerania from the river Oder eastward, Dantzic, Elbing, and Koningsberg; also to Copenhagen and Elsinore, and to Finland, Gothland, Bornholm, and Oeland. This charter was confirmed by another from Charles I. in 1629 (*b*).

(*a*) Anderson.   (*b*) Anderson.

IN the same stat. 25. *Car.* 2. the following provisions were made for laying open a very considerable part of this trade: It was declared lawful for any native or foreigner at all times to have free liberty to trade into and from Sweden, Denmark, and Norway; notwithstanding the charter to the Eastland merchants, or any other charter; and further, that every person being a subject of this realm might be admitted into the fellowship of merchants of Eastland, on paying forty shillings and no more *(a)*; which latter provision made the trade to the other parts within the limits of the charter easily accessible.

THE *Russia Company* subsisted by virtue of a charter granted by Philip and Mary in the first and second year of their reign, which was confirmed by a private statute passed in the eighth year of queen Elizabeth. The charter was granted to them under the stile of *The Merchants Adventurers of England for the Discovery of Lands, Territories, Isles, Dominions, and Seigniories unknown, and not before their late Adventure or Enterprise by Seas or Navigation*

(a) Sect. 5. 6.

*commonly frequented* (a). In the statute they were described by the name of *The Fellowship of English Merchants for Discovery of new Trades.* The extent of their rights under the statute was, the sole privilege of trading to and from the dominions and territories of the emperor of Russia lying northward, north-eastward, and north-westward from the city of London; as also to the countries of Armenia Major or Minor, Media, Hyrcania, Persia, or the Caspian sea. It was said in stat. 10. & 11. *Will.* 3. c. 6. to be commonly called *The Russia Company.*

In the reign of king William it was thought this trade might be considerably enlarged, if the admission of persons into the Company was made more easy; and that it would be very proper to ascertain the fee of admission, which had not been done either by the charter or statute. It was accordingly enacted by the statute just mentioned, that every subject of this realm might be admitted into the Company upon payment of five pounds only (b).

(a) See Hackluyt, Vol. I. p. 258 to 274, for the charter and other matters relating to the Russia Company.
(b) Sect. 1, 2.

THE

THE trade to the Levant subsisted under a charter granted in the third year of king James I. confirmed by letters patent of the thirteenth year of Charles II. The incorporation was by the name of *The Governor and Company of Merchants of England trading into the Levant seas.* The qualifications for admission to this Company were these: they were to be mere merchants; and no person residing within twenty miles of London was to be admitted, unless he was made free of the city. The fee of admission was by the charter of James I. twenty-five pounds for those under twenty-six years, and fifty pounds for those above that age. The greatness of this fee, and the peculiarity of the description of candidates, were thought unnecessary restraints; and by stat. 26. *Geo.* 2. c. 18. it was enacted, that every subject of Great Britain may be admitted, upon proper application, into *the Turkey Company,* upon paying the sum of twenty pounds, and no more *(a)*; and all persons free of that Company may, separately or jointly, export from Great Britain to any port or place within the limits of the letters patent, in any British or plantation-built ship, navigated according to law, to any person be-

PART II.
13. CAR. II. TO
A. D. 1783.
EUROPEAN
TRADE.

The Turkey Company.

*(a)* Sect. 1.

ing a freeman of the Company, and a Christian subject, and submitting to the direction of the British ambassador and consuls any goods not prohibited to be exported, and import in like manner from any place within the said limits raw silk, or any other goods purchased within those limits, and not prohibited by law (a).

The limits of this trade were mentioned very generally in the first charter granted in 1581; the liberty there given was, "to trade to Turkey." In the second charter in 1593, the trade is specified more particularly; namely, " to Venice, Zante, Cephalonia, Candia, and other Venetian territories; the dominions of the Grand Seignior by land and sea, and through his countries over-land to the East Indies." These charters were both temporary; the first for seven, the second for twelve years (b).

No parliamentary provision was made for opening the Hamburgh trade. This, the oldest of our trading Companies, and heretofore more usually called *Merchants Adventurers*, had taken warning from the re-

(a) S. A. 3.

(b) Whether the limits continued the same under the charter of king James and king Charles II. I do not know, not having been able to see either.

peated

peated complaints made of their monopoly, (the laſt of which was in 1661) and had facilitated the admiſſion by private regulations made by themſelves. Add to this, it was, like the Hudſon's Bay Company, without any parliamentary ſanction; and had not been able even during the reigns of Charles II. and James II. to protect its excluſive privileges againſt the ſeparate adventurers (*a*).

AMONG the information which is to throw light upon the foregoing proviſions, we find ſome few deciſions of courts. The European trade ſtood principally upon the eighth ſection of the Act of Navigation, and the prohibition contained in the Statute of Frauds reſpecting the Netherlands and Germany. What we have to ſay reſpecting the articles of the European trade being wholly confined to thoſe contained in this ſpecial prohibition, it will be more convenient to diſpoſe of them firſt, and then we may proceed to conſider the eighth ſection.

PITCH is one of the articles prohibited by ſtat. 13. & 14. *Car.* 2. c. 11. to come from the Netherlands; but when *white pitch*, the product and manufacture of Germany, was

(*a*) Anderſon.

imported

imported from Rotterdam, it was held by Mr. *Warde* (a), that if it had been the constant usage ever since the act to allow it to be so imported, that might give some light to the intention of the law that this commodity had not been looked upon as any sort of pitch; for if it was agreed to be a sort of pitch, he considered it as undoubtedly prohibited.

THE following is another instance where usage was permitted to over-rule the strict sense of the wording in this act of explanation. This act prohibits the importation from the Netherlands and Germany of all wines, except Rhenish. In point of practice, several other wines, besides Rhenish, had been brought from the Netherlands and Germany, as Moselle and Neckar wines. The extent of the prohibition as to this point was submitted to the law-officers; and it was the opinion of *Sir Thomas Trevor*, that wines of the growth of Hungary are not restrained by this statute from being imported from the Netherlands and Germany: for, in his opinion, the exception in favour of Rhenish wine extended to all wines of the

(a) 19 October 1692.

growth

growth of Germany or the emperor's dominions *thereabouts*, and was not to be confined to the strict literal sense of the words, namely, to such wines as grow on the borders of the Rhine, but must be taken according to the common acceptation of the word, by which all wines of the growth of Germany or the emperor's dominions were generally called Rhenish; which construction was fortified, in his judgment, by the usage, since the making of the statute, of allowing other wines of the growth of Germany to be so imported.

SIR JOHN HAWLES agreed in this opinion as far as regarded all wines of Germany; but he thought Hungary wine could not be imported within the meaning of this act, Hungary being a country distinct from Germany, though under the dominion of the emperor; and he thought Hungary wine a *casus omissus* in the act. We have seen the Legislature by stat. 1. *Ann.* st. 1. c. 12. s. 112. have put Hungary wines, if imported from Hamburgh, on the same footing in point of duty as Rhenish wine, or wines of the growth of Germany; which settled the doubt as to importation from *Hamburgh*, but left the rest of Germany and the Netherlands as they were before. But now,

now, by stat. 22. Geo. 3. c. 78. wines being the growth, production, or manufacture, of Hungary, the Austrian dominions, or any part of Germany, may come from the Austrian Netherlands, or any place subject to the emperor or the house of Austria, on the same duty as Rhenish wine; as also organzine thrown silk upon the same duty as if imported from Italy.

'By the same statute, all drugs of the growth, production, or manufacture of Hungary or Germany (which, says the act, had been theretofore usually imported from Rotterdam upon the low duties), laden or shipped at any place in the Austrian Netherlands, or at any port in Germany, and imported from thence in British-built shipping, are to be taken as imported directly from the place of their growth, production, or manufacture, and are to pay duties accordingly (a). Silk and drugs are not among the prohibited articles; and these provisions about duties are not strictly a part of our subject; but they are so combined with the other matter of this statute, that I could not avoid mentioning them.

Grocery being one of the articles prohibited to be brought from the Netherlands

(a) Sect. 1.

and Germany, some annifeed imported from Hamburgh had been seized; annifeed being classed in the Book of Rates under the head of Grocery. It was contended by the merchants, that the parliament could not have meant to prohibit the importing of any article from the place of its growth; and they concluded grocery wares to be, sugar white and brown, sugar-candy and loaf-sugar, spices, and other goods manufactured in Holland, or imported from *their* plantations, or trade abroad; and that as to raisins, currants, and other goods, the growth of other countries, they were sufficiently prohibited by the Act of Navigation; that annifeed, being used only in physic, was not properly rated as grocery ware in the Book of Rates; that grocery ware means what is used in a kitchen; and that many articles, as French and pearl barley, which are more properly grocery than annifeed, being for the use of families, were daily imported from Hamburgh, but would not have been permitted, if the Act had not been so understood.

This question being submitted to *Sir Edward Northey* (a), he was of opinion,

(a) 19 March 1702-3.

that

that it was very reasonable to restrain the general words of this prohibition to such goods concerning which there was a doubt after making the Act of Navigation, whether they were prohibited by that act to be imported from Holland and Germany; and not to construe it according to the utmost extent of the words, so as to prohibit any goods to be brought from those places (though comprized under the general words) concerning which there was never made any doubt. A doubt, says he, had been made, whether the fourth section of the Act of Navigation prohibited European goods, or only the goods of Asia, Africa, and America, to be imported from any other place than the place of their growth, production, or manufacture; and that doubt occasioned the provision in question concerning Holland and Germany. And in regard the doubt was of European goods imported from Holland or Germany not of the growth of those places, and there never was any doubt concerning importing from those places goods of their own growth, and the practice having been since the act so to import annifeeds of the growth of Hamburgh, he thought it not reasonable to disturb the merchants in making

ing such importation; which to him seemed not to be the intent of the prohibition. But he thought anniseeds were certainly grocery, being so declared in the Book of Rates.

IN a more extensive sense, Holland has been sometimes considered as included in Germany. It must have been in this sense, that juniper-berries of Germany had been usually admitted from Rotterdam on the low duty, as coming from the place of their growth; and *Sir Dudley Ryder* (*b*) thought this usage might be maintained, however he might decide on it, if it were *res integra*. It is with the same latitude in words, that the inhabitants of the United Provinces are by us called *Dutch*; which appellation belongs properly only to those of Germany (*c*).

(*b*) 16 May 1750.

(*c*) Germany is *Deutchland*, and a German is called *ein Deutcher*. Those we call *Dutch toys* are properly so called, for they are made at Nuremberg in Germany, and are really *Deutsche waaren* (or rather *Nurnbergische waaren*, as they are termed in Germany), though they are vulgarly supposed, from the abuse of the term in this country, to be made in Holland.

SOME

SOME French wines having been bought in Holland, by the Queen's direction, for her own use, it became a question, Whether they could be imported from thence, contrary to this stat. 13. & 14. *Car.* 2. ? And it was held by *Mr. Powis*, *Mr. Northey*, and *Mr. Harcourt* (a), that her majesty might lawfully import such wines for her own use. They recommended that the importation should be in the Queen's own ships, a sign manual being given to the captains and commanders directing them to receive the wines on board, bring them to England, and deliver them to the storekeeper of her majesty's wines. But *Sir James Montague* (b) declared his opinion, that he could not advise such wines should be bought in Holland, and imported from thence, contrary to stat. 13. & 14. *Car.* 2.; but he thought the Queen should give orders under her sign manual to some agent to buy the wines out of some neutral ship, and to order them to be put on board some of her majesty's ships, to be brought into her majesty's own cellar or warehouse: the Queen not being, as he conceived, prohibited from

(a) 9 June 1708.   (b) 5 June 1708.

importing

importing French wines, under the act then in force.

The town of Dunkirk having been a part of the Netherlands, and for many years annexed to the crown of France, came by treaty into the poffeffion of our crown. It was made a queftion at that time how this place was to be confidered with refpect to the Acts of Navigation; and *Sir Edward Northey* (a) was of opinion, that although Dunkirk changed its owner, yet it remained a part of the Netherlands within ftat. 13. & 14. *Car.* 2; and although it might have a different confequence, if Dunkirk were abfolutely yielded to her majefty, and thereby became part of her dominions, yet in being put into her majefty's poffeffion provifionally only, on agreement made between her majefty and the French king, French wine could not be imported from thence, but was reftrained by the prohibition of that ftatute.

Thus far of the Prohibition in the Act of Frauds. We come now to confider the provifions in the eighth fection of the Navigation Act. The only part of this claufe which

(a) 1 Auguft 1712.

has

has given rise to much discussion is that which relates to the shipping in which it is to be carried on.

A DIFFICULTY arose from comparing this and the ninth section with the sixth section of stat: 13. & 14. *Car.* 2. c. 11. and it was made a doubt, whether a Dutch-built ship English owned and navigated could import wines from France, or timber from Norway. And it was held by *Mr. Browne*, *Mr. Warde*, *Mr. Roger North*, and *Mr. Pollexfen (a)*, and afterwards by *Sir Edward Northey (b)*, that such importation was no cause of forfeiture, but merely subjected the goods to aliens duties.

BY stat. 12. *Car.* 2. a foreign ship truly belonging to the people of England, and made free by the oath of the owner, as directed by that act, and manned with a master and three-fourths of the mariners English, might lawfully import the goods in question, and pay only such duties as the importer of them in English-built ships should pay. Several other privileges by that act are allowed to foreign-built ships owned by

(a) March 1689.    (b) 28 November 1701.

English,

English, made free and manned as beforementioned; and by that act some goods from some places are allowed to be imported in English-built ships. It was designed by stat. 13. & 14. *Car.* 2. c. 11. sect. 6. to lessen the privilege allowed to foreign-built ships, though owned, made free, and manned as allowed by the former act (but it was not intended totally to forbid the trading in foreign ships owned by the English); and for that purpose the act directed an account to be transmitted to the custom-house of all foreign-built ships made free in any of the ports of England; and provided, that only such as should be in the list sent to the custom-house, and by them to the court of exchequer before Dec. 1662, should enjoy the privilege of a ship *belonging* to England:
" But to me, says Sir *Edward Northey*, it is
" plain, it did not take away all the privileges
" allowed to foreign ships made free; for it
" did not take away the method, directed by
" the Act of Navigation, of making a foreign
" ship free;" but as to foreign ships not in the list, and freed after Dec. 1662, they were to be deemed as aliens' ships; not absolutely, but only so far as to make the goods imported in them liable to all duties to which aliens' ships were liable by the Act of Navigation,

tion, and which are mentioned in the ninth section of that act. And it seemed plain to him, the parliament did not intend that goods imported in a foreign ship owned and manned by the English, and made free after Dec. 1662, should be forfeited; for that was absolutely repugnant to the conclusion of the clause, *but shall be liable to all duties that aliens' ships are liable unto.*

AN opinion was once entertained and delivered in court from great authority, that the words in this section were meant to declare, that the commodities of Russia and the enumerated articles should be imported in foreign ships, but that they should be English-manned.

IN the case of *Scott v. Schwartz*, which happened in 13. *Geo.* 2. (*a*) it was contended by the counsel for the crown, and admitted and reasoned upon at length by the *Chief Baron Comyns*, that the words expressing the ships in which Russia goods should be imported, *such as belong to the people thereof, &c.* must mean the people of Russia, and not the people of England; and that the policy

(*a*) Comyns, 677.

of that provifion was, that Ruffia fhips
fhould be the bringers of thofe articles, but
they fhould be navigated by Englifh mafters
and mariners; and comparing it with the
wording refpecting the importation of articles from Turkey, which requires the fhip
to be *Englifh-built*, it was faid, that
the manning of Ruffia fhips with Englifh
mariners was a policy extremely beneficial to Englifh navigation, and fuch as
both countries would find an advantage in;
but that it was forefeen, that Turkifh fhips
would hardly be fuffered by the Mahometans to be navigated by Italian failors, nor
would it be proper for Chriftian powers to
condefcend to fuffer it; and therefore the
act requires in that cafe, that where the mariners were Englifh, the fhip alfo fhould be
fuch. This feems to have been the decided
opinion of the *Chief Baron* upon that
occafion (a).

But furely a very little verbal criticifm
would have drawn from thefe words a different conftruction. For, in the firft place, it
is not only the goods of Ruffia that are in
queftion, but alfo various other enumerated
goods, which are not expreffed to be the

(a) Ibid. 684.

produce of any particular country; and therefore, when we admit that *ships belonging to the people thereof* may, when referred to Ruffia, have an antecedent to which they may refer, it may be afked, What *people* are referred to, where no *country* is mentioned as the place where the enumerated goods are produced? fo that in all cafes, except that of Ruffian commodities, this conftruction, put upon thefe words, leaves them without effect or meaning.

In the next place, this conftruction feems to be taken contrary to the obvious method of tracing the antecedent referred to. For the words being, *that no goods, &c. of Ruffia, &c. nor any mafts, &c. fhall be imported into England, Ireland, Wales, or Berwick, in any fhip or veffel whatfoever, but in fuch as do truly and without fraud belong to the people thereof, or fome of them, as the true owners and proprietors thereof, and whereof the mafter and three-fourths of the mariners at leaft are Englifh,* the natural conftruction is to refer *the people thereof* to the laft antecedent, *England, Ireland, Wales, and Berwick,* and not to *Ruffia.*

LASTLY,

LASTLY, upon comparing this description of the ships, and the manning of them, with other descriptions of ships in the same act, it appears to be the same form of words as is used in various places, in the former part of the act, to describe English shipping. It is used, in the first section, to describe the shipping for the plantation-trade; in the third section, to describe those that are to bring the commodities of Asia, Africa, and America; it is nearly repeated in the fourth section; and as much of it as regards ships, is used in the fifth section relating to the fishery; it is likewise used in several parts of the act subsequent to the eighth section. Indeed this is the sense in which this provision was understood on a subsequent occasion. In the case of *Scott v. D'Acbez*, in 16. & 17. *Geo.* 2. *Lord Chief Baron Parker* lays down the law in that sense, without noticing the determination to the contrary, or that there was any doubt ever entertained upon the subject (*a*).

THE exception at the close of this section has occasioned some discussion: *Except only such foreign ships as are of the built of the coun-*

(*a*) Parker, 27-29.

*try or place of which the goods are the growth, &c. or of such port where the goods can only be, or most usually are first shipped for transportation, and whereof the master and three-fourths of the mariners at least are of the said country or place.* The most material doubt upon these words was, whether they applied only to the latter part of the section relating to currants and the Turkey-trade, or extended to the whole of the section. It was maintained by the crown-lawyers in the beforementioned case of *Scott v. Schwartz*, that it was confined to the Turkey trade; but this was over-ruled by the *Chief Baron Comyns*, who clearly thought the exception extended to the whole section; upon the consideration, that the goods of Russia and the enumerated goods, as well as currants and the commodities of Turkey, are all declared in the ninth section to be aliens' goods, if they are imported in other than English shipping.

THE Danes and Swedes being at war, it became a question, In what light prize-ships taken by one or other of those powers should be considered? Sir *Edward Northey* (a) was of opinion, that a Danish ship being taken a

(a) 24 Feb. 1710.

prize

prize by the Swedes, and condemned in the court of admiralty in Sweden, the property was altered, and any British subject might lawfully purchase such ship; and such ship being owned by British subjects might import timber from Sweden; but Swedes being owners of such a ship could not import timber from thence, such ship not being of the built of Sweden; which opinion seems well founded: for though prize-ships with us are favoured in the same manner as British-built, this is by special provision in an act of parliament; and nothing similar being enacted with regard to ships taken prize by any foreign power, that circumstance, of their being taken *prize*, cannot make them of the *built* of that country, as the law expressly requires them to be.

WHERE English-built ships were sold to foreigners, and navigated by them, there had been a difference of opinion, and of practice, as to the qualification of such ships; some holding, that they were qualified under this section of the Act of Navigation; others, that they were not.

AN English-built ship sold to subjects of the Duke of Tuscany imported oil from Naples.

Naples. It was held by *Mr. Browne* (a), that the ship might legally be admitted to an entry without incurring any forfeiture; for though in strictness the letter of the Act of Navigation seemed against it, yet the intention and design of it was plainly otherwise; for it could not in reason be presumed to be the intention of the law-makers, when legislating for the encouragement of English-built shipping (which was the great design of the law) to take from it that liberty and privilege which British-built shipping had before, and put our ships built here in a worse condition than those built in Italy; and the ninth section directing the payment of aliens' duty explained, as he thought, their meaning to be so.

Such is the first opinion to be found upon this point; but some few years after, we find *Sir Edward Northey* delivering a contrary opinion (b); for he lays it down, without any doubt or qualification, that wine of the growth of Italy might not be imported from Leghorn in an English-built ship owned and manned by the subjects of the Duke of Tuscany; for the parliament did

(a) 2 May 1693.  (b) 6 March 1702-3.

not intend that any foreigners should import, unless in English ships manned with English, any goods even of the produce of their own country, except they built ships for importing them; in which case only, they are allowed to import their goods in their own ships, manned with a master and three-fourths of the mariners of their own country; but they cannot trade in ships they buy, and do not build.

So where an English-built ship was taken prize by the French, and afterwards was employed to import French wines, with a master and mariners French, Sir *Edward Northey* held the importation to be contrary to the Act of Navigation (a).

This opinion of Sir *Edward Northey* seems not to have been maintained by his successors without some mixture of doubt. Thus in 1740, where a British-built ship, the master and mariners Portuguese, imported fruit and oil from Portugal, Sir *Dudley Ryder* and Sir *John Strange*, who were consulted on the legality of this importation, thus express themselves: It seemed to them a case

(a) 16 May 1715.

wherein,

wherein, by the letter of the act, the ship and goods would be forfeited; but they were not so clear, that it was within the intent. The end of the act was to encourage British shipping and navigation, and therefore it required the importation to be in British ships, except in the reasonable instance of the country sending their own goods in their own ships, which was allowed. In this case, if it was a Portuguese ship, there could be no objection; and they did not see how Great-Britain was hurt by a Portuguese sending goods in a British-built ship; which answered one view of the act in encouraging our shipping, though not the other with regard to the navigation (*a*).

The policy of this exception in favour of foreign shipping was very ably examined in the before cited case of *Scott v. D'Arbez*, where an English ship having become French property imported French wine and vinegar from France, the master and three fourths of the mariners being French.

In favour of this ship it was objected, that the main design of the act was, that the

(*a*) 20 December 1740.

English,

English, and not foreign nations, should be carriers, and therefore they may carry as well in foreign-built ships, being their property, as in ships of the built of their own country, if they qualify them according to the tenth section, and navigate them with a master and three-fourths of the mariners English; and this is enforced in the eleventh section. Again, if a foreign ship may have the privilege of an English ship, *pari ratione*, or rather *à fortiori*, an English ship, being foreign property, should be intitled to the like privilege, taking the encouragement of ship-building to be the second consideration of the act. For, in the present case, our own timber and workmen were employed, and we had the benefit of rigging and furniture; whereas, if she had been French-built, she would have been duly qualified to have imported those articles, and we should not have had the advantage of building and equipping.

To these objections it was answered, and resolved by the *Chief Baron Parker*, that they were indeed specious, but were founded on a supposition, that we could have prohibited the importation of European goods in foreign bottoms; but as that could not be
done

done with safety to our trade, the force of the objections vanished.

It was seen, said he, that many countries in Europe, as *France*, *Spain*, and *Italy*, could more easily buy ships than build them: that, on the other hand, countries like Russia, and others in the North, had timber and materials enough for building ships, but wanted sailors. It was from a consideration of this inaptness in most countries to accomplish a complete navigation, that the parliament prohibited the importation of most European goods, unless in ships owned and navigated by English, or in ships of the built of and manned by sailors of that country of which the goods were the growth. The consequence would be, that foreigners could not make use of ships they bought, though English subjects might. This would force them to have recourse to our shipping, and the general intent of the act, to secure the carrying-trade to the English, would be answered, as far as it possibly could. On the other hand, if foreign property had been sufficient to qualify ships, foreigners might have bought ships where they pleased, and manned them with their own sailors; and then not only the freight, but the employment

ment of our sailors, would have been lost to England; and preventing this must greatly counterbalance any advantage that could accrue to England from the building and equipping ships for foreign use; which too, being a secondary consideration in making the act, was not to defeat the primary one (a).

THE *Chief Baron* remarked, that with all the desire the parliament had to encourage English shipping, and notwithstanding they had, with that view, required the productions of our own colonies, and those of Asia, Africa, and America, to be imported only in English shipping; yet they wisely foresaw, that if they restrained the importation or exportation of European goods, unless in our own ships, and manned with our own seamen, other States would do the same; and this in its consequences would amount to a prohibition of all such goods; which would be extremely detrimental to trade, and in the end defeat the very design of the act (b). This exposition of the Act of Navigation is certainly the true one.

(a) Parker, 30, &c.        (b) Ibid.

DOUBTS

*Of the Country where Foreign Ships built.*

DOUBTS had arisen, Whether the *country* or *place* where foreign ships were built so as to be properly qualified under the exception in the eighth section, was to be construed in a more extensive or more limited sense; whether it depended on the *geography* of the country, or the dominion and *sovereignty* of it, as it stood at the time the Act of Navigation was passed?

THOSE who held it should be construed with a view to the geography of European countries, alledged, the practice of the custom-house was to consider the third and fourth sections geographically, and to give the words *country* and *place* there used a very extensive construction. Thus goods of foreign plantations in America had been allowed to be imported from the British colonies; the products of one part of Africa had been imported from another part of Africa, and they were still deemed to come from the place of their growth. They urged, that the construction of the Prohibition in the Act of Frauds (which was said to be made for explaining the Act of Navigation) had been also geographical; for that clause had been understood not to affect such other countries, not in Germany, as were subject either to the

the emperor, or any other sovereign prince of the empire.

NOTWITHSTANDING this reasoning, it seems to have been the opinion of the crown-officers very early, that the construction of this act should turn upon sovereignty, and upon a sovereignty that existed at the time the Act of Navigation was made. This appears from the following case.

THE king of Sweden having subdued, and being in possession of, the whole dukedom of Courland, receiving its revenues, and doing other acts of sovereignty, some tar of the growth of that country was imported in a Swedish-built ship, owned and manned by Swedes, from a port in Courland; and Sir *Ed. Northey* (a) was of opinion, this importation was not legal, as the king of Sweden was not in possession of that country at the time when the Act of Navigation was passed.

THE practice of the custom-house seems to have been formed partly upon the idea,

(a) 19 May 1703.

that the same sovereignty constituted the same country, without regard to its having been so at the time of making the Act of Navigation, and partly with an eye to the local situation and geography of places.

Thus we are told, in the year 1757, that *Dantzic* ships had, time out of mind, been freighted with goods from any port of *Prussia* for Great-Britain or Ireland; and the limits of the country called *Prussia* had been considered to reach from the port of *Colberg* on the south-west, to the port of *Memel* on the north-east of *Dantzic*; and accordingly *Dantzic* ships had imported goods of *Memel* and *Colberg*, and the intermediate ports; and ships from any of these ports had brought to Great-Britain Dantzic goods from *Dantzic*, in the same manner as *Dantzic* ships; and such ships had, without any difficulty, been reported as belonging to the real port to which they belonged, and the cargoes as brought from the place from which they really were brought; and all the ports from *Colberg* to *Memel* had been in this manner deemed ports of *Prussia*. But in 1755 a cargo from Memel arriving at Liverpool in a Dantzic ship, a doubt was started

started as to the legality of the importation; yet on application to the commissioners they directed the collector to admit the goods to an entry, and the same was afterwards done with regard to other ships.

But the commissioners caused this point to be laid before the law officers, in order to have the law upon the subject thoroughly ascertained; and we find, in August 1756, the following opinion of *Mr. Murray*, then attorney-general (a). He held, that the words *country or place*, as well as the scope and meaning of the act, confine the importation to such foreign ships as are built at and navigated by the people of Memel, or some other part of Ducal Prussia. He did not take the reason of the exception to have been geographical but political; because we could not hinder the people of any country from carrying their own commodities. This reason he thought did not hold as to importations in English ships from Asia, Africa, America, or elsewhere; and therefore in such importations greater latitude might have been allowed. He observed, that the master and three-fourths of

(a) 19 August 1756.

the mariners muft be of the country or place; but *Ducal Pruffia* could not be faid to be the *country* of a Pole.

SOME few months after, the fame point was laid before the fucceeding law-officers, Mr. *Henley* and Mr. *Yorke (a)*, who declared, they concurred in opinion with Mr. *Murray*, that goods the growth, product, or manufacture of Ducal Pruffia could not be imported in fhips belonging to Polifh Pruffia.

A QUESTION of this fort arofe upon a cafe ftill more nicely circumftanced. The province of Eaft Friefland came to the king of Pruffia by inheritance, and he had been in poffeffion of it for about thirty years. Stettin is a part of Pruffian Pomerania. The inhabitants of Eaft Friefland and Stettin are, therefore, equally fubjects of Pruffia, and navigate under Pruffian colours. It was made a queftion, Whether fhips of Eaft Friefland might import timber from Stettin and other Pruffian ports? And it was held by Mr. *Thurlow*, then attorney-general, that the apparent object and exprefs provifion of the Act of Navigation was to take from the

(*a*) 5 May 1757.

ships of other nations the employment of carriers to this, permitting them however to bring in their own goods, either of manufacture or produce. The circumstance of one country, which was severed in 1660, being united by conquest or descent, did not seem to him to change the law of England; but the subjects of that country would still be confined to the importation of their own produce or manufactures only; for which reason he thought East Friesland, under the circumstances above stated, was not intitled to import timber the growth of the rest of Germany.

AGAIN, where a ship of Stettin brought timber from Memel, and *Mr. Thurlow* was again consulted on this point, he said, generally speaking, it appeared to him, that two countries, which became united under one sovereign by descent or conquest, preserving however, in all other respects, their separate character, are not one and the same country, in the sense of the Act of Navigation: as, if Spain and the Netherlands should again descend to the same prince, they would still remain distinct for the purpose of trade, and no Spanish ship could import hither the enumerated articles from Ostend.

*PART II.*
*12. CAR. II. TO*
*A.D. 1783.*
*EUROPEAN*
*TRADE.*

Oftend. But perhaps two countries might be so united by changing and new-modelling their constitutions into one, as to bring the whole within the description of this law; as if an union were established similar to that which makes Great Britain one kingdom.

*Stat. 22. Geo. 3. c. 78.*

But these questions were at length determined by a provision in stat. 22. Geo. 3. c. 78. by which act a remedy was applied to this and other supposed defects in our navigation laws.

It was therein enacted, that any person might import into Great Britain any sort of timber, or of the said articles, from any foreign place in Europe, in a ship *the property* of subjects under the same sovereign as the country of which such goods are the growth, product, or manufacture, although the country or place where such ship was *built,* or to which she *belongs,* was not under the dominion of such sovereign at the time of passing the Act of Navigation *(a)*. But such goods are liable to aliens and all other duties, as before this act *(b)*. By this provision a doubt respecting countries that

(*a*) Sect. 3.   (*b*) Sect. 4.

were

were diſtinct, but had the ſame ſovereign, was removed. Secondly, It was the property, and not the built, of the ſhip that was to be regarded. Thirdly, The property was not confined to the *very* country or place of production, as the built was by the old law, but might be of ſubjects under the ſame ſovereign.

THE immediate object of this proviſion was to enable his Pruſſian majeſty's ſubjects to import Pomeranian merchandize in Eaſt Frieſeland ſhips. But it led to conſequences of greater extent; and it was found neceſſary afterwards to correct this innovation upon the Act of Navigation, by a proviſion made in ſtat. 27. *Geo.* 3. as will be ſeen hereafter.

THE requiſite of *the maſter and three-fourths of the mariners being of the ſaid country or place* led to ſome diſcuſſion. Where a Dutchman was maſter of a Dantzic ſhip, and it appeared that he had been made a free burgher of Dantzic, *Mr. Dodd* was of opinion, that this qualified him ſufficiently to be maſter (*a*). And on a ſubſequent occaſion (*b*), where a Ruſſian ſhip was

(*a*) In 1706.   (*b*) In 1712.

navigated

navigated with half English, Dutch, and Danes, who were alledged to have been married in the Russian dominions, Sir Ed. Northey was of opinion, that supposing these English, Dutch, and Danes, to be settled inhabitants in Russia, and naturalized there, they were of that country, within the meaning of the Act of Navigation. Notwithstanding these opinions had shewn, that great latitude was meant to be allowed in ascertaining this qualification, there was afterwards a disposition to contract the meaning of the description. This point was brought forward in the beforementioned case of *Scott v. D'Achez*, when it underwent a complete discussion, and was finally determined.

In order to ascertain the extent of this description, it was upon that occasion considered, that the requisite, when applied to English shipping, *that the master and three-fourths of the mariners should be English*, was explained by the act itself. Thus, in sect. 2. it is said, that no alien born, *unless naturalized or made denizen*, should use the trade or employment of a merchant or factor in any part of his majesty's dominions in Asia, Africa, or America. Again, by sect.

sect. 6. no persons are to load for carrying coastways goods on board any bottom of which a stranger born is owner, *unless he has been made a denizen, or been naturalized.* From these it was collected, that none were to be esteemed *English*, within the meaning of this act, but such as are natives, or are naturalized, or made denizens; from whence it was inferred, that the words *those of other countries* being set in opposition, as it were, to the word *English*, the mariners so described should be *natives* of the country, or at least that which is tantamount.

OTHERS said, that these words did not seem to be placed in such designed opposition as to call for the above inference; that the law in this country respecting aliens was of feudal origin, was peculiar to this country, and was not a measure to be taken for determining the law of any other country, and prescribing what should denominate persons *to be of such country.* If we look into the act itself for assistance, we find, that the section now in question speaks of ships *belonging to the* PEOPLE *of those countries,* and then goes on to require the master and three-fourths of the mariners to *be of that country:* it seemed as if it meant to say, *of the people* of that country. The fourth section, which speaks of fish *usually fished for and caught by the* PEOPLE *of England, Ireland, and Wales*, must denote the *inhabitants* of those countries generally, whether natives or not. The same where it says, *fish when imported into England, &c. not being caught by vessels belonging thereto, nor cured by the* PEOPLE *thereof*, should pay double aliens customs; it must mean the *inhabitants* thereof generally; for it could not be supposed, that if the fish were cured and dried by natives *not* inhabitants, they would be excused by the double duties. Again, the sixteenth section speaks of *fish caught by* THE PEOPLE *of Scotland*; need it be enquired, Whether such fish were caught by the natives of Scotland?

UPON the whole, it was judged to be the design of the act, that no foreign ships should import any of the goods enumerated and described in this section, if mariners were brought from any foreign kingdom to navigate them. It does not precisely define, *who* shall be the people of the country, but certainly gives a larger signification than what can be meant by the word *natives (a)*.

(a) Comyns Rep. 686, 687, 688.

SUCH was the reasoning upon this expression in section 8. in the case of *Scott v. Schwartz* beforementioned. This was the case of a ship, Russia-built, from Riga, navigated by a master who was born out of the Russian dominions, but who had, seven years before, been admitted a burgher of Riga, and had ever since continued so, residing there when not engaged in voyages. There were eleven mariners, four of whom were born in Russia; the fifth was born in Ireland, there bound apprentice to the master, and as such went with him to Riga; for three or four years before the seizure he served on board this ship, and sailed in it from Riga on the present voyage. The other six were born out of the dominions of Russia; but one had resided at Riga for eight years next before the seizure; another five years; another four years; another seven years; and the last four had, during the same period, sailed from Riga in that and other vessels. It was understood there was no such thing as naturalization known in Russia.

THE *Chief Baron Comyns* was of opinion, that the master being a burgher, and having taken an oath of allegiance to the empress, as was proved on the trial, there was hardly anything more cogent than this to denominate a man *of a country*; he must be a subject of the empress. As to the other four mariners, he thought them *to be people of the country*, within the meaning of the act; first, because the act seems to intend nothing more than fixed and settled inhabitants there; and a residence of four or five years might well satisfy that expression: secondly, because it seemed to answer the intent of the act; which was not so much to create difficulties to other countries to find mariners amongst themselves, as to prevent their supplying themselves with them from other countries than England (a): thirdly, because by the civil law such a residence gives a country a right to the resident's service: *Qui originem ab urbe Roma habent, si alio loco domicilium constituerunt, munera ejus sustinere debent* (b); fourthly, because in the present case it was not found by the special verdict that these persons had ever any habitation or residence out of the empress of Russia's dominions,

(a) *Vide ant.* 226. the Chief Baron Comyns's opinion upon navigating Russian ships with English mariners.

(b) Dig. l. 50. tit. 4. lex 3.

and

and what does not appear is not to be intended. It was found that they had made several voyages from Ruffia, but it did not appear that they had made any voyage from any other country; fo that they might properly be faid to be mariners of Ruffia, but not of any other country: and as the act fpeaks of mariners of the country, and does not fay mariners *born in* the country; and as *mariner* is a denomination they muft acquire, for they cannot be born mariners, if therefore they were of that country while they were mariners, and never were mariners of any other country, they feem to fatisfy the words and intent of the act (*a*).

Upon the whole it was faid, that it would be almoft impracticable, and make commerce very hazardous, if a merchant was to fearch out the nativity of every mariner he employed, and in cafe of miftake or mifinformation was to forfeit his fhip and cargo; and therefore the court decided in the above manner (*b*), as no fuch conftruction (fays the report) appears hitherto to have been made of the act.

(*a*) Comyns, 689, 690, 691.    (*b*) Ibid. 693.

On

On the other hand, where a Scotchman, who had been made a burgher of Stockholm, was the master of a Swedish ship, navigated with Swedish mariners, *Sir Philip Yorke* (a) apprehended this would not intitle him to be considered as a Swede in Great-Britain, his native country: with regard to his own country, he continued a natural-born British subject, and would, in his opinion, still continue a good British master to navigate a British-built ship with British mariners; which seemed to shew that he could not be considered here as a Swedish master to navigate a Swedish ship. But as this was a new case, he thought it would be hard to take advantage of the forfeiture.

If a ship comes out of a foreign country properly manned, and the men die in the voyage, and others, of England or Holland are taken in to supply their places, this case of necessity will prevent the forfeiture. An allegation that the men deserted, is liable to suspicion, and is not so likely to be received as an excuse. It should seem, that if they were not full three-fourths mariners of the country, and

(a) 3 August 1732.

the master properly qualified, when they came out of the *country* or *place*, nothing that may be done afterwards to qualify the navigation ought to be admitted.

HAVING thus taken a view of the importation of goods from all parts of the world, we come now to two confiderations which apply to all the foregoing trades; namely, to the exception which, in the opinion of lawyers, it was judged proper to make in the case of *prize-goods* imported contrary to the requisites of the Acts of Navigation; and, secondly, to the nature of *importation*, and what circumstances have been deemed necessary to constitute a transaction on which so much hazard of penalties and forfeitures depends.

IT had been an established doctrine in the custom-house, that general prohibitions upon trade did not operate with respect to goods taken as prize: in consequence of this it had been the practice, when goods had been condemned as prize at Gibraltar, in Ireland, or in any of his majesty's dominions abroad, to permit them to be imported into England, notwithstanding they would have been forfeited, if brought hither

hither from those places in the common way of trade; and the duties have in such cases been permitted to be taken even where the goods, though condemned, were discharged by a sentence of reversal. But in a case where an East India ship of great value had been captured and carried into Ireland, the commissioners, before they allowed the importation, wished to have the opinion of the law-officers; when Mr. Henley (a) declared it to have been established upon very solid grounds, that the acts prohibiting importation of particular commodities are applicable only to importations in a course of trade; and he held, that English merchants purchasing the cargo of this ship in Ireland might import it into England, as they would stand in the place of the captors; and the commissioners were not justified by any laws, either regarding the nation in general or the East India Company in particular, in refusing to permit the importation and entry of such a cargo.

Thus far may prize-goods be considered upon general reasoning; but a shorter

(a) 1 March 1757.

answer

answer to such questions is, that prize-goods are specially excepted by sect. 15. of the Act of Navigation; which provision is not referred to in any of the law opinions on this point.

YET where goods the product of a British plantation were taken prize by the French and carried into France, and the merchants in England, to whom they had been consigned, meant to purchase them if they could be permitted afterwards to import them, *Sir Dudley Ryder* (a) held, however reasonable this might be in itself, the Act of Navigation was so plain upon the point, that if those goods should be imported from France, they would, in his opinion, be forfeited, and the commissioners licence or warrant to admit them to an entry, as was proposed, would not dispense with the forfeiture.

IN carrying into execution these laws of navigation, it became material to ascertain what amounted to an *importation*. The following cases will throw some light upon this point.

(a) 14 May 1745.

AT a time when the importation of French goods was prohibited, a ſhip laden with French wines from Spain to Ireland was driven into Plymouth by ſtreſs of weather, and it was ſubmitted to the law-officers, Whether this was an importation? Sir *Robert Sawyer* delivered his opinion, that where a ſhip was bound to a foreign port, and in purſuing her courſe to ſuch port was driven into an Engliſh port, it would be no importation; but where ſhe was bound to an Engliſh port, or came with a deſign to land the goods in England, and in her courſe thither, but by ſtreſs of weather, ſhe put into another port, he conceived it a forfeiture. Sir *George Treby* (a), upon the ſame occaſion, ſays, a mere involuntary importing by diſtreſs of weather is not an importation againſt this prohibitory act; for though ſuch importing is not excepted by expreſs words of the act, yet it is underſtood to be excepted by that equity which is allowed in interpreting ſtatutes; but this exception is not to be extended to caſes, where there is a *mala fides* and a poſitive intent to break the law, for that takes away all title to ſuch equity and favour. In this

(a) 5 March 1691-2.

caſe

case there is an importation coupled with a purpose to break the law, for they only differ in the circumstance, of going to one prohibited place instead of another; but the substantial part, besides what happened to be done, was actually intended; and it was in his judgment no better than if a ship designing to bring French goods into the Isle of Man, or Jersey, or Dartmouth, should, from extremity of weather, put into Liverpool, or Guernsey, or Plymouth.

But this case was submitted to the opinions of eminent lawyers more than once. Sir Robert *Sawyer* (*a*) gave another opinion, where he declares, that the coming of the ship into port by stress of weather is no importation within the act; and the intention to go to Ireland could work no forfeiture. Mr. *Constantine Phipps* also held, that although the master's declaration that he was bound for Ireland, was an evidence that he intended to commit an offence against the prohibitory act, yet such intention should not subject the ship and goods to forfeiture; for the merchants and owners might have

(*a*) 28 March 1692.

altered

altered their voyage, and ordered the ship to some other port, and a bare intention to break the act of parliament is not punishable; nor can the intention make any alteration in this case in strictness of law, for the only point in issue upon the information would be, *Whether the goods were imported contrary to the act?* and he never knew that the coming in of a ship by stress of weather was ever construed an importation. *Mr. Warde* and *Sir Francis Pemberton* both agree in holding the intention to go to Ireland as not altering the case, and that the coming in by stress of weather could not be an importation.

THE coming in by stress of weather seems to have been generally held to be no importation under the Act of Navigation. Where a ship loaded with teas was driven into Yarmouth harbour, *Sir Philip Yorke* (a) clearly held it not a case to proceed upon; and he seems to have paid no regard to the circumstances which shewed the ship to be bound to Newcastle, contrary to the declaration of the master, who alledged he was bound for North Bergen.

(a) 18 September 1731.

AGAIN,

AGAIN, where a Dutch ship was stranded on the coast of Sussex with goods the product of Surinam; *Sir Philip Yorke (a)* was of opinion, that the goods might be admitted to an entry, if the commissioners of the customs were satisfied they were fairly stranded, without any fraudulent intent to evade the Act of Navigation; for the prohibition in that act was not an absolute prohibition of the importation, but only a qualified one, as in case they were imported in *ships* not duly navigated, or from any place not being the place of their growth, production, or manufacture; or from the ports where they had not been usually first shipped for transportation; and stat. 5. *Geo.* 1. c. 11. s. 13. has declared all stranded goods should be liable to the same duties, as if they had been regularly imported. As to the frauds that might be committed under the colour of stranded goods, the commissioners might always exercise their judgment, whether it was a case where the goods should be admitted to an entry.

WHERE a prize-ship laden with sugars was carried into Montserrat to be con-

(a) 27 November 1729.

PART II.
12. CAR. II TO
A. D. 1783.
EUROPEAN
TRADE.

demned, and was from thence, without unloading, carried to Antigua, this was held by *Sir Dudley Ryder* (a) not to be such an importation at Montserrat as to subject the sugars to the duty imposed on the importation of such sugars in that island.

BEFORE the Hovering Act, when small vessels loaded with brandy used to come into port in the night, in moderate weather, without any urgent necessity, *Sir Edward Northey* (b) held, if it should appear such vessels came into port with intent to unload, such coming in would be an importation, although no bulk was broken; but such intent must be fully and plainly proved by some attempt to sell, or put out of the vessel any of the goods. On a subsequent occasion it was laid down by *Sir Dudley Ryder* (c), that the mere coming within the limits of a port, without any intent to break bulk or unlade, is not looked upon as an importation within any of the acts, either to make the customs become due, or subject the ship or goods to forfeiture, or to oblige the master to report or make an entry, or to require a coast-cocket.

(a) 5 June 1738.　　(b) 26 December 1716.
(c) 19 April 1748.

UPON

UPON this head of *importation* there are a few, and but few, determinations of courts. There was an information of feizure of goods in a ship that was twenty miles below the *Hope*, but within the limits of the port of London: a new trial was moved for upon a doubt, Whether this could be faid to be an importation? But the new trial was refufed; and it was therefore concluded the court judged this to be an importation (*a*).

WHERE a ship carrying teas from Oftend to Lifbon came into the port of Cowes to mend her bowfprit, fhe was feized by the officers; after which fome goods were run by the failors. The *Chief Baron (b)* held this not to be an importation within the Act of Navigation, and that fuch running did not amount to a forfeiture, becaufe after the feizure the fhip was in the power and controul of the officers; but the jury gave a verdict for the forfeiture, thinking the *coming into Cowes* was only a pretence, and the *running afterwards* declared the firft intent to have been fraudulent (*c*).

(*a*) Bunb. 79.   (*b*) Anno 1727.   (*c*) Ibid. 236.

It had been usual on the trial of informations for forfeiting goods illegally imported, to produce the master of the ship as a witness for the defendant; and no objection was made to his competency (especially if there was no information for forfeiture of the ship) till a case which happened in 1723, when it was insisted that the ship, as well as goods, was forfeited; and the objection was held to be good. Accordingly in 1724, at the trial of an information on stat. 9. & 10. *Will.* 3. ch. 10. s. 3. for importing India silks, the master of the ship being offered as a witness for the defendant, he was refused by *Lord Chief Baron Eyre* because, although no prosecution had yet been commenced, he was *liable* to one (a).

In the case of *Idle v. Vanneck* it was contended for the defendant, who was prosecuted for bringing goods from *Rotterdam*, not being the place of their growth, that the goods were brought either by the passengers or the mariners without the knowledge or privity of the master, and it was hard to subject the master, and much more the owner, to a loss for a cause of forfeiture

(a) Bunb. 140.

which

which they could not prevent; and they relied on ſtat. 27. *Ed.* 3. c. 19. and ſtat. 38. *Ed.* 3. c. 8. But *Lord Chief Baron Pengelly* ſaid, his preſent thoughts were, that *knowledge* in the maſter was not neceſſary; for the act is an expreſs prohibition without any limitation or qualification, and the fact proved came directly within the deſcription of the act; the forfeiture was upon the goods themſelves, and not upon the perſon; the intention of the law was to ſupport trade; and therefore it might be preſumed, all perſons would take the utmoſt care, trade ſhould be carried on without fraud. The owner is to take care what maſter he employs; and the maſter what mariners and what paſſengers he takes in; and being *exercitor navis,* and having the entire controul of the ſhip, he may ſearch and examine when and where he will. No damage accrues to the owner, for he may recover againſt the maſter for the forfeiture of the ſhip accruing by his default; and (as he thought) the maſter might recover againſt a paſſenger who cauſed a forfeiture. There is more reaſon the owner ſhould ſuffer, as he had the benefit of the freight which occaſioned the forfeiture. The maſter is to report, and therefore is obliged to see what he does report.

SUCH was the opinion delivered by the *Chief Baron*, though he meant to reserve the point for the opinion of the court; but it turned out not to be necessary, for the jury found that the defendant *had* actual knowledge of the fact.* On a motion for a new trial, all the Barons agreed in opinion that notice in the master was not necessary to create a forfeiture upon this act; though for a small matter they thought it would be hard a ship should be condemned (*a*).

ON a subsequent occasion, in 1733, this distinction was made upon the point by *Lord Chief Baron Reynolds*; namely, Whether the goods so brought were part or not part of the cargo? and therefore, if mariners or passengers *privately* bring over a *small parcel* of goods, they are not to be looked upon as part of the cargo, and it would be hard the ship should be forfeited for such a cause (*b*).

NOTWITHSTANDING this question seemed thus to be settled, it was moved again in

(*a*) Bunb. 238.   (*b*) Ibid. 232.

6. GEO. 3.

6. *Geo.* 3. in *Mitchell v. Torup*, being an information on the fourth section of the Act of Navigation, for an importation of 221 lb. of teas from Norway, which were found by the jury to have been put on board by the mariners without the knowledge, privity, or consent of the master, mate, or owners. Upon that occasion a very full opinion was given by the *Lord Chief Baron Parker*.

He observed, that the words of the act in the first, second, third, and fourth sections were all equally negative, absolute, and prohibitory; they operate both on the goods and the ship, and there is not a syllable that hints at the privity or consent of the master, mate, or owners. The reason of penning the section in these strong terms was, to prevent as much as possible its being evaded; for if the privity or consent of the master, mate, or owners had been made necessary, the provisions of the act would have been defeated.

In expounding acts of parliament where words are express, plain, and clear, they ought to be understood according to their genuine and natural signification, unless by such exposition a contradiction or inconsistency

fiftency would arife by reafon of fome fubfequent claufe, from whence it might be
inferred the intent of the act was otherwife:
now the fubfequent claufes of this act do
not contradict, but enforce the natural import of the words of the fourth claufe; which
appears by the twelfth, thirteenth, and fourteenth fections; and when this act was
under the confideration of the Legiflature at
feveral fubfequent periods, as at the times of
making ftat. 14. *Geo.* 2. c. 36. ftat. 17. *Geo.* 2.
c. 36. and ftat 25. *Geo.* 2, c. 32. no relaxation was made by any of thofe acts, fo as to
make the privity or confent of the mafter,
mate, or owners, neceffary to a forfeiture.

To the objection made by the defendant,
that the penalty or forfeiture impofed by
the fourth fection, is only applicable where
there is fome crime or guilt, and none can
be imputed to the mafter, mate, or owners,
without their privity, he anfwered, that
though penalties and forfeitures, generally
fpeaking, are the confequence of fome crime
or guilt, yet neither of them neceffarily im-
ply the one or the other, though punifh-
ment always does: which he illuftrated by
the examples of a fword belonging to an innocent man being forfeited, if a murder
had been committed with it; fo of deodands;
and

and by stat. 4. *Will.* & *Mary*, c. 8. the horses of innocent owners, upon which robberies are committed, are forfeited; and there are various forfeitures of a similar nature in the revenue-laws, as those of boats, carriages, horses, cattle, and other things. And by this fourth section, the forfeiture is not upon the person, but on the ship, not *in personam* but *in rem*.

He said, it had been suggested to him, that informations had been constantly drawn in this form from the first passing of the act, without alledging any privity; and as it is not necessary to prove more than is laid, he said, the finding of the jury, who in this case found that the importation was without the privity of the master, mate, or owners, was nugatory and void, not being comprized in the issue.

To the stat. 38. *Ed.* 3. c. 8. for protecting ships from being forfeited for a small thing put into a ship without knowledge of the owner, he answered, that the Navigation Act was passed subsequent, is an express prohibition, without restriction or limitation, and has altered the law, by excluding the privity, as the most effectual means to prevent the mischief. Indeed ships are

are now forfeited for much smaller quantities, *viz.* 6lb. and 20lb. by stat. 9. *Geo.* 2. c. 35. stat. 3. *Geo.* 3. c. 22. s. 5. stat. 5. *Geo.* 3. c. 43. yet he thought, if the quantity was so small as not to be discoverable by reasonable care and search, it might be proper for the consideration of the jury; and they neither would nor ought, in such a favourable case, to find a forfeiture of a ship; for *de minimis non curat lex.*

To the objection rested on stat. 27. *Ed.* 3. c. 19. " that no merchant should forfeit his " goods for the trespass and forfeiture of his " servant," he answered in like manner, that the Navigation Act was subsequent to it. He repeated, that the owners are to take care what master they employ, and the master what mariners; that in the present case, negligence was plainly imputable to the master, who is to report the cargo; and if he had searched, as the officers did, he would have found the tea, and so might have prevented the forfeiture.

HE said, the authorities were wholly in favour of this opinion; the Chief Barons at Nisi Prius had uniformly so acted; *Chief Baron Montague* in *Foster v. Philips* in 1722;

*Chief*

Chief Baron *Gilbert* in *Gatehouse v. Aycock* in Trinity 1725; *Chief Baron Pengelly* in *Idle v. Vanneck* beforementioned, where the Barons agreed with him on a motion for a new trial; and he observed, that the stat. 27. & stat. 38. *Ed.* 3. were cited upon that occasion. He noticed the distinction made by *Chief Baron Reynolds*, whether the goods were a part of the cargo, or not; which he recognized, but thought it did not apply to the case before him, for the quantity was not so small as to excuse the forfeiture of the ship (*a*).

Notwithstanding these judgments against the application of stat. 38. *Ed.* 3. c. 8. to the Act of Navigation, and other acts passed since, it seems now to be the prevailing opinion, that this statute is not repealed by subsequent acts, however absolute in their prohibition, and that it ought to have its influence in construing cases of forfeiture. But stat. 27. *Ed.* 3. c. 19. is not considered in the same light. Instances frequently occur, where forfeitures arise from the conduct of the clerk; but to allow this as a plea, would open a door to all sorts of fraud.

(*a*) Parker 227.

fraud. The opinion of the custom-house on these two laws may be inferred from the collection they have printed of the laws of the customs, which they conceive to be in force; they have inserted stat. 38. *Ed.* 3. but stat. 27. *Ed.* 3. they have excluded.

This is all that I have been able to collect, for illustrating the rules laid down in the Act of Navigation and of Frauds for the conduct of the European trade. And having now taken a view of the policy pursued, for rendering the foreign trade of the whole world subservient to the increase of our shipping and navigation, I shall draw the reader's attention to another part of the subject; and present to him the instances in which this spirit of prescribing the mode of carrying on foreign trade has been compelled to yield, and the execution of our navigation laws have been suspended, lest, in the attempt to enforce them, our commerce might be extinguished, or greatly endangered.

The laws of Navigation, like other laws, have given way to necessity; and have been suspended in time of war. During the dread of continual danger from an enemy

enemy at sea, it is well if foreign trade can be carried on at all; it is no time to be curious as to the built of the ship that is employed in it, how it is navigated, or whence it comes. At such conjunctures it has been usual, more or less, to suspend the Acts of Navigation: the first instance of this was in the Dutch war in the reign of Charles II.

IT was then done, as was common in *those* times, by the prerogative exercised by the crown, of dispensing with laws upon urgent occasions. On the 6th of March 1664, it was found necessary to issue an order of council for suspending the Act of Navigation wholly, as far as regarded the import and export of Norway, and the Baltic Sea; and as far as regarded Germany, Flanders, and France, provided the merchants and the owners of the ships were natural-born subjects: it was further permitted to any one of a nation in amity to import from any parts, hemp, pitch, tar, masts, salt-petre and copper, and to pay duty only as natural-born subjects. English merchants were permitted to employ foreign ships in the coasting and plantation trade, but they were to comply with the restriction of shipping

ping in, and bringing their cargoes to, England or Ireland.

THIS was letting loose at once most of the restrictions belonging to our Navigation system, and throwing it among the rest of Europe, to make the best of it, during the time we were unable to follow up the plan we had proposed to ourselves. In the war of 1740, when we had a war with both France and Spain, it was again necessary to relax from the strictness of our navigation laws; but it was endeavoured to be done in such a way as would facilitate the carrying-on of our trade, without wholly giving up the favourite object of British shipping; and this was by permitting foreigners to become owners of British ships, and to trade as British subjects.

THE colour stated in the preamble of the statute made upon this occasion is, that the selling British-built ships to foreigners is a beneficial branch of trade, and ought to be encouraged; and that it is highly reasonable ships so sold to, or being the property of foreigners, should enjoy the same privilege in these kingdoms, as if they were of

the

the built of the respective countries from whence they came.

This was accordingly done by stat. 17. Geo. 2. c. 36. which enacted, that the goods enumerated and described in the eighth section, might be imported into Great-Britain, Ireland, Guernsey, Jersey, or the colonies or territories in Asia, Africa, or America, in shipping built in Great-Britain, or Ireland, so as the master and three-fourths of the mariners at least were British, or of the country or place of which the goods were the growth, production, or manufacture. But goods so imported in ships the property of foreigners, although British-built, were to pay alien and other duties, the same as if the ship was foreign-built *(a)*. This relaxation of the Act of Navigation was to continue only during the war. In the war with France beginning in the year 1756, the like law was passed, to continue during that war; and again in the year 1779 *(b)*, during the continuance of the then subsisting hostilities with France.

(*a*) Sect. 1, 2.
(*b*) Stat. 29. *Geo.* 2. c. 34. sect. 19. stat. 19. *Geo.* 3. c. 28.

In the last war, during the hostilities between this country and the two crowns of France and Spain, it was found expedient to relax the Navigation Acts.

ACCORDINGLY, by stat. 19. *Geo.* 3. c. 9. permission was given to bring organzined thrown silk of the growth or production of Italy, from any port or place, in any ship, notwithstanding stat. 2. *Will. & Ma.* st. 1. c. 9. This was not to extend to the silk of Turkey, Persia, the East-Indies, or China.

IT was enacted by stat. 20. *Geo.* 3. c. 45. that any person free of the Turkey Company might import into Great Britain or Ireland, any goods or commodities which had theretofore been usually imported from Turkey or Egypt, or from any place within the dominions of the Grand Seignior within the Levant Seas, in any ship built in or belonging to Great Britain or Ireland, and navigated according to law; or in any ship *belonging* to any kingdom or state in amity with his majesty, navigated by foreign seamen, from any port or place whatsoever, upon the same duties as if imported in British ships directly from the place of their growth, production, or manufacture. But if if the importation was in foreign-*built* ships, the goods were to be subject to aliens' duties *(a)*.

AGAIN, any goods or commodities which had been usually theretofore imported from any port or place in Europe, within the streights of Gibraltar (except such as might theretofore be imported only from such ports or places as are within the dominions of the Grand Seignior), might be imported by any person whatsoever into Great Britain or Ireland, from any port or place whatsoever, in like manner, in any British or foreign ship, with the like distinction; only that drugs imported by any person not free of the Turkey Company were to pay the same duties, as if imported not directly from the place of their growth and production *(a)*.

THIS act was to continue in force till 1 June 1781; but it was then re-enacted, to continue during hostilities with France, Spain, and Holland.

IT was also found necessary to provide for other articles of import, by removing

*(a)* Sect. 1.   *(a)* Sect. 3.

the restraints of the Act of Navigation. Thus, by stat. 21. *Geo.* 3. c. 19. flax or flax-feed might be imported from any country or place, in any ship belonging to a state in amity, and navigated with foreign seamen. The same of orchilla weed and cobalt, by stat. 21. *Geo.* 3. c. 62.; and of wool, barilla, jesuits-bark, and linen yarn, by stat. 21. *Geo.* 3. c. 27.; by which act, any goods or commodities of the growth, production, or manufacture, of the colonies or plantations belonging to Portugal, might be imported in any ship belonging to Portugal, from any port or place in Portugal, or the Western Isles, commonly called Azores or Madeira Islands. Again, by stat. 23. *Geo.* 3. c. 1. all sorts of corn, grain, meal, and flour of wheat, rice, and barley, might be imported from any country or place, in foreign ships belonging to any state in amity; and so of rice, paddy, Indian-corn, Indian-meal, and maize, by stat. 23. *Geo.* 3. c. 9.

In these temporary expedients we may trace the progressive increase of British shipping. In the Dutch war of 1664, the nation were obliged at once to abandon the Baltic trade, and to admit foreign ships into the coasting and plantation trade. But in the

the war of 1740 we made no other concession than that of admitting foreigners into the ownership of British-built ships, and to navigate with foreign seamen for carrying the European commodities to this country, and to the plantations. This was also done in the war of 1756, and in the last war. However, in the last war, pressed as our trade was on all sides, we were compelled to yield a little further. Many articles of the trade of Asia, Africa, and America, were permitted to be brought from any place, in any ships belonging to a nation in amity. But in neither of these wars, not even in the last, when we had the maritime powers of both worlds to cope with, Spain, France, Holland, and America, did we allow foreign ships to participate in the coasting or in the plantation trade.

CHAPTER

## CHAPTER IV.

#### THE COASTING TRADE.

PART II.
―――
12.CAR. II. TO
A. D. 1783.
COASTING
TRADE.

THE next object in the Act of Navigation is *the Coasting Trade*. It enacts, that no person shall load, or cause to be loaden and carried, in any bottoms, ships, or vessels, whatsoever, whereof any stranger born (unless such as shall be denizens or naturalized) be owner, part-owner, or master, and whereof three-fourths of the mariners at least shall not be English, any fish, victual, wares, goods, commodities, or things, of what kind or nature soever, from one port or creek of England, Ireland, Wales, the islands of Guernsey or Jersey, or the town of Berwick, to another port or creek of the same, or of any of them, under pain of forfeiting the goods and ship; one moiety to the king, and the other moiety to the informer (*a*).

(*a*) Sect. 6.

By this provision, foreign *property* was excluded from the coasting trade. By stat. 1. *Jac.* 2. c. 18. it was meant to exclude from this trade foreign-*built* ships. Every foreign-built ship or vessel bought, and brought into the kingdom of England, Wales, or the town of Berwick, to be employed in carrying goods and merchandize from port to port, is to pay at the port of delivery for every voyage, over and above all other duties, five shillings *per* ton; one moiety to the chest of Chatham, the other moiety to the Trinity Company (*a*). A duty of twelve-pence *per* ton was to be paid by those foreign ships already employed in the coasting trade (*b*).

These two provisions make the whole of the law of Shipping and Navigation, as far as regards the coasting trade.

(*a*) Sect. 1.   (*b*) Sect. 2.

CHAPTER

( 280 )

## CHAPTER V.

#### THE FISHERIES.

*Certain Sorts of Fish foreign-caught to pay double Aliens' Duty—The Herring, North-Sea, and Westmony Fisheries encouraged—The Greenland and Newfoundland Fisheries free of Duty—Importation of Fish foreign-caught in foreign Ships prohibited—The Newfoundland Fishery—All Fish bought of Foreigners prohibited—Allowances on salted Fish British-caught and cured—Bounties in the Greenland Fishery—Bounties in the Newfoundland Fishery—And in that of the Gulf of St. Laurence and Labrador—Bounties in the Southern Whale Fishery—The Society of the Free British Fishery instituted.*

PART II.
12. CAR. II. TO
A. D. 1783.
FISHERIES.

THE last means of employment for shipping provided for by the Act of Navigation, are *the Fisheries*. With respect to these it was ordained, that any sort of ling, stock-fish, pilchards, or any other kind of of dried or salted fish, usually fished for, and caught by the people of England, Ireland, Wales, or the town of Berwick, or any sort of cod-fish or herring, or any oil or blubber made of any kind of fish whatsoever, or any whale-fins or whale-bones which shall be imported into England, Ireland, Wales, or the town of Berwick, not having been caught in vessels truly and properly belonging thereunto, as proprietors and right owners thereof; and the said fish cured, saved, and dried, and the oil and blubber (and such blubber to be accounted and pay as oil) not made by the people thereof, imported into England, Ireland, or Wales, or the town of Berwick, shall pay double aliens' duty *(a)*.

THE first provision after that in the Act of Navigation for favouring the fisheries, was by a clause *(b)* in stat. 13. & 14. Car. 2. c. 11. where a duty, since called the *Mediterranean duty*, being imposed on under-sized ships trading into the Mediterranean, an exception was made in favour of ships, one moiety of whose full lading was fish only; and in such case, the fish exported, and any

*(a)* Sect. 5.   *(b)* Sect. 36.

goods

goods and merchandize imported in the same ship for that voyage, were not to be subject to any other duty of tonnage or poundage for them than were theretofore accustomed (*a*). And by stat. 9. *Geo.* 2. c. 33. that moiety must consist of fish taken and cured by his majesty's subjects only (*b*).

Two years after another provision was made, for the purpose principally of encouraging the herring, and *North-Sea, Ifland,* and *Weſtmony* fisheries. It was enacted, by stat. 15. *Car.* 2. c. 7. that no fresh herrings, fresh-cod, or haddock, coal-fish, or gull-fish, should be imported into England, Wales, or Berwick, but in English-built ships or vessels, or those *bond fide* belonging to England, Wales, or Berwick, and having a certificate as required by that act, and whereof the master and three-fourths at least of the mariners are English; and which had been fished, caught, and taken, in such ships, and so navigated, and not bought or had of any strangers born, or out of any strangers bottoms, under pain of forfeiting the fish and the vessel (*c*). By the same act a duty was laid on salted or dried

(*a*) Sect. 36.   (*b*) Sect. 3.   (*c*) Sect. 16.

dried fish, imported, and fished or caught, in any other ship or veſſel than of the built, or belonging to, England, Wales, or Berwick, having a certificate, and navigated as before-mentioned *(a)*.

BY ſtat. 18. *Car.* 2. c. 2. no ling, herring, cod, or pilchard, freſh or ſalted, dried or bloated, or any ſalmon, eels, or congers, taken by foreigners, aliens to this kingdom, was to be imported or expoſed to ſale in this kingdom, under pain of forfeiture *(b)*. This was a temporary act, but was made perpetual by ſtat. 32. *Car.* 2. c. 2. ſect. 2. by which act it was provided, that the importation of ſtock-fiſh and live eels ſhould not be thereby prevented, but they might be imported by anybody *(c)*.

AGAIN, by ſtat. 25. *Car.* 2. c. 6. aliens are to pay for fiſh caught by Engliſhmen and exported in Engliſh ſhipping, whereof the maſter and three-fourths of the mariners are Engliſh, no greater ſubſidies and cuſtoms than natives *(d)*. This alſo was a temporary act.

*(a)* Sect. 17.   *(b)* Sect. 2.   *(c)* Sect. 7.
*(d)* Sect. 3.

By stat. 25. *Car.* 2. c. 7. encouragement was given to the Greenland and Newfoundland fisheries, by permitting all persons, whether natives or foreigners, to import train-oil or blubber of Greenland and the parts adjacent, of Newfoundland, or any other of his majesty's colonies, made of fish, or other creatures living in the sea, and whale-fins caught and imported in ships truly and properly belonging to England, Wales, or Berwick, without paying any custom or other duty. Duties were laid upon those articles, if taken and imported in shipping of the colonies; a lower duty if taken by shipping of the colonies, and imported in shipping of England, Wales, or Berwick; and a very high one, amounting to a prohibition, if they were of foreign fishing. And because it was necessary to encourage harpooners, it was permitted, for a limited time, to navigate with one moiety harpooners, and to have one moiety only of the rest of the mariners English, and to enjoy the same privilege as if they were three-fourths English, provided the captain was English (*a*). Such ships were always to victual in England, Wales, or Berwick,

(*a*) Sect. 1.

which

which was to be attested by the collector of
the port, and they were to proceed directly
on their voyage (*a*).

*Importation of Fish foreign-caught in foreign ships prohibited.*

IN a subsequent act, the prohibitions were
not confined by a special enumeration as
before, but extended to *all* fish. Thus, by
stat. 10. & 11. *Will.* 3. c. 24. no fish (except
stock-fish and live eels) taken or caught by
any foreigners, aliens to this kingdom (except protestant strangers inhabiting within
this kingdom) is to be imported in any
foreign ship, vessel, or bottom, not being
wholly English property, and exposed to sale
in this kingdom, under pain of forfeiting the
fish and ship (*b*). This was not to prohibit
the importation of anchovies, sturgeon, botargo, or cavear (*c*).

*Newfoundland Fishery.*

THE fishery at Newfoundland came under
consideration of parliament in the same sessions, when an act was passed (*d*), containing a variety of regulations for securing the
advantages to be derived from this distant
fishery. For this purpose it was declared,
that all his majesty's subjects residing within

(*a*) Sect. 2.   (*b*) Sect. 13.   (*c*) Sect. 14.
(*d*) Ch. 25.

the

the realm of England, or the dominions thereunto belonging, should have the free trade and fishery to and from Newfoundland, and take bait and fish there and in the seas and islands adjacent; which was designed for removing the obstacles that might be thought to lie in the way of a free fishery, from various charters heretofore granted of that island, as well as of other parts of America; and that no alien, not residing within England, Wales, or Berwick, should take any bait, or use any sort of trade or fishing there (*a*). Because doubts had arisen, whether whale-fins, oil, and blubber, taken by ships belonging to the Company of Merchants of London trading to Greenland were not subject to an additional duty of 12d. imposed by stat. 8. & 9. *Will.* 3. c. 24. and stat. 9. & 10. *Will.* 3. c. 23. (although all manner of fish English-taken were excepted) it was declared by this act, that all such whale-fins, oil, and blubber, and also all whale-fins, oil, and blubber, of English fishing, taken in the seas of Newfoundland, or any of the seas belonging to his majesty's plantations or colonies, and imported by the king's subjects in English shipping, should

(*a*) Sect. 1.

be

be free of those duties, as all fish of English-taking (*a*).

THE protection of the English fisheries came again before parliament; when, upon confideration of stat. 15. *Car.* 2. c. 7. and stat. 18. *Car.* 2. c. 2. beforementioned, and the evasions those provisions suffered by the fraudulent practice of persons who traded in English smacks buying, when out at sea, great quantities of fish caught by foreigners, and then bringing it into our ports (a practice which had been complained of and provided against in former times (*b*)); it was enacted by stat. 1. *Geo.* I. st. 2. c. 18. that no herring, cod, pilchards, salmon, or ling, fresh or salted, dried or bloated, nor any gril, mackerel, whiting, haddock, sprats, coal-fish, gull-fish, congers, nor any sort of flat fish, nor any sort of fresh fish whatsoever, shall be imported or exposed to sale in that part of this kingdom called England, which shall be taken by, bought of, or received from, any foreigner, or out of any strangers bottoms, except protestant strangers inhabiting within this kingdom; nor shall any person give or exchange any goods or things for fish so taken. A penalty of 20l. or twelve

(*a*) Sect. 17.    (*b*) Vid. ant. 28, 29.

months

*Fish bought of Foreigners prohibited.*

months imprisonment, is laid on the master of the smack or vessel importing fish contrary to this act (*a*); which by stat. 9. *Geo.* 2. c. 33. is made 100l. on every person offending against the act, and 50l. on the master of the vessel. The penalties of stat, 1. *Geo.* 1. are not to extend to eels, stock-fish, anchovies, sturgeon, botargo, or caveare (*b*).

The effect of stat. 10. & 11. *Will.* 3. c. 24. having made lobsters and turbot very dear, permission was given as well to foreigners as to British to import lobsters or turbots, whether of foreign or British catching, in the same manner as before that statute (*c*).

The fisheries had now become objects of great national concern; and after various experiments for their encouragement, at one time by prohibiting foreign-caught fish, at another by allowing an importation free of duty to fish British-caught; the parliament, in making regulations for the revenue on salt, had, at different times, made certain allowances on the export of salted fish, which operated in the nature of a bounty

(*a*) Sect. 1, 2.    (*b*) Sect. 3.    (*c*) Sect. 10.

on the fisheries (*a*). The principal of these is stat. 5. *Geo.* 1. c. 18. by which allowances were to be paid by the collector of the salt duties on the exportation from Great Britain of the following sorts of fish British-taken, *viz.* on pilchards or shads, seven shillings *per* cask; cod-fish, ling, or hake (except dried cod-fish, ling, or hake, commonly called haberdine), of a certain size, five shillings *per* hundred; wet cod-fish, ling, or hake, two shillings *per* barrel; dried cod-fish, ling, or hake, commonly called haberdine, three shillings *per* cwt.; salmon, four shillings and sixpence *per* barrel; white herrings, two shillings and eightpence *per* barrel; full red herrings, one shilling and ninepence *per* barrel; clean shotten red herrings, one shilling *per* barrel; dried red sprats, one shilling *per* last (*b*).

PART II.
12. CAR. II. TO A. D. 1785.
FISHERIES.
Allowances on salted Fish British-taken and cured.

THE first experiment made by bounties was this on the exportation of British-caught fish; the next was to encourage the fitting out in order to catch; and it was begun in the whale-fishery. The allowing of whale-fins, oil, and blubber, to be imported duty-free (*c*),

Bounties in the Greenland Fishery.

(*a*) Stat. 10. & 11: *Will.* 3. c. 44. f. 14. to 20.
(*b*) Sect. 6.
(*c*) *Vid.* stat. 12. *Gm.* 1. c. 26. and stat. 5. *Geo.* 2. c. 28.

not being found sufficient for regaining this beneficial trade, which was judged by the parliament to be in danger of being intirely lost, and of going into the hands of foreigners who used to bring great quantities of oil to this kingdom, it was thought adviseable to try what could be done by giving a bounty on the *return* of ships from that fishery. Accordingly by stat. 6. *Geo.* 2. c. 33. a bounty of twenty shillings *per* ton was given on all British ships of two hundred tons and upwards, proceeding from Great-Britain on the whale fishery to the *Greenland Seas*, or *Davis's Streights* and the adjacent seas, manned and navigated according to law. Such ships were to have proper equipments of men, harpooners, boats, and other requisites for the fishery, and were to do their utmost endeavours to take whales, or other creatures living in the sea (and on no other design), and to import the whale-fins, oil and blubber, thereof into Great-Britain. Various regulations were devised relative to the fitting out, and the return of such ships, for securing the object of the act. This act was to continue as long as stat. 12. *Geo.* 1. c. 26. and stat. 5. *Geo.* 2. c. 28. on which these articles depended for being duty-free. By stat. 22. *Geo.* 2. c. 45. s. 3. an additional bounty

of

of twenty shillings was given for a limited time; and various other regulations were made for promoting the fishery; which bounties and regulations were continued by stat. 28. *Geo.* 2. c. 20. to the 25th of December 1764. By the same act, no bounty was to be paid for more than four hundred tons in one ship, and it was allowed to ships under two hundred tons.

In stat. 11. *Geo.* 3. c. 38. the whale-fishery was again taken up; the same bounties and the same indemnities in point of duty were given; and at the same time a detail of regulations was devised for carrying the design of the act into execution. This act was to continue for fifteen years: it corresponded with the former policy; only the bounties of forty shillings were to expire at the end of five years, when they were to continue at thirty shillings for five years, and for the last five years they were to be only twenty shillings (*a*); and the benefits of this act were extended to ships fitting out from the American colonies, under similar regulations to be observed at the time of their

(*a*) Sect. 3.

fitting

fitting out (*a*). This act continued in force till the 25th of December 1786.

THE same act held out, for the space of fifteen years, an encouragement to the fishery in the Gulf and River of *St. Lawrence*, and in the seas on the coasts of the American colonies, by allowing the importation in ships belonging to his majesty's subjects of whale-fins taken from whales of those fisheries, free of all custom or subsidy except that granted by stat. 25. *Car.* 2. c. 7. (*b*).

AN exception, that had been made from the prohibition against foreign salt by stat. 2. & 3. *Ann.* c. 14. in favour of cod-fish, ling, or hake, caught and cured at Newfoundland or Iceland, was followed by stat. 13. *Geo.* 3. c. 72. which allows, subject to stat. 10. & 11. *Will.* 3. c. 25. and under certain restrictions, the importation in British-built ships of the same fish caught and cured in *Chaleur Bay*, or any other part of the *Gulf of St. Lawrence*, or on the coast of *Labrador*.

IT was now intended to give the like encouragement by bounties to these fisheries,

(*a*) Sect. 14.    (*b*) Sect. 17.

as had been before given to those of *Greenland* and *Davis's Streights*. This was begun by stat. 15. *Geo*. 3. c. 31. which gives bounties for eleven years to ships employed in the British fishery on the banks of Newfoundland, being British-built, and owned by the king's subjects residing in Great-Britain or Ireland, or Guernsey, Jersey, or Man, of fifty tons burthen or upwards, navigated with not less than fifteen men, three-fourths of whom besides the master were the king's subjects. They were to clear out from Great-Britain; to catch not less than ten thousand fish on the Banks, and land them on the southern or eastern side of Newfoundland, before the 15th of July; then make another trip to the Banks, and return in like manner to the island with the same cargo: the first twenty-five of such ships were to have forty pounds each, the next hundred ships twenty pounds each, and the next hundred ships ten pounds each *(a)*.

THE same act gave the following bounties for the same term of eleven years, for five ships employed in the whale-fishery in the Gulf of St. Lawrence, on the coast of

*(a)* Sect. 1.

Labrador,

Labrador, or Newfoundland, or in any seas to the southward of the *Greenland Seas* and *Davis's Streights*. Every such ship was to be British-built, owned by the king's subjects residing in, and navigated by three-fourths of the king's subjects of, Great-Britain, Ireland, Guernsey, Jersey, or Man; was to clear out from one of those places; and was to take and kill one whale at least in the fishery above described, and return in the same year to some port in England with the oil of the whale or whales so taken: the ship which should arrive with the greatest quantity of oil in the same year, was to have five hundred pounds; with the next greatest quantity, four hundred pounds; with the next, three hundred pounds; the next, two hundred pounds; and the next, one hundred pounds (*a*).

AGAIN, the importation duty-free of train-pil, and blubber, and whale-fins in English ships, by stat. 25. *Car.* 2, c. 7. which had been by a subsequent act extended to British ships, was now extended to ships belonging to Great-Britain or Ireland, or Guernsey, Jersey, or Man (*b*).

(*a*) Sect. 3.   (*b*) Sect. 9.

SHIPPING AND NAVIGATION.

THE act did not stop here; but went on to extend to Ireland the advantages of stat. 11. *Geo.* 3. c. 38. so that any ship might proceed from Ireland on the whale-fishery to the *Greenland Seas*, and *Davis's Streights* and the adjacent seas, being British-built, and owned by the king's subjects of Ireland, and the master and three-fourths of the mariners being the king's subjects of Ireland (*a*). These Irish ships were put under the same regulations as ships going from Great-Britain.

PART II.
12. CAR. II. TO
A. D. 1783.
FISHERIES.

THE whale-fishery aimed at in this statute to be carried on southward of the *Greenland Seas* and *Davis's Streights*, was the first glimpse of what has since been called *the Southern Whale Fishery*, and which in the following session of parliament appeared to the Legislature in a more distinct view. For in stat. 16. *Geo.* 3. c. 47. we are told, that *a valuable whale-fishery had been lately discovered in the seas to the southward of the latitude of* 44 *degrees North*. But it being found necessary that ships going to that fishery, should fit out at a different season of the year than that mentioned in stat. 15. *Geo.* 3. c. 31. the same bounties were allowed to five ships which

Bounties in the Southern Whale Fishery.

(*a*) Sect. 21, 22, 23.

were

were to sail between the first day of August and the first day of November in every year, and having taken at least one whale, were to return to *England* with the oil thereof before the first day of August following; and such oil might be landed without payment of any duty.

A DOUBT having arisen, whether whales taken in 64 degrees and a half northern latitude were within the meaning of stat. 15. *Geo.* 3. c. 31. and to be deemed as taken and killed in a sea to the southward of the *Greenland Seas* and *Davis's Streights*; it was declared by stat. 20. *Geo.* 3. c. 60. that the *Greenland Seas* and *Davis's Streights* should be deemed to extend to the latitude 59 degrees 30 minutes north, and no further; and the bounties given by that act were not to apply to whales taken and killed in any sea to the southward of the *Greenland Seas* or *Davis's Streights* exceeding 44 degrees of north latitude; which made a division of the whale-fishery into three descriptions; namely, that of *Greenland* including *Davis's Streights*, the *Southern*, and the one lying between those two. By the same act an allowance was made for the times of fitting out, in consideration

sideration of the hostilities then subsisting (*a*).

In the mean time the Greenland fishery called for the aid of the Legislature. It was found, that since the bounty granted by stat. 11. *Geo.* 3. c. 38. had been reduced by the lapse of the first five years from forty shillings *per* ton, the number of vessels employed in that fishery had been much diminished: to prevent therefore this fishery entirely falling, a bounty of twenty shillings *per* ton was added for five years by stat. 22. *Geo.* 3. c. 19. to the twenty shillings *per* ton then due by the former act. Because by stat. 15. *Geo.* 3. c. 31. and stat. 16. *Geo.* 3. c. 47. the ships to be intitled to the bounty must be the whole property of persons residing in that part of the king's dominions from whence they cleared out, which prevented any co-partnership between persons residing in Great-Britain and Ireland, it was declared by stat. 18. *Geo.* 3. c. 55. s. 8. that the property might belong to those residing in Great-Britain *or* Ireland.

While so many experiments were making to promote and extend the British whale-fishery,

(*a*) Sect. 2.

fishery, the one which was carried on upon our own coasts was not neglected by the Legislature. This, from its vicinity, and the supply it furnished towards the food as well as employ of the industrious poor, might, perhaps, be considered as deserving a more particular attention.

*The Society of the Free British Fishery instituted.*

To give stability and vigour to this species of fishery, his majesty was authorised by stat. 23. *Geo.* 2. c. 24. intituled, *An Act for the Encouragement of the British White Herring Fishery*, to incorporate certain persons under the stile of *The Society of the Free British Fishery*, to continue for twenty-one years from the date of the charter. To co-operate with the exertions of this Society, a bounty of thirty shillings *per* ton was granted for fourteen years to all persons, whether Members of that Society or others, being owners of decked vessels from twenty to eighty tons, built and fitted out for and employed in those fisheries, which had proceeded from some port of Great-Britain manned and navigated according to law. The Society so incorporated were impowered to raise a capital of 500,000 l.; 'and as an encouragement to become a subscriber to such stock, an allowance of three *per cent.* was to be paid by Government for fourteen years

years for all the money actually employed in the fishery (*a*). To encourage still more such subscriptions, persons subscribing 10000l. might carry on the fishery under their own management by the stile of *The Fishing-Chamber* of such city or town where they chose to establish themselves, and should be intitled to the allowance of three *per cent.* (*b*).

SOME amendments were made in this statute by stat. 28. *Geo.* 2. c. 14. by which, among other things, the bounty and allowance were continued three years beyond the original term of fourteen years (*c*). The bounty of thirty shillings *per* ton being judged insufficient, it was discontinued by stat. 30. *Geo.* 2. c. 30. and in lieu thereof was granted another of fifty shillings *per* ton for the same term of years.

THESE acts being suffered to expire, the parliament interposed again in favour of this fishery. By stat. 11. *Geo.* 3. c. 31. a bounty of thirty shillings *per* ton was again granted for the space of seven years to the owners of decked vessels from twenty to eighty

(*a*) Sect. 40.   (*b*) Sect. 18.   (*c*) Sect. 4.

tons burthen, fitted out and employed in the British White Herring Fisheries; which bounty was further continued by stat. 19. Geo. 3. c. 26. for seven years more.

WE must place among the regulations concerning the fisheries, the prohibition that was laid on the inhabitants of a great part of the American colonies from coming to the fisheries in those seas. By stat. 15. Geo. 3. c. 10. if any vessel being the property of the subjects of Great Britain, not belonging to and fitted out from Great-Britain or Ireland, or the islands of Guernsey, Jersey, Sark, Alderney, or Man, should be found carrying on any fishery on the Banks of Newfoundland, the coast of Labrador, or within the River or Gulf of St. Lawrence, or upon the coast of Cape Breton or Nova Scotia, or any other part of the coast of North America, or having on board materials for carrying on such fishery, the vessel with her tackle and fish in her should be forfeited, unless the master could produce a certificate from the governor of Quebec, Newfoundland, Saint John, Nova Scotia, New York, New Jersey, Pennsylvania, Maryland, Virginia, North or South Carolina, Georgia, East or West Florida, Bahamas,

or

or Bermudas, shewing that such vessel had fitted out from one of those colonies in order to proceed on that fishery (*a*). An exception was made in favour of those who had cleared out before a certain day for the whale-fishery only. A special exception was made in favour of the people of the island of *Nantucket* employed in the whale-fishery only; and in favour of the people of *Marshfield* and *Scituate*, in the province of Massachusett's Bay, employed in the mackerel, shad, and alewife fisheries only (*b*).

(*a*) Sect. 7.  (*b*) Sect. 9, 10, 11.

CHAP-

## CHAPTER VI.

### OF BRITISH SHIPS.

*How English-built Shipping to be understood—
Foreign Ships, English-owned, to be registered
—English Ships to be English-built—The
Plantation Register Act, Stat. 7. & 8. Will. 3.
c. 22.—Of Registers lost or mislaid—When
foreign Seamen employed—Ships made free by
Letters Patent—By Private Acts—By the
Commissioners of the Customs—Of Prize Ships
—Of Master and Mariners naturalized.*

PART II.

12. CAR. II. TO
A. D. 1783.
BRITISH
SHIPS.

HAVING considered the various branches of trade and employment for shipping, which are noticed in the Act of Navigation, and are thereby subjected to certain rules and regulations in order to promote the increase of British shipping and navigation, we come to the remaining part of this famous statute which relates to the *ship* itself, and the qualifications that constitute a British ship. But before we enter upon this,

it

it will be proper to look back, and bring together into one view the various qualifications of shipping that are required by this act for different employments.

In the *plantation-trade* it requires shipping to *belong* to the people of England, Ireland, Wales, or Berwick, *or* to be of the *built* of and belonging to the plantations; so that if the ship were owned by persons in the mother-country, it was not material where it was built; but if it was owned by some person in the plantations, it must also have been built there.

As to the trade with Asia, Africa, and America, not being plantations of this country, the ship might be *owned* by any one in England, Ireland, Wales, or Berwick, or in the plantations, but nothing is said of the built. In the fourth section the act speaks of goods of foreign growth, which, it supposes, are to be brought in *English-built shipping*, or *other shipping* belonging to some of the aforesaid places (viz. England, Ireland, Wales, Berwick, and the plantations); but the act had before said nothing of goods that are to be brought in *English*-built shipping, no built being

being spoken of but the built of the *plantations*, and that for the plantation-trade. For the trade of Asia, Africa, and America, nothing is said of the built, but merely of the ownership.

In the European trade the importation of goods the growth, production, or manufacture of Russia, and of the other goods (except currants) enumerated in the eighth clause, is to be in ships *owned* in England, Ireland, Wales, or Berwick; but currants and goods the growth, production, or manufacture of Turkey, are to be brought in English-*built* shipping, and nothing is said of the ownership. In the coasting trade no stranger is to be *owner* or part-owner of a ship, but nothing is said of the built. In the fishery, the ship must be *owned* in England, Ireland, Wales, or Berwick. In all these trades the circumstance of the master and three fourths of the mariners being English, is invariably required; but in the fishery nothing is said of the master and mariners.

It appears, therefore, that in three instances only did the statute require that the ship should be of any particular *built*; namely, for the plantation-trade it must be plantation-built, if the owner lived in the plantations; and for bringing currants and Turkey commodities it must be English-built. In all other instances, whether in the plantation-trade, the trade with Asia, Africa, or America, the European-trade, coasting-trade, or the fisheries, it was sufficient if the ship *belonged* to persons in England, Ireland, Wales, or Berwick, as owners. When we consider that the plantation-trade might be carried on by ships *owned* in England, Ireland, Wales, and Berwick; and that currants and Turkey commodities might be brought by foreign-built ships of that country, there existed no sort of trade where the law required absolutely the employment of *English-built* shipping. But there were several instances in which the law required shipping to be *owned* in England, Ireland, Wales, or Berwick; and in all, except the fishery, a ship so owned was to be navigated by a master and three-fourths of the mariners English.

From all this it is clear, that the object the parliament immediately proposed to itself was, *to increase the number of seamen, and encourage the* PURCHASING *of ships by merchants.* The building of ships in England was rather looked to as a consequence to follow

follow from the operation of these and other causes.

*How English-built Shipping to be understood.*

I SHALL now state the regulations made by this act on the *built*, *ownership*, and *navigation* of English, or, as they are now termed, British ships. The first of these is, to explain the sense in which *English-built shipping* is to be understood. It is to be understood, says the act, of shipping built in England, Ireland, Wales, the islands of Guernsey or Jersey, or the town of Berwick-upon-Tweed, or in any the lands, islands, dominions, or territories to his majesty in Asia, Africa, or America, belonging, or in his possession: and where English-built shipping is mentioned in the Book of Rates as intitling goods to any ease, abatement, or privilege, in point of duties, it is always to be understood with the proviso that the master and three-fourths of the mariners at least are English; and wherever it is required that the master and three-fourths of the mariners should be English, they are to be such during the whole voyage, unless in case of sickness, death, or being taken prisoners in the voyage; which facts are to be proved on the oath of the master or other chief officer of the ship (*a*).

(*a*) Sect. 7.

## SHIPPING AND NAVIGATION.

*Foreign Ships, English owned, to be registered.*

In order to prevent foreign ships passing for English, which was termed the colouring of foreign ships, it was ordained, that no foreign-built ship or vessel should pass as a ship belonging to England, Ireland, Wales, or the town of Berwick, and have the privileges thereof, until the person claiming the property thereof made appear to the chief officer of the customs in the port next to the place of his abode, that he was not an alien; and should take an oath before such chief officer that such ship was *bonâ fide*, and without fraud, bought by him for a valuable consideration, expressing the sum, as also the time, place, and persons from whom it was bought, and who were his part-owners, if any (which part-owners were to take the same oath before the chief officer of the customs of the port next to their abode), and that no foreigner directly or indirectly had any part, interest, or share therein; upon which oath the officer of the customs was to give a certificate under his hand and seal, whereby the ship might pass as belonging to that port. The officer was to keep a register of such certificates, and to return a duplicate thereof to the chief officer of the customs at London for those in England, Wales, and Berwick, and at Dublin for such as should be in Ireland; together with the name of the person from whom the ship was bought, the sum paid for her, and the names of the part-owners, if any (*a*).

ANY officer allowing the privilege of a ship belonging to England, Ireland, Wales, or Berwick, until such certificate was produced, or such proof on oath made; or who should allow such privilege to such ship coming into port and making entry until examination whether the master and three-fourths of the mariners were English; or who should allow such privilege to a foreign-built ship bringing in commodities the growth of the country where it was built, without examination and proof whether it was a ship of the *built* of that country, and that the master and three-fourths of the mariners were of that country; or if any governor should allow a foreign-built ship to load or unload before such certificate produced, and examination made whether the master and three-fourths of the mariners were English; such officer or governor should, for the first offence, be put out of his place (*b*).

(*a*) Sect. 10.   (*b*) Sect. 11.

BY this act a duty of five shillings *per* ton was laid on all ships belonging to the subjects of France that loaded or unloaded goods, or took in, or set on shore, passengers here, to be paid as long as a duty of fifty sous was continued on the shipping of England lading in France (*a*); which duty ceased by the treaty of Utrecht.

PART II.<br>13. CAR. II. TO<br>A. D. 1783.<br>BRITISH<br>SHIPS.

IT has been seen, that the Act of Navigation was confined, except in two instances, to encouraging *property* in shipping, and not the *built* of them, in this country, and the other parts of the English dominions. But in the next year the parliament went a step further, and took away the privilege of English ships from all those that were not English-built as well as English-owned. By stat. 13. & 14. *Car.* 2. c. 11. sect. 6, the collectors and other officers of the customs, in all the ports of England, were called upon to give an account to the collector and surveyor in the port of London of all foreign-built ships in their ports, owned and belonging to the people of England, and of their built and burthen, for which certificates had been made by

English Ships to be English-built.

(*a*) Sect. 17.

virtue of the Act of Navigation, The collector and surveyor were to make a list of all such ships, attested under their hands, and transmit it to the court of exchequer before 1 December 1662. This list became a record of great use to enable them to carry into execution the provision that followed;

WHICH was, that no foreign-built ship, namely, no ship not built in some of his majesty's dominions in Asia, Africa, or America, or which should not have been bought before 1 October 1662, and expressly named in the beforementioned list, should enjoy the privilege of a ship belonging to England or Ireland, although owned or manned by English, except such ships only as were taken at sea by letters of marque or reprisal, and condemned in the court of admiralty as lawful prize: but all such foreign-built ships were to be deemed aliens' ships, and be liable to duties as such.

IT was further declared, in explanation of the Act of Navigation, that wherever, by that act, it was required that the master and three-fourths of the mariners should be English, the meaning was, they should be the king's subjects of England, Ireland, or the plantations; and the number was to be accounted according to what they had been during the whole voyage (*a*).

In the same act encouragement to building large ships was held out. First, If merchandize was exported from any port of this kingdom, in a ship capable of two hundred tons upon an ordinary full sea, to any port or place of the Mediterranean beyond the port of *Malaga*, or goods were imported from those ports or places in any ship or vessel not having two decks, and carrying less than sixteen pieces of ordnance mounted, with two men for each gun, and other ammunition proportionable, there was to be paid one *per cent:* over and above the duties of tonnage and poundage otherwise payable (*b*). But fish, as has been before noticed, might be exported from any of the king's dominions into any such ports of the Mediterranean, in any English ship or vessel whatsoever, provided one moiety of her full lading be fish only; and in such case wares or merchandize might be imported in the same ship for that voyage, without paying other

(*a*) Sect. 6.   (*b*) Sect. 35.

duties of tonnage and poundage than were before accuftomed (*a*).

SECONDLY, For encouraging the building of good and defenfible fhips, a bounty was given for the term of feven years to perfons building fhips of three decks, or two decks and a half with a forecaftle, and five foot between each deck, mounted with thirty pieces of ordnance at leaft (*b*). The fame act made provifion for better recovering the tonnage-duty of five fhillings on French fhipping (*c*).

THE next act on the fubject of fhips was the beforementioned ftat. 1. *Jac.* 2. c. 18. made in the reign of a prince who, among other peculiarities, was diftinguifhed from his predeceffors in being an experienced fea-officer, and full of attachment and zeal for the fea-fervice. We have before feen, that by this act all foreign-built fhips and veffels thenceforward bought and brought into the kingdom of England, Wales, or town of Berwick, to be employed in carrying goods or merchandize from port to port, were to pay at the port of delivery

(*a*) Sect. 38.   (*b*) Sect. 37.   (*c*) Sect. 24.

for every voyage, over and above all other duties, five shillings *per* ton; one moiety to the Chest at Chatham, the other moiety to the Trinity Company (*a*). A duty of twelvepence *per* ton was to be paid by those foreign ships already employed in the coasting-trade (*b*).

THE next regulations made respecting the built of ships were in stat. 7. & 8. *Will.* 3. c. 22. which has been already an object of consideration, under the head of the plantation-trade. It was meant to prevent the frauds committed by colouring foreign ships under English names. This was to be effected by a more strict registering than had yet been attempted. No ship or vessel was to be deemed or pass as a ship of the built of England, Ireland, Wales, Berwick, Guernsey, Jersey, or any of the plantations in America, so as to be qualified to trade to, from, or in, the plantations, until the person claiming property therein should register it in the following manner.

IF the ship belonged, at the time of registering, to any port of England, Ireland, Wales,

---

(*a*) Sect. 1.    (*b*) Sect. 2.

Wales, or Berwick, then proof was to be made on oath of one or more of the owners before the collector and comptroller of that port; if in the plantations, or in Guernsey or Jersey, then before the governor, together with the principal officer of the revenue residing in the plantation or island; which oath, according to the form given in the statute, being attested by the governor or custom officer, who administered it under their hand and seal, after having been registered by them, was to be delivered to the master of the ship for the security of her navigation; and a duplicate of the register was to be transmitted immediately to the commissioners of the customs in the port of London, in order to be entered in a general register to be there kept. Any ship trading to, from, or in, the plantations, and not having made proof of her property, as here directed, was to be forfeited as a foreign ship, unless she was a prize condemned in the high court of admiralty (*a*). And such prize ships were required to be specially registered, mentioning the capture and condemnation instead of the time and place of building, with proof upon oath that the

(*a*) Sect. 17, 18.

entire

entire property was English, otherwise such prize was not to be allowed the privilege of an English ship (a).

An exception was made in favour of fisher-boats, hoys, lighters, barges, or any open boats or other vessels, though of English or plantation built, whose navigation was confined to the rivers or coasts of the plantation or place where they traded; all which were not to be registered; the registering being to be confined to ships that cross the seas to or from England, Ireland, Guernsey or Jersey, and the plantations, and from one plantation to another (b).

No ship's name, when registered, was to be afterwards changed, without registering the ship *de novo*; which was also to be done on any transfer of property to another port, and delivering up the former certificate to be cancelled, under the beforementioned penalties. And if there was any alteration of property in the same port, by the sale of one or more shares in any ship after registering thereof, such sale was always to be acknow-

(a) Sect. 20.     (a) Sect. 20.

ledged

ledged by indorsement on the certificate of the register, before two witnesses, in order to prove, that the entire property in such ship remained to some of the subjects of England, if any dispute should arise thereupon (a). Such are the provisions of this act for registering ships; which subject has been re-considered, and new-cast in the Register Act passed lately.

THE treaty of union with Scotland, which admitted that nation to a participation in all the advantages of our trade and commerce, communicated to their ships the privileges belonging to English ships. By the fifth article of that treaty, all ships or vessels belonging to the queen's subjects of Scotland at the time of ratifying the treaty, though foreign-built, were to be deemed and pass as ships of the built of Great Britain, the owner, or, if there were more owners, one or more of them, making oath of the same; and that the ship did, at the time of making the deposition, wholly belong to them; and that no foreigner, directly or indirectly, had any share, part, or interest therein. This oath was to be taken before the officer

(a) Sect. 21.

of the cuſtoms at the port next the abode
of the owner; it was to be regiſtered and
delivered to the maſter, and a duplicate
tranſmitted to the chief officer of the cuſtoms
at the port of Edinburgh, to be there entered in a regiſter, and thence ſent to the
port of London, to be there entered in the
general regiſter of trading ſhips belonging
to Great Britain.

THE proviſion made by the Plantation
Regiſter Act, ſtat. 7. & 8. *Will.* 3. for
regiſtering *de novo,* and for making an indorſement on the certificate, in caſes where
the property was changed, had not been
obſerved with ſuch ſtrictneſs, but that the
certificates of the regiſter of ſeveral ſhips had
been ſold to foreigners; and ſuch certificates
being delivered to the purchaſers, the ſhips
of foreigners, under colour thereof, had
been admitted to trade to and from the
plantations. To prevent this it was enacted,
by ſtat. 15. *Geo.* 2. c. 31. that no ſhip or
veſſel required by that act, or by the ſtat.
5. *Ann.* c. 8. for the union of the two kingdoms, to be regiſtered, and carrying goods,
wares, and merchandize, to or from any of
the plantations in America, or to or from
one plantation to another, ſhould be permitted

mitted to trade, or be deemed qualified for that purpose, within the meaning of those acts, until the master, or person having the charge of such ship or vessel, should upon oath before the governor or collector of the customs of the plantation where he arrived, give a just and true account of the name and burthen thereof, and of the place from whence she came, with other particulars contained in the form of oath given in the act. And if any ship load or unload goods, wares, or merchandize, in the plantations, before such proof made, the ship should be forfeited and prosecuted, the same as if she had not been registered according to stat. 7. & 8. *Will.* 3. (*a*).

Of Registers lost or mislaid.

AGAIN, because masters of ships frequently *lost* or *mislaid* certificates, to the great prejudice of owners, who thereby lost their voyages, and the benefit of registering their ships *de novo*, the following regulations were made. If it happened in the plantations, the master or person having the charge of the ship might make oath before the governor or collector of the customs where the ship should happen to be, " that the ship was,

(*a*) Sect. 1.

as he believes, registered for the plantation-trade, and had a certificate granted at such a port, but that it is lost or mislaid, and that he cannot find it, nor knows where it is, or what is become of it; that it has not been, nor shall be, with his privity or knowledge, sold or disposed of to any person whatsoever; that he and three-fourths of the mariners navigating the ship are British subjects; and that the ship does now, as he believes, belong wholly to British subjects; and that no foreigner, to his knowledge or belief, has any share, property, or interest therein." The master is likewise to give security in £500. if the ship is of one hundred tons burthen, and so in proportion for greater burthens, that the ship was duly registered for the plantation-trade; and that the register, if found, shall be delivered up to the commissioners of the customs to be cancelled; that no illegal use has been, or shall be, made of it; that the ship wholly belongs to British subjects, and no foreigner has any share in it. Then upon such oath and bond the governor and collector shall freely, and without fee, give a certificate under their hands and seals of his having made such oath and given such bond; and thereupon the ship shall have

liberty

liberty to trade for that voyage only, and the officers taking such oath and bond are to transmit an account thereof to the commissioners of the customs (a).

But a certificate *de novo* was still necessary in cases where the urgency of the single voyage was provided for; and for obtaining that, the master and one of the owners were to make proof to the satisfaction of the commissioners of the customs, if the owners lived in Great Britain, Ireland, Guernsey, or Jersey, and of the governor or collector of the customs in the plantations, if she was registered in the plantations, and none of the owners resided in Great Britain, Ireland, Guernsey, or Jersey, upon oath of the loss of the certificate, and also of the name, burthen, built, property, and other particulars required by stat. 7. & 8. *Will.* 3. and before the same persons as was required in case of original registers; and shall give security in £500. if the ship is of one hundred tons, and so in proportion if of more, to the collector of the port to which the ship belongs, that the original certificate has not been, nor shall be, fraudulently disposed of,

(a) Sect. 2.

SHIPPING AND NAVIGATION.

or used contrary to law; and that when found, it shall be delivered up to the commissioners of the customs to be cancelled. In such case, the commissioners of the customs, and the governor and collector in the plantations, are to permit such ship to be registered *de novo*; and a certificate thereof is to be delivered to the owners, as directed by stat. 7. & 8. *Will.* 3. mentioning it to be granted by virtue of this act, instead of a former certificate: such new register is to have the same force and effect as the original register and certificate; and a duplicate thereof is to be transmitted to the commissioners of the customs *(a)*.

THIS law for new registering, where the certificate was lost, was followed by stat. 20. *Geo.* 2. c. 45. by which prize-ships, legally condemned, are to be considered as British-built ships, and to have all the privileges and advantages thereof, and be subject to all the rules and regulations to which British ships are subject *(b)*.

BY stat. 7. *Geo.* 3. c. 45. ships and vessels built in the isle of Man, and owned by the

*(a)* Sect. 3.    *(b)* Sect. 9.

Y                king's

PART II.
12. CAR. II. TO
A. D. 1783.
BRITISH
SHIPS.

king's subjects in that island, are to pass as ships of the built of Great Britain, upon one of the owners registering such ships, and making proof of the built and property before the king's receiver-general there, or his deputy, in the form directed by stat. 7. & 8. *Will.* 3.

NOTWITHSTANDING the express manner in which the property of English-built ships was, by the regulations concerning registers, meant to be confined to natural-born subjects, yet it was found that foreigners still continued to own shares of ships, which on that account could not obtain registers under stat. 7. & 8. *Will.* 3. To remedy this it was enacted by stat. 13. *Geo.* 3. c. 26. that no foreigner, or other person not being a natural-born subject, shall be entitled to, or shall purchase, or contract for, any part or share of any British ship or vessel belonging to natural-born subjects, without the consent in writing of the owner or owners of three-fourth parts in value at least of such ship or vessel first obtained, and indorsed on the certificate of the register before two witnesses; otherwise such agreement, purchase, and sale shall be void.

THE

THE last provision made within the present period of the history of shipping was stat. 18. *Geo.* 3. c. 56. for opening the plantation-trade to Ireland; and by that act it was ordained, that all ships and vessels built in Ireland, and owned by his majesty's subjects residing in any part of the British dominions in Europe, should be deemed British-built, and intitled to the like privileges, in all respects, as ships built in Great Britain: and all ships belonging to his majesty's subjects residing in Ireland, and not British-built, should be intitled to the same privileges in all parts of his majesty's dominions as ships belonging to his majesty's subjects residing in Great Britain, and not British or Irish built *(a)*.

THE necessities of war, which obliged the parliament to relax the rules of the Navigation Act in regard to the trade to and from this country, made it expedient, sometimes, to deviate from them in the manning and navigating of British ships. Thus by stat. 6. *Ann.* c. 37. f. 19. during the continuance of the then war, privateers, or merchant or trading ships, might be navigated by foreign seamen, or mariners,

(*a*) Sect. 9.

not

*When foreign Seamen employed.*

not exceeding three-fourths of the mariners at one time employed, and the other fourth were to be natives, or naturalized subjects of Great Britain; sudden death, and the hazards and casualties of the sea excepted. A foreigner so serving for two years, was to all intents and purposes to be deemed a natural-born subject *(a)*.

THE queen was also impowered to grant a licence to buy or procure in foreign parts ships, not exceeding twenty, for privateering; and such ships, after the war, were to have the privilege of ships British-built *(b)*.

THE liberty to employ foreign seamen was renewed in the war of 1740, by stat. 13. *Geo.* 2. c. 3. when a general power was lodged in the crown, in case of a declaration of war, at any future time, to permit by royal proclamation all merchant ships, and other trading vessels and privateers, to be manned with foreign mariners and seamen in the manner provided by this act; and upon the publishing of such proclamation, this act is to be deemed in full force, and continue so during the whole of such war *(c)*. A

*(a)* Sect. 19. 20.   *(b)* Sect. 21.   *(c)* Sect. 4.

temporary

temporary permission was given in the year 1755, before hostilities had begun, to employ foreign seamen, in the same proportion (a). A similar law was passed in 1779, when actual hostilities subsisted (b); in both which acts there was a saving of the king's power to issue proclamations under stat. 13. Geo. 2. c. 3.

We come now to such information as can be collected on the subject of British shipping, and which will contribute to illustrate the regulations that had been made by parliament on that head.

As often as the Legislature made new provisions, which had the effect of shutting out from the privileges of British shipping any number of ships liable to disqualification, attempts were made to get them restored, by application to extraordinary remedies. In the time of Charles II. when the prerogative of the crown to dispense with acts of parliament was considered as a part of the constitution, the privileges of an English ship used to be granted sometimes by letters patents under the great seal, and sometimes

(a) Stat. 28. Geo. 2. c. 16. (b) Stat. 19. Geo. 3. c. 14.

by

*PART II.*
*35. CAR. II. TO*
*A. D. 1763.*
*BRITISH*
*SHIPS.*

by the king's sign manual alone. This practice was very common; and at one time it was carried to such an extent of abuse, as to become an object of enquiry before the Committee of Council for the Affairs of Trade and Plantations; when it appeared that the king's signature had been surreptitiously obtained in various instances for this purpose. The sign manual was preferred, as the less expensive mode, and several ships used to be put in the same instrument. The usage and the law upon this point is illustrated by the following curious opinion of *Sir William Jones*: He declared himself of opinion, that a warrant under his majesty's sign manual would not be sufficient for making a ship free; but he thought the king, by letters patent under his great seal, might dispense with the statute, and grant to the owners such privilege, with a *non obstante* to the statute; and he thought the privilege might be granted, by the same letters, to several ships.

*By private Acts.*

WHEN this prerogative of the crown had been declared illegal by the Bill of Rights, such indulgences could not be obtained but by act of parliament; and before the Legislature could be induced to interpose in favour

favour of particular ships, it became necessary to lay before them some claim of merit, or some very special circumstances of hardship, as reasons to prevail with them to dispense with the general law. There are instances of this sort where the parliament has been induced to consent to private acts for the relief of individuals; and there are more, where they have refused to grant any relief at all.

In the year 1689 a petition was presented to the house of commons by persons who had purchased many ships in foreign parts, to employ them in the coal and east-country trade. They alledged, that while they were at sea some few persons had procured stat. 1. *James* 2. whereby their ships would after the 29th of September 1689, be excluded from the coal-trade. It was moved to bring in a bill for the relief of such persons; and upon a division, and a slight majority (*a*), leave was given; but the bill was never presented (*b*).

Nothing more was heard of such applications, till after passing stat. 7. & 8. *Will.* 3.

(*a*) 54 to 43.   (*b*) 10. Vol. Com. Journ. 208.

by which a more vigilant system was established, and interloping ships were less likely to escape unnoticed. We find, that from the ninth year of king William as far as to the eighth year of queen Anne, there was hardly a session without some bill passing, to confer on a disqualified ship the privileges of an English ship. But these, all together, do not amount to more than twenty-six instances. These special acts of parliament granted the privilege either generally, or in a qualified manner, for some particular sort of trade.

But in the eighth year of queen Anne, a petition was presented from the shipowners of the port of London, complaining of the many bills that had been brought into the House, and of some then depending, for making free foreign ships; and alledging, that having, on the faith of the Acts of Navigation, laid out considerable sums in building ships, at a much greater rate than they could be built for abroad, they thought themselves intitled in this point to the protection of the House. This petition was followed by others from shipwrights, sail-makers, and other persons employed in different branches of trade connected with the building

building and equipping of ships in the port of London, and other maritime towns (*a*).

THESE petitions seem to have had the intended effect, for from that time to the present day there appear no more bills of this sort; nor even any petition for a bill, except one, recently after passing stat. 26. Geo. 3. c. 60. when a petition was presented, stating that two ships had been begun to be built in Maryland by the petitioners, who had laid out nearly half of the money expended in buying rigging and other fitting-out in Great-Britain. A bill was permitted to be brought in, and was read a first time, but upon a motion for reading it a second time it was rejected (*b*).

A PRACTICE, however, had obtained at the custom-house, of allowing the privileges of an English-built ship to those of foreign built, in the particular case of a ship having undergone very considerable repairs in this kingdom, so as to amount nearly to a rebuilding. The origin of this practice does not appear; but the first instance to be

---

(*a*) 16. Vol. Com. Journ. 148. 150, 151. 154. 156. 159.
(*b*) 7 March, 11 May, 16 May, 26 May 1786.

found of any sanction given to it by the opinion of a law-officer is in 1711, which was about two years after the parliament had declined to entertain applications for special acts to grant this privilege to foreign ships. This is an opinion of *Sir Edward Northey*, who, without making any question about the legality of the thing, answers shortly, that the ship in question was to be deemed an English-built ship. Another opinion of his, two given by *Sir Philip Yorke*, others by *Sir Dudley Ryder*, and succeeding law-officers, are equally short. The only principle to be extracted from them is, what results from the consideration of the expence incurred in the repairs. The following are instances of repairs that were judged sufficient to intitle the ships to be made free.

A FLY-BOAT, become unfit for service, was in that condition bought by an English merchant, who caused her to be rebuilt with a new keel, as appeared by an affidavit of facts (*a*). Another, similarly circumstanced, not worth two hundred pounds when bought, was new-built with a new

(*a*) 22 March 1711.

keel,

keel, and other work to the amount of seven hundred pounds (*a*). A French prize was bought for one hundred and forty-one pounds; the owners laid out upon her above twelve hundred and eighty pounds in repairing the body and hull, so that the greatest part of her false keel was new made; she was all new planked and new sheathed from the keel to her wale, her upper works intirely new, her masts all English, and she had been thirteen years in the English service (*b*). A ship was bought two years before, ready rigged and equipped for a voyage, for six hundred pounds; there had been laid out in putting on an under keel and other shipwright's work, four hundred and eighty-six pounds one shilling and two-pence, as appeared by the affidavit of the shipwright and smith (*c*). A ship was built at Archangel for six hundred and seventy-four pounds four shillings and ten-pence, as appeared by a deposition annexed; there was since laid out in this kingdom in putting in a new oak keel, and other shipwright's and smith's work, eight hundred and fifty-eight pounds eighteen shillings and three-pence, as appeared by the bills and affidavits (*d*).

(*a*) 18 February 1714.   (*b*) 28 July 1725.
(*c*) 27 May 1726.   (*d*) 21 February 1737.

BUT

BUT this practice, which had usage alone to support it, and was evidently against the express meaning of the Act of Navigation, and stat. 7. & 8. *Will.* 3. was viewed with jealousy. We find in the year 1749 an opposition was endeavoured to be made against it by the commissioners of the customs, who expressed themselves dissatisfied with the usage, and especially with what was said to be the prevailing notion in the Long Room, namely, that if a *foreign-built ship*, bought by British subjects only, did not cost above one-third of the whole expences in fitting her out (the remaining two-thirds being laid out upon her in Britain), she was to be deemed a British-built ship to all intents and purposes, although there was not a single passage in any act of parliament to warrant such a position.

AT that crisis the commissioners were consulted by the Scotch commissioners on the following case arising upon this sort of question: A foreign-built ship, stranded within the port of Aberdeen, was purchased by some merchants for one hundred and seventy pounds, who, as appeared by proper vouchers, expended in recovering and repairing her with British materials, two hundred and sixty-

sixty-five pounds; part of the repairs consisting of a new keel, and new keel-stone. The solicitor of their board thought she was intitled to be deemed a British-built ship; but that board, considering the granting of plantation-registers as a matter of great delicacy, had declined adopting the solicitor's opinion.

THE English commissioners, being thus called upon for their advice, caused the whole to be laid before the law-officers, that it might be fully considered, and the rule of conduct finally settled.

ON this occasion it was declared by Sir *Dudley Ryder* (a), that if the matter was *res integra*, there might be a reasonable ground of doubt; but he took it to have been long understood to be the law and settled practice, that a foreign-built ship greatly repaired here, and with a new keel, at a much greater expence than the prime cost, did become intitled to be registered as a British-built ship, though the precise proportion of one expence to the other was not settled: the true foundation of this was,

(a) 10 November 1749.

that such a sort of repair might be reasonably looked upon as a re-building. And he said, the circumstance of a new keel was no otherwise material, than as that was probably considered among ship-builders, and persons conversant in the trade, to be material in distinguishing between a repair and rebuilding. And he thought the facts in the case from Scotland were such as should intitle the ship to a register.

This opinion seems to have put an end to all further doubt; and it continued the practice to allow such ships a plantation-register, upon the bills being laid before the Attorney-General verified by affidavit; the putting a new keel, however, being considered usually as the strong circumstance to denominate it a rebuilding.

The privileges of a British-built ship were conferred on ships taken prize, and legally condemned, by the general laws of shipping, and by statutes passed at various times during the continuance of hostilities.

It is only upon such temporary acts that any information is to be collected respecting prizes.

THE

THE effect of such a capture was considered in the following case: A French ship was taken prize and condemned. It was afterwards recaptured by the French, and then sold to a Spanish merchant, and was employed to import the commodities of Spain with a Spanish master and mariners. It was a question, Whether this was a legal importation? An act had been passed for the encouragement of English ship-building, stat. 29. *Geo.* 2. c. 34. (*a*), which dispensed, during the war, with stat. 12. *Car.* 2. c. 18. sect. 8. and allowed the articles there enumerated to be imported in British-built shipping owned and navigated by foreigners of the place where the goods were the growth, and giving the privilege of a British-built ship to all prizes taken. It depended on the construction of this act 29. *Geo.* 2. whether the ship which became intitled to the privileges of British-built by the capture, continued to retain that quality when sold to the Spaniard. It was thought by *Mr. Starkie* (*b*), that the importation was good; but this being a new case, and one which did not fall in with that part of the preamble which takes notice of the beneficial branch of trade

(*a*) Sect. 18, 19, 20.  (*b*) 4 March 1758.

arising

arising from selling British-*built* ships to foreigners; and as this ship after the capture was sold by the French, who then had the property in her, to a Spanish merchant, by which no advantage could accrue to this country; he thought it deserved great consideration. *Mr. Pratt*, in an opinion given by him, seems to think the importation was good, and that the re-capture made no difference in the case. In a similar case of French prize, where the sale was made by the captors to a Spaniard, it was held by *Mr. Norton* (a), that she was legally qualified to import the goods of Spain, being navigated by Spaniards under the prize act, the same as if she was really British-built.

*Of Master and Mariners naturalised.*

THE *manning and navigating* of English or British ships has given occasion to some points of discussion. It was a question, Whether a Dutchman, made a denizen of Ireland, was *English* within the first section of the Act of Navigation, so as to be master of a ship? *Sir William Jones* (b) held, that both a master and mariner born in Ireland, or any other of the king's dominions, and having his habitation or residence there,

(a) 22 Feb. 1758.  (b) 10 July 1676.

was

was as much English within the intent of this act, as if he were born in England; for this word *English*, when applied to masters and mariners, is as large as when applied to shipping; and this seemed to him to be clearer from the words, *that the master and three-fourths be* ALSO *English*; which words seem to make the word *English* bear the same sense in both relations. He thought a foreigner born being made a denizen of Ireland, if he had his habitation and residence there, was as much *English* as if born there; for by his denization he was become part of *the people*, and one of the king's subjects there. Yet he thought a denizen of Ireland or England, and indeed a natural-born subject of either, not having his habitation there, was not *English* within the intent of this act; for the former words are, not *belonging to* ENGLISH *or* IRISHMEN, but *to the people of* ENGLAND *or* IRELAND; and the word *English* with the latter words must be understood in the same sense. He also thought that a native of Scotland, if he inhabited in England, was to be accounted English or Irish within the Act of Navigation explained by the Act of Frauds, viz. stat. 12. *Car.* 2. c. 18. f. 7. and stat. 13. & 14. *Car.* 2. c. 11. f. 6. and also within

Z the

the Act of Trade, stat. 15. *Car.* 2. c. 7. s. 17.

WE find this question was again moved at the distance of twenty years, when *Sir John Hawles* gave an opinion upon it. A considerable doubt arose from the explanatory act stat. 13. & 14. *Car.* 2. c. 11. s. 6. which declares, that wherever the Act of Navigation requires the master and three-fourths of the mariners to be English, it should be understood, that any of his majesty's subjects of England, Ireland, or his plantations, should be accounted English, and no other. To this he answers, that whatever might have been the intent of the parliament by that clause, yet since, by law, a man born in Scotland is a subject of England; and since the two kingdoms, as to matters of privilege, while they remain united and have the same king, are accounted but one nation, this clause will not exclude a Scotchman from the privilege of an English subject.

THE word *English*, he said, must, in the Act of Navigation, be construed according to the rules of the common law in like cases; and since the union of the two crowns, at least

least at this day, says he, it has been undoubtedly held, that persons born in Scotland shall have the same privileges as persons born in England as to purchasing freeholds, taking lands by inheritance, and other matters. He thought it must be the same where any act of parliament gives a privilege to a Scotchman; for a Scotchman will be English in privilege, though a native of Scotland: and wherever this act mentions *a subject of England or Ireland*, he thought the words *England or Ireland* redundant, and so should be rejected, and certainly would not exclude a Scotchman without negative words.

But where the case of a Scotchman residing in Ireland was submitted to the opinion of *Mr. Warde*, he refers to the Act of Frauds, as containing the description of the master and mariners; and says, he apprehends that a man, though born in Scotland, yet having from his tender years been educated, married, and a settled housekeeper in Ireland, might well be understood to be one of his majesty's subjects of Ireland, and so within the meaning of the Explanatory Act; from which it should seem he considered this point as resting entirely on those

those words, and not turning upon the general principles laid down by *Sir John Hawles*. He also seems to think, that being a *housekeeper* in Ireland added strength to the case, for that is wholly his own wording, there being no such fact in the statement laid before him. Such circumstances seem to have been thought of weight, and had been stated to *Sir John Hawles*; but he thought it made no alteration in the case, whether such Scotchman was a housekeeper or lodger, single or married.

A SIMILAR doubt arose after the Union, Whether a Scotchman living in England ought to be accounted as a subject of Scotland within the meaning of the fifth article of the Union, stat. 5. Ann. c. 8. by which *all ships and vessels belonging to* HER MAJESTY'S SUBJECTS OF SCOTLAND *at the time of ratifying the Union, though foreign-built, are to pass as British-built?* And *Sir Simon Harcourt* (a) held that he ought to be so considered.

(a) 10 June 1707.

PART

# PART III.

## INTRODUCTION.

THE settlement made by the peace in 1783, had a considerable effect upon the system of law respecting Shipping and Navigation. A revulsion which converted a great part of our American colonies into independent States, that had shipping and commerce of their own, gave a new appearance to the trade of America. It became expedient to accommodate the law to the existing state of circumstances by some new regulations, which the exigency of the moment might suggest.

THE American trade became thus a new subject, and called for the best attention that the Legislature and his majesty's Government could bestow upon it. Connected in some measure with this change in America,

rica, the *regiſtering* of Britiſh ſhipping and the *fiſheries* preſented themſelves as objects of very important concern. Theſe three heads, therefore, of our ſubject, namely, *The Plantation Trade*, *The Fiſheries*, and *Britiſh Shipping*, will be ſeen to undergo very great modification during the ſhort period that elapſed from the peace in 1783 to the year 1792, and much more than in any former period of ten times its duration.

INDEED almoſt the whole that has been done of this ſort has been accompliſhed within a ſtill ſhorter period; for it is principally ſince the year 1785 that the great regulations reſpecting the fiſheries and Britiſh ſhipping have been brought forward. At that time his majeſty was pleaſed to appoint a committee of council for the conſideration of all matters relating to trade and foreign plantations, and ſoon after to place at the head of it a noble lord whoſe ſervices to this country in affairs of commerce and navigation have already had effects ſo ſolid and extenſive, as to promiſe to be remembered when praiſe will have no appearance of flattery. It is to the ſuperintendance and authority of this committee, and

and to the great knowledge and unwearied exertions of the noble lord at the head of it, that we are indebted for the very important improvements in the law of shipping and navigation made during this short lapse of time.

## CHAPTER I.

### THE PLANTATION TRADE.

*The American Intercourse Bill, Stat. 23. Geo. 3. c. 39.—The Newfoundland Supply Bill—Stat. 28. Geo. 3. c. 6.—Intercourse with the West Indies—With the American Colonies—The American Orders in Council—Doubt thereupon removed by an Explanatory Order—Free Port Act.*

PART III.
FROM THE PEACE 1783, TO A.D. 1795.
PLANTATION TRADE.

NOTWITHSTANDING the American colonies had been separated from this country, and their independence acknowledged by the peace of 1783, we cannot avoid placing them, with regard to their trade, among our plantations. This seems suitable as well to the consequences, as to the crisis of their transition from the state of colonies to that of foreign States, which happened at this period; the Government of this country having imparted to them many of the advantages and easements in trade,

and

and in duties, that are enjoyed only by the British plantations.

THE first parliamentary regulation that applied to the United States, was made with a view of giving effect to the peace: this was by opening the trade and *intercourse* which stood prohibited by stat. 16. *Geo.* 3. c. 5. enforced by stat. 17. *Geo.* 3. c. 7. These two acts were accordingly repealed by stat. 23. *Geo.* 3. c. 26. It then remained to make a new disposition of the trade applicable to the new situation. The country belonging to the United States now ceased to be a part of the British plantations, and fell back into the class of American dominions that were not intitled to any special privileges in matters of trade. They no longer were intitled to come to the British plantations, nor could the goods and commodities of their country be imported into Great-Britain but in British ships.

To adhere to the strictness of this rule, and exclude American ships belonging to the people of the New Sovereignty, now acknowledged by us, would have manifested such a want of disposition to conciliate, as was not consistent with the recent treaty

treaty of peace; and something was to be devised that would bear a resemblance to the course of trade that had long subsisted. It was soon seen that this adjustment required a more minute investigation than the pressure of the moment would allow; the parliament therefore, instead of laying down any permanent rule for regulating this complicated and hitherto unexplored subject, conferred on his majesty a discretionary power to make such order therein, as he from time to time should be advised to make. It was enacted by stat. 23. *Geo.* 3. c. 39; for the purpose of opening a commercial *intercourse* (for this term, introduced by the prohibitory acts, was now continued to express the American trade) with the United States, that it should be lawful for the king in council, by orders to be issued from time to time, to give such directions and make such regulations with respect to duties, drawbacks, or otherwise, for carrying on the trade and commerce between the people and territories belonging to the crown of Great Britain and those of the United States, as to him in council should appear most expedient and salutary (*a*).

(*a*) Sect. 3.

To free American ships from the checks to which they were before subject, as ships bringing plantation goods, it was at the same time ordained, that no manifest, certificate, or other document whatsoever, should be required for any ship belonging to the United States arriving from thence at any port in this kingdom, or upon entering or clearing out from any port in this kingdom for any port in the United States, except the bonds that are required for duly exporting and not relanding goods intitled to a drawback or bounty, or prohibited to be used in this kingdom (*a*). Where a certificate is necessary for discharging a bond entered into for landing goods in the United States, a certificate under the hands and seals of any officers appointed by the United States for that purpose shall be sufficient; and if none such are appointed, then of any magistrate there, certifying, that no such officer has been appointed, and that oath was made before him by the master, that the goods were duly landed (*b*).

PART III.
FROM THE PEACE 1783, TO A.D. 1792. PLANTATION TRADE.

This act being experimental, and to serve the necessity of the moment, was to

(*a*) Sect. 1.   (*b*) Sect. 2.

continue

continue only for a few months; but it was afterwards further continued by two acts made in the next sessions of parliament, namely, stat. 24. *Geo.* 3. st. 1. c. 2. and c. 15. It was again further continued by two acts passed in the second session of 24. *Geo.* 3. (*a*), and by another passed in 25. *Geo.* 3. and so on to the 28. *Geo.* 3. by an annual act of continuance, without any alteration except the following; namely, in stat. 24. *Geo.* 3. c. 45. the parliament united to the discretionary power they had conferred on the king for regulating the trade and commerce with the United States, the same power to regulate the trade and commerce with the British colonies in America, as far as regarded iron, hemp, sail-cloth, and other articles of the produce of any place bordering on the Baltic, which might be lawfully exported from this kingdom. This regulation went on, hand in hand with the other for the general intercourse, in the annual acts of continuance.

SOME doubt had arisen as to the legal mode of enforcing a due execution of the power lodged in his majesty by stat. 23. *Geo.* 3.

(*a*) C. 1; and c. 23.

c. 39.

c. 39. To remove this it was enacted by stat. 27. *Geo.* 3. c. 7. (one of the annual continuing acts) that if any goods or commodities, the growth or production of the United States, should be imported into the West-India Islands, other than such, and in such manner, as by law, or by that act, or by order of his majesty in council, should be permitted, they should be forfeited, together with the ship *(a)*. The forfeiture was extended by stat. 28. *Geo.* 3. c. 5. sect. 2. to the export from this kingdom of the beforementioned articles from the Baltic, and to the import of American articles from the United States into this kingdom.

In the same act the following temporary regulation was made respecting the intercourse between the United States and our West-India Islands, in addition to that made under stat. 23. *Geo.* 3. c. 39. In order that no provisions or lumber, being the growth or production of the United States, should be imported from the foreign islands, it was enacted, that no flour, bread, rice, shingles, or lumber of any sort, should be imported from a foreign West-India Island; with a

(*a*) Sect. 4.

proviso,

PART III.
FROM THE
PEACE 1783,
TO A.D. 1792.
PLANTATION
TRADE.

provifo, that governors, in cafe of neceffity, might, with the advice of their councils, authorize the import of fuch articles for a limited time.

The New-
foundland
Supply Bill.

ANOTHER exception to the power given to the king by ftat. 23. *Geo.* 3. c. 39. was contained in ftat. 25. *Geo.* 3. c. 1. which was made for regulating the trade between the United States and the ifland of Newfoundland. By that act, no goods or commodities whatfoever were to be imported into Newfoundland, or the adjacent iflands, from the United States, except bread, flour, and live-ftock, and that only in British-built fhips, owned by the king's fubjects, and navigated according to law, and which fhould have cleared out within feven months before the importation from fome part of the king's dominions in Europe, and obtained a licence, according to the form prefcribed in the act, from the commiffioners of the cuftoms in England or Scotland, or the commiffioners of revenue in Ireland. This was to continue to 25 March 1786; and from thence it was continued, by ftat. 26. *Geo.* 3. c. 1. to 25 March 1788. By ftat. 26. *Geo.* 3. c. 1. Indian-corn was added to the other articles permitted to be fo imported.

THUS

THUS stood the law in the beginning of the year 1788, respecting the intercourse between this kingdom and the United States, and between the colonies and the United States. As to the former, it depended on an annual order of council, grounded on stat. 23. *Geo.* 3. c. 39. continued and amended by subsequent acts, as beforementioned; the nature of which annual orders in council I shall defer speaking on for the present. As to the latter, it depended upon the same order, saving the branches of it which the parliament had taken out of the hands of the king: first, By stat. 25. *Geo.* 3. and 26. *Geo.* 3. with regard to the import of bread, flour, Indian-corn, and live-stock, from the United States to Newfoundland; and, secondly, by stat. 27. *Geo.* 3. c. 7. with regard to the circuitous importation of lumber and provisions from thence, through the foreign West-India Islands, into our own. These laws were now upon the point of expiring, when the parliament, having again to declare its annual judgment upon the intercourse with the United States, deemed it proper to make a permanent law for settling one great portion of this trade. The annual act for Newfoundland was left to expire. The annual intercourse act, stat.

stat. 23. *Geo.* 3. c. 39. was continued by stat. 28. *Geo.* 3. c. 5. so far only as extended to the trade and commerce carried on between this kingdom and the territories of the United States; which at once let fall the regulation concerning the circuitous import of lumber and provisions, and the whole of the order in council founded on it, which respected the trade between our colonies and the United States. This latter was put into an act, which was intended to be permanent. As the intended regulation was to contain the substance of what had been the policy of the orders in council, and had now had the experience of five years of practice, added to the light which some discussion had now thrown upon the new position in which the two countries stood with relation to each other, it was thought it might safely be formed into a standing law, instead of floating any longer on an order of council, that must be renewed every year.

This gave rise to stat. 28. *Geo.* 3. c. 6. which contains the whole of the present law respecting the intercourse between the British colonies and the United States. The provisions of this act may be divided into such as as relate to the West-Indies, and such as relate to the colonies in North America.

PART III.
FROM THE PEACE 1783, TO A. D. 1791.
PLANTATION TRADE.
Intercourse with the West-Indies.

FIRST, with regard to the West-Indies, it ordains, that no goods or commodities whatever shall be imported or brought from any of the territories belonging to the United States into any of his majesty's West-India Islands (in which description the Bahama and the Bermuda or Somers Islands are included), under the penalty of forfeiture, together with the ship importing them, except only the following articles; namely, tobacco, pitch, tar, turpentine, hemp, flax, masts, yards, bowsprits, staves, heading-boards, timber, shingles, and lumber of any sort; horses, neat-cattle, sheep, hogs, poultry, and live-stock of any sort; bread, biscuit, flour, peas, beans, potatoes, wheat, rice, oats, barley, and grain of any sort; such commodities being of the growth or production of any of the territories of the United States (*a*); and these are not to be brought but by British subjects, and in British-built ships, owned by his majesty's subjects, and navigated according to law, under the same penalty of forfeiting the ship and cargo (*b*).

(*a*) Sect. 1.  (*b*) Sect. 2.

THUS

PART III.
FROM THE
PEACE 1783,
TO A.D. 1794.
PLANTATION
TRADE.

Thus far of the imports to the West-Indies; next as to the exports from thence. It is permitted to export from the West-India-Islands to the territories of the United States any goods or commodities whatsoever which were not, at the time of passing the act, prohibited to be exported to any foreign country in Europe; and also sugar, molasses, coffee, cocoa-nuts, ginger, and pimento: but those articles, or any other (except salt from *Turks Islands*), are not to be exported but by British subjects, and in British-built ships owned by his majesty's subjects, and navigated according to law, under the penalty beforementioned *(a)*. In such cases, where a bond would be required on the exportation of goods to a British colony in America, a bond is to be given, on the exportation of such goods, for the due landing of them in the United States, to be discharged by a certificate under the hand and seal of the British consul, or any officer appointed by the United States (or of some magistrate, certifying that there is no such officer), and that oath has been made by the master, that the goods were duly landed *(b)*.

(*a*) Sect. 3.  (*b*) Sect. 4.

Such

SUCH is the plan of policy settled by parliament for the intercourse with our West-India Islands. But, notwithstanding all American ships were thus excluded from the general trade to and from the West-Indies, it was thought adviseable to admit them to a particular branch of trade, which needed more than ordinary encouragement: this was, the making of salt at *Turks Islands*, which are among the *Bahama* Islands. Any ship belonging to the United States coming in ballast, but not otherwise, may enter the ports of those islands for the purpose of lading with salt, but for no other purpose, under the penalty beforementioned *(a)*. The master of such ship is to make entry upon oath, declaring the built of the ship, how manned, who is master and owner, and the purpose of his coming; and is to answer questions touching those particulars, if put by the officers of the customs, on pain of forfeiting £100. *(b)*. A tonnage duty of two shillings and sixpence is imposed on such ships, to be ascertained by admeasurement; and it is to be paid before any salt is laid on board *(c)*.

PART III.

FROM THE PEACE 1783, TO A.D. 1792. PLANTATION TRADE.

(*a*) Sect. 5.    (*b*) Sect. 6.    (*c*) Sect. 7, 8.

To prevent the communication thus permitted with *Turks Iflands* being made a channel of illicit trade, no goods or commodities whatever are to be exported from *Turks Iflands* to any part of the British dominions in America or the Weft-Indies, or laid on board any veffel in thofe iflands, except falt; nor to Great Britain or Ireland, except falt, and alfo fuch goods and commodities as may by law be imported into this kingdom from all other countries whatfoever, free of all duties, under the penalty of the forfeiture beforementioned.

The next provifion in this act is to obviate the circuitous trade that had been provided againft in the annual act of 2ⁿ. *Geo.* 3. None of the articles permitted in the former part of the prefent act to be imported directly from America, are to be brought from any ifland in the Weft-Indies under the dominion of any foreign European fovereign or ftate, under the penalty of the forfeiture beforementioned (*a*). However, in cafes of public emergency or diftrefs, the governors of any of the iflands may, with the advice and confent of their council, authorize the

(*a*) Sect. 10.

importation

importation of those articles for a limited time from any such foreign island, for the supply of the inhabitants; but such importation must be by British subjects, and in British-built ships, owned by his majesty's subjects, and navigated according to law *(a)*. Such is the whole of this act, which relates to the West-Indies.

SECONDLY, it ordains, with regard to the American colonies, that no goods or commodities whatever shall be imported from the United States into the provinces of *Nova Scotia* or *New Brunswick*, the *Island of Cape Breton, St. John's*, or *Newfoundland*, or into any country or island within their respective governments, under the penalty of the same forfeiture *(b)*. However, in cases of public emergency and distress, the governors of all those places (except Newfoundland) may, with the advice and consent of their council, authorize the importation of scantling, planks, staves, heading-boards, shingles, hoops, or squared timber, of any sort; horses, neat-cattle, sheep, hogs, poultry, or live-stock of any sort; bread, biscuit, flour, pease, beans, potatoes, wheat, rice, oats, barley, or grain of any sort, for a limited

*(a)* Sect. 11.   *(b)* Sect. 12.

limited time, from the United States, for the supply of the inhabitants.

AND, with regard to *Newfoundland*, his majesty in council may by order from time to time authorize, or by warrant under his sign manual impower the governor of Newfoundland to authorize, in case of necessity, the importation of bread, flour, Indian corn, and live-stock, from the United States for the supply of the inhabitants and fishermen, for the then ensuing season only; which importation is to be conformable to such regulations and restrictions as shall be specified in such order, or warrant: and such special importations, whether to *Nova Scotia* and the other places, or to *Newfoundland*, must be by British subjects, and in British-built ships, owned by his majesty's subjects, and navigated according to law (*a*).

FURTHER, no goods or commodities whatever are to be imported from the United States by sea or coastwise into the province of *Quebec*, or the countries or islands within that government, or up the

(*a*) Sect. 13.

River

River St. Lawrence, under the penalty of the forfeiture beforementioned (*a*).

THE import of American articles from the foreign islands, which the governors might under this act permit occasionally for the supply of the inhabitants, was soon converted into a traffic of importing, and then exporting to others of our own islands. This being contrary to the design of the measure, it was provided by stat. 29. *Geo.* 3. c. 56. that such exportation, or the putting on board any ship, boat, or vessel, or bringing to any quay with intent to export, should be punished with a forfeiture of the articles in question, and of the ship, boat, or vessel (*b*). The better to guard against such exportation, no articles of the same sort that may be lawfully exported, are to be shipped till the exporter has made oath, that none of them were imported, under such permission, from a foreign island (*c*). By stat. 31. *Geo.* 3. c. 38. these provisions are extended to any foreign colony or plantation on the *continent* of *South America*.

IT now remains to consider the orders in council, that were made from time to time for carrying into execution the powers

(*a*) Sect. 14.   (*b*) Sect. 1.   (*c*) Sect. 2.

lodged

PART III.
PEACE 1783,
TO A.D. 1792.
PLANTATION
TRADE.

lodged in his majesty by stat. 23. *Geo.* 3. c. 36. for regulating the trade with America; and which were reserved for this place, that they might not interrupt the train in which it was convenient to arrange the foregoing statutes, all belonging to the same subject.

THE first order was made 14 May 1783; by which it was directed, that oil, and unmanufactured goods and merchandize, the growth or production of the United States, might be imported directly from thence into this kingdom, either in British or American ships, upon payment of the same duties as if imported from a British plantation in America; and that there should be the same drawbacks, exemptions, and bounties on merchandize exported from Great-Britain to the United States, as on the like goods exported to a British plantation in America; and American ships that had come into port since 20 January 1783, were to be admitted to an entry, and entitled to the benefit of this order.

THE act under which the above order was made having expired, and a new act passed to the same effect, a new order was thereupon made. This order was dated 6 June 1783, and varied somewhat from the former. Instead

stead of the general words there used, it enumerated the articles that were to be admitted upon the plantation-duty; namely, pitch, tar, turpentine, indigo, masts, yards, and bowsprits. It further directed, that tobacco might be landed from thence, on paying the old subsidy, and then be warehoused, upon bond, with the allowance for payment of the further duty according to the acts in force.

THIS variation in the orders of council, issued within less than a month one from the other, shews how unsettled men's minds were, and how unprepared to agree upon any permanent system for governing the American trade.

As yet, nothing had been done to regulate the trade between our colonies and the United States; but on 2 July 1783, an order came out for that purpose; by which permission was given to export rum, sugar, molasses, coffee, cocoa-nuts, ginger, and pimento, by British subjects, in British-built ships owned by his majesty's subjects, and navigated according to law, from the West-India islands to the United States, on payment of the same duty, and subject to the like

like regulations, as if they were exported to a British colony in America.

Such was the limited intercourse which his majesty's government thought it expedient to allow between the United States and the British colonies. An order was issued on 5 September 1783, to facilitate this intercourse, by directing, that bonds given on clearing out from Great-Britain or the West-Indies, and carrying the above-mentioned goods to the United States, should be discharged upon the like certificates as are required by the Act of Navigation, stat. 12. *Car*. 2. c. 18. f. 19. to discharge bonds given in Great-Britain for the due landing of any other goods in the United States; and direction was given that all bonds taken since the date of the former order, should be discharged on the like certificate.

By an order of 5 November 1783, an amendment was made in the order of 6 June 1783, respecting the importation of tobacco, by directing, that in case of importation into the ports of London, Bristol, Liverpool, Cowes, Whitehaven, or Greenock, the importer might be allowed to give bond for the

the old subsidy, as well as the further duties due, in the manner and with the allowances mentioned by the acts on that subject; and if such tobacco should be taken out of the warehouses, at any of those ports, to be exported, the bonds should be discharged in the manner mentioned in the acts of parliament on that subject. Some doubt arising concerning the allowance here made, an order came out on 19 November 1783, whereby it was declared, that the said order should not extend to the making any allowance for payment of the old subsidy; and the port of Glasgow was added to those named in the said order of 5 November 1783.

ON 26 December 1783, a new order was issued, containing, for the first time, the whole regulation for the American trade, both with Great-Britain and with the colonies; and this order is particularly deserving of notice, as the subject was there thrown into that form in which it has continued, with very little variation, ever since.

IN this order, there is another variation in the description of the articles; that is, oil, which had been a permitted article in the first,

first, but not enumerated in the second order, was not expressly excepted; and the general description of *unmanufactured goods*, used in the first order, was now added to the articles enumerated in the second order; to which general description was added a guard, to prevent goods, otherwise prohibited, from coming in under this permission; the words run thus: " any unmanufactured goods, " or merchandize, the importation of which " into this kingdom is not prohibited by " law (except oil), and any pitch, tar, " turpentine, indigo, masts, yards, and " bowsprits." The regulation about tobacco was retained, together with the last alteration made for taking away the allowance for prompt payment of the old subsidy.

THE orders that had hitherto been made for the intercourse between the United States and our colonies, went no further than to permit the *exportation* from the West Indies of certain articles to the United States. The present order went a step further, and laid down a rule for the *importation* of certain articles from the United States. It was ordered, that pitch, tar, turpentine, hemp, flax, masts, yards, and bowsprits, staves, heading-

heading-boards, timber, shingles, and all other species of lumber; horses, neat-cattle, sheep, hogs, poultry, and all other species of live-stock, and live provisions; pease, beans, potatoes, wheat, flour, bread, biscuit, rice, oats, barley, and all other species of grain, being the growth, and production of any of the United States, might be imported by British subjects in British-built ships, owned by his majesty's subjects, and navigated according to law, from any port of the United States to any of his majesty's West India islands, the Bahama islands, and the Bermuda or Somer islands. The export from the West Indies was continued on the same footing as by the former order; and the whole of the regulations of the present order were made to extend to all goods imported from and shipped for exportation to the United States since 20 December 1783.

THE orders issued on 18 June and 30 July 1784 (the act under which the first of them was made continuing only to 1 August) conformed precisely with the one of the former year just mentioned. On 27 August in the same year, there came out a fresh order, grounded on the act passed that session of of parliament respecting goods of the Baltic. By this order the same drawback was allowed on exportation of foreign hemp, or iron, to the British colonies, or to the United States, as are allowed by law on their exportation to other foreign ports. By an order made 24 November 1784, the port of *Lancaster* was added to the other ports for warehousing tobacco imported from the United States.

THE act passed in the sessions 1784, was made to continue to 5 April 1785; the acts passed after that were in like manner annual; and so were the orders of council made upon them. The annual order made 8 April 1785, pursued the order of the former year precisely; besides which was added, for the first time, a regulation for the trade between the United States and the British colonies in North America. It was ordered, that no goods or commodities being the growth or manufacture of the United States, should be imported into the provinces of *Nova Scotia* or *New-Brunswick*, and their respective dependencies, except horses, neat-cattle, sheep, hogs, poultry, and all other species of live-stock, and live provisions; pease, beans, potatoes, wheat, flour,

flour, bread, bifcuit, rice, oats, barley, and all other fpecies of grain; alfo lumber of every fort; and thefe were to be imported by Britifh fubjects only, and in none other than Britifh-built fhips, owned by his majefty's fubjects, and navigated according to law, and only during fuch time as the governors of thofe provinces fhould, with the advice of their council, declare the fame by proclamation to be neceffary for the fupply of the inhabitants: further, no goods or commodities whatfoever, being the growth or manufacture of the United-States, were to be imported into the ports of the province of Quebec.

AN order was made 15 February 1786, for allowing the warehoufing of rice upon the fame terms as were prefcribed in former orders with regard to tobacco, preferving the fame diftinction between the ports there named and others.

IN the annual order made 24 March 1786, were contained fome few variations from the former. The exception from the enumerated articles, which had hitherto been confined to oil, was now extended to blubber, whale-fins, and fpermaceti; and the word

*oil*

oil was changed into *fish-oil*; the importation might be either in British-built ships owned by his majesty's subjects, and navigated according to law; or if in American ships, might be until 1 Jan. 1787 in ships *belonging* to the subjects of the United States, and whereof the master and three-fourths of the mariners were subjects of the United States: but if after 1 Jan. 1787 they were American ships, they were to be ships *built* in the United States, and owned and navigated as before-mentioned. These two alterations were, no doubt, suggested by the discussions that were now frequently had on the subject of the Southern Whale-fishery, and the shipping and navigation of the country, and which led to the forming two bills that were passed into laws in the then session of parliament. Conformably with the ideas then prevailing, the expression of *British ships* was changed into *British-built ships*.

An act having been passed in the last session of parliament respecting the importation of tobacco, the former directions on this head were dropped in the present order, and that article was directed to be imported in conformity to the regulations of stat. 25. *Geo.* 3.;

25. *Geo.* 3.; but the special wording on that subject was retained and transferred to the article of rice. In the part that regulates the trade between the West India islands and the United States, tobacco is added as an article that may be imported from America *in the fair and lawful way of barter and traffic* " between the people of " the United States and those of the West " Indies," as permitted by stat. 25. *Geo.* 3. just mentioned.

In the annual order made 4 April 1787, an addition was made to the enumerated articles, which now run in this order: *pig-iron, bar-iron,* pitch, tar, turpentine, *rosin, pot-ash, pearl-ash,* indigo, masts, yards, bowsprits; and conformably with the policy begun in the last annual order, if the importation was in American ships, they were to be *built* in the countries of the United States, and owned and navigated as required in the former order. Again, the following articles were added to the enumerated articles allowed to be imported into *Nova Scotia* and *New Brunswick,* rather with the view of better explaining, as it should seem, what came under the word *lumber,* namely, every sort of squared timber, scantling, planks,

planks, boards, ſtaves, heading-boards, ſhingles, and hoops. In other reſpects this order conformed with the one of the foregoing year, and the annual order made 19 March 1788 conformed with that of 1787 juſt mentioned, except that every thing relating to the Weſt Indies and the Britiſh colonies was left out, thoſe regulations being introduced into ſtat. 28. *Geo*. 3. paſſed that ſeſſion of parliament.

THE annual order made 3 April 1789, purſued that of the foregoing year in every thing, only that *wheat*, which had been prohibited by an order of council dated 25 June 1788, on account of an alarm about the Heſſian fly, which was ſuppoſed to have infeſted the American crop, was added to the articles excepted from importation. The annual order made in April 1790 contained no alterations from that of the foregoing year, but that *wheat* was no longer among the excepted articles.

SOME doubt had been ſtarted upon the meaning of the American order, which applied to it in all its changes from the firſt iſſue of it to the laſt; namely, What was to be be the construction as to those articles imported from the United States which were not enumerated or described in the order? And upon examining the order itself, a doubt was raised upon the wording. Some contended, that the words towards the close of the first section, *and no other*, were to be understood as referring to the *articles*; and then the meaning would be, that no other *articles* than those enumerated and described should be admitted at all. Others contended, that *no other* referred to the *duty*; and the meaning was, the articles enumerated should pay the duty there specified, and *no other* duty: and they held, that those articles that were excepted, and all other articles from the United States, should be imported upon *the general duty* to which they would be subject, if coming from any other place. The latter is most probably the sense in which the words were used by the framers of the first order; it was certainly the sense in which they had been construed at the custom-house. But to remove all doubt, it was thought proper, that an order of council should be made for explaining this doubt, and putting beyond all dispute the words of an instrument, that contained the law for governing the whole trade with the United States. This was accordingly done by an order made 6 Oct. 1790; in which likewise was removed an ambiguity to which the word *oil* was subject, from the printer having interposed a comma between that word and the word *fish*.

THE provisions of this explanatory order are as follow: That oil made from fish or creatures living in the sea, and blubber, whale-fins, and spermaceti, and also all other goods and merchandize, the importation of which into this kingdom is not by law prohibited, being the growth, production, or manufacture of any of the territories of the United States, and not enumerated or described in the annual order, may be imported upon payment of such duties of custom and excise as are payable on the like goods and merchandize imported from countries not under the dominion of his majesty, according to tables *A.* and *D.* and *F.* in the consolidation act, or any subsequent law; and where different duties are there imposed on the same goods coming from different countries not under the king's dominion, then upon the lowest of such duties; and such goods are to be intitled to drawbacks, according to those tables.

THE

SHIPPING AND NAVIGATION. 373

THE annual order issued 1 April 1791 was worded conformably with this explanation; and the order issued 1 April 1792 is a literal copy of that of the preceding year; and upon this order the trade with the United States is now carried on *(a)*.

PART III.
PEACE 1783,
TO A.D. 1792.
PLANTATION
TRADE.

ANOTHER point in the present policy with regard to the plantations, is to encourage the trade that can be carried on by means of free-ports in the West-Indies. For this purpose the act of 6. *Geo.* 3. which had been dropped, as far as regarded the free-ports in the island of *Dominica*, ever since stat. 21. *Geo.* 3. and was now upon the point of expiring *in toto*, was repealed by stat. 27. *Geo.* 3. c. 27. as far as regarded importation or exportation, or the admission of vessels, or the duties payable thereon *(b)*. The repealing act then goes on to make regulations *de novo*, adding to the number of ports before opened, restricting the commodities admissible to certain enumerated articles, and limiting the tonnage of the shipping.

Free Port Act.

*(a)* See the American order in the Appendix.
*(b)* Sect. 1.

Bb 3  THUS

Thus wool, cotton-wool, indigo, cochineal, drugs of all sorts, cocoa, logwood, fustic, and all sorts of wood for dyers use, hides, skins, and tallow, beaver, and all sorts of furs, tortoise-shell, hard-wood or mill-timber, mahogany, and all other woods for cabinet-ware, horses, asses, mules, and cattle, being the growth or production of any colony or plantation in America, belonging to, or under the dominion of, any foreign European sovereign or state; and all coin and bullion, diamonds or precious stones, may be imported from such colonies or plantations into the ports of *Kingston*, *Savannah la Mer*, *Montego Bay*, and *Santa Lucea*, in the island of *Jamaica*, the port of *St. George* in the island of *Grenada*, the port of *Roseau* in the island of *Dominica*, and the port of *Nassau* in the island of *New Providence*, one of the *Bahamas*. Such importation must be in some foreign sloop, schooner, or other vessel, not having more than one deck, and not exceeding the burthen of seventy tons, and must be owned and navigated by the subjects of some foreign European sovereign or state (*a*); and the same description of persons and ships may export from those

(*a*) Sect. 4.

ports rum being the produce of a British island, negroes brought into those islands in British-built ships, owned, navigated, and registered according to law, and all manner of goods that had been legally imported into those islands, except masts, yards, or bowsprits, pitch, tar, turpentine, and tobacco, and also except such iron as shall have been brought from the British colonies or plantations in America *(a)*. The legality of such importation is to be first made appear to the satisfaction of the officer of the customs *(b)*.

THE enumerated articles so imported may be exported to Great Britain or Ireland, under the same regulations as are laid down in the Act of Navigation, stat. 12. *Car.* 2. c. 18. and stat. 22. & 23. *Car.* 2. c. 26. and also in stat. 20. *Geo.* 3. c. 10. which laid open the colony-trade to Ireland *(c)*.

No goods or commodities of the growth, production, or manufacture of Europe, or the East-Indies, or other places beyond the Cape of Good Hope, are to be exported from the islands of Grenada or Dominica,

*(a)* Sect. 4.   *(b)* Sect. 5.   *(c)* Sect. 6.

or the Bahama Islands, to any other British colony or plantation in America or the West-Indies *(a)*. The regulations of this act are enforced by the usual forfeiture of the ship and goods. No fee or reward is to be taken by the officers of the customs for any such foreign vessels, or the goods and merchandize imported or exported therein *(b)*.

Two alterations have since been made in this act. It being found that the limitation in the tonnage of the vessels was too great a restraint on the trade, it was taken off by stat. 30. *Geo.* 3. c. 29. but the vessels are still limited to one deck. Again, it being found that persons who inhabited within the limits of countries admitted by us to belong to European sovereigns, but who did not hold themselves to be *subjects* of such sovereigns, were anxious to participate in this trade, it was, by stat. 31. *Geo.* 3. c. 39. sect. 7. extended to vessels owned by any persons *inhabiting* such countries on the continent of America.

(a) Sect. 7.  (b) Sect. 8.

The stat. 27. *Geo.* 3. like the former Free Port Act, was a regulation of experiment, and was to continue in force only till 1 September 1792, and from thence to the end of the next sessions of parliament. It is now continued, by an act of the present session; and by another act of the present session, sugar and coffee, the produce of any foreign country or plantation, may be imported into the port of Nassau, and into any other port in the Bahamas, or Bermuda Islands, that shall be approved by his majesty in council, under the regulations of the Free Port Acts of 27. *Geo.* 3. and 30. *Geo.* 3.

CHAPTER

## CHAPTER II.

### TRADE WITH ASIA, AFRICA, AND AMERICA.

*PART III.*
*PEACE 1783,*
*TO A. D. 1792.*
*TRADE WITH ASIA, AFRICA, AND AMERICA.*

THE only regulation made since the peace in 1783, which affected the general policy established by the Act of Navigation with regard to this trade, is a section (*a*) in stat. 27. *Geo.* 3. c. 19. which regards the African Trade, and makes it lawful for any person to import or bring into Great Britain from Gibraltar, in any ship or vessel which before 1 May 1786 did truly and without fraud belong to his majesty's dominions, or was of the built of his majesty's dominions, and was navigated and registered according to law, any goods, wares, or merchandize, being the growth or production of the dominions of the emperor of Morocco, and which shall have been imported into Gibraltar directly from any of those dominions

(*a*) Sect. 11.

not

not lying to the fouthward of the port of *Mogadore*, in fhips or veffels belonging to, or of the built of, his majefty's dominions, as before defcribed, navigated and regiftered according to law, or in fhips or veffels belonging to the fubjects of the emperor of Morocco, upon payment of the fame duties as if imported directly from Africa (*a*). But fuch goods are to be accompanied with a certificate from the governor of Gibraltar, fhewing they were brought into Gibraltar in the above manner (*b*).

The following alteration concerned the affairs of the African Company. The fort of *Senegal* had been ceded to France by the peace of 1783; and the French king guaranteed to Great Britain the poffeffion of fort *James* and the river *Gambia*, both lying between the port of *Sallee* and *Cape Rouge*. It was now thought more beneficial for the trade, that the forts, fettlements, and factories, between the port of *Sallee* and *Cape Rouge*, which by ftat. 5. Geo. 3. c. 44. had been vefted in the king, fhould be re-vefted in the Company. This was accordingly done by ftat. 23. Geo. 3. c. 65. The fame freedom of trading there was, notwithftanding, continued to all the king's fubjects.

(*a*) Sect. 11.    (*b*) Sect. 12.

CHAPTER

## CHAPTER III.

#### THE EUROPEAN TRADE.

THE only provisions made during this last period that can properly be classed under the head of regulations respecting the European Trade, are in a clause in stat. 27. *Geo.* 3. c. 13. and another in stat. 27. *Geo.* 3. c. 19.

THE first of these was for carrying into execution the commercial treaty with France. Two of the articles that were the objects of that treaty were wine and olive-oil, both which were, by the Act of Frauds, stat. 13. & 14. *Car.* 2. c. 11. prohibited to be imported from the Netherlands. This stood in the way of the adjustment now made by the treaty; and to remove this obstacle it was enacted (*a*), that French wines might be imported in casks from any place in the

(*a*) Sect. 22.

European dominions of the French king, in such manner, and under such regulations, as they might then by law be imported from France; and also French wines in bottles or flasks, as well for sale as for private use, in the same manner, and under such regulations, as they might then be imported from France for private use: and also, that olive-oil the product or manufacture of France, or of any place in the European dominions of the French king, may be imported from any part of the Netherlands belonging to, or under the dominion of, the French king, in British-built ships or vessels owned, navigated, and registered according to the laws in force on or before 10 May 1787, or in French-built ships or vessels owned by, and belonging wholly to, the subjects of the French king, and whereof the master and three-fourths of the mariners at the least are the subjects of the French king. This regulation expires with the treaty in the year 1900.

The last of these clauses (*a*) was made in order to do away the injury which the Navigation Act suffered from the provision lately made by stat. 22. *Geo.* 3. c. 78. in favour of

(*a*) In stat. 27. Geo. 3. c. 19.

foreign

foreign shipping. Under that act, foreign shipping were qualified to import the articles enumerated and described in the eighth section of the Act of Navigation, if they were of the built, or belonged to any other country than that of their growth or production, provided it was a country under the same sovereign. This made an opening that gave offence to the jealous defenders of the policy of the Navigation Act; and it was accordingly meant to be repealed, without its being so expresly declared, by the following provision; namely, that the goods or commodities so enumerated or described in the Act of Navigation, being of the growth, production, or manufacture of Europe, *may* be imported into Great Britain, under the regulations of that act, and of stat. 13. & 14. *Car.* 2. c. 11. and stat. 6. *Geo.* 1. c. 15. either in ships which before 1 May 1786 truly and without fraud wholly belonged to his majesty's dominions, or which are of the built of his majesty's dominions, and registered according to law, or in ships the built of any country or place in Europe belonging to, or under the dominion of, the sovereign or state in Europe of which such goods or commodities are the growth, production, or manufacture, or of such ports where

where those goods can only be, or most usually are, first shipped for transportation, with a master and three-fourths at least of the mariners belonging to such country, place, or port, and in no other ships whatsoever (*a*).

By this act, the ships are required to be of a certain built, as by the old law, but the built need not be of the very country of production, only of *some* country under the same sovereign; which latter point so far agrees with the liberality of the statute meant to be otherwise corrected by this; and by the wording of this part it applies also to countries circumstanced like those that were not under the same sovereign at the time when the Act of Navigation was passed.

It was intended by this act to restore the law to the state it was in under the eighth section of the Act of Navigation, as altered by the prohibitory clause in stat. 13. & 14. *Car.* 2. c. 11. and stat. 6. *Geo.* 1. c. 15. But the penning of this act seems to do more. Thus, under the words of this act, currants and Turkey commodities,

(*a*) Sect. 10.

being

being the growth, production, or manufacture of Europe, may be imported either in ships *belonging to*, or ships built in, Great Britain, or in ships of the country; but by the eighth section they may not be imported but in British-*built* ships, or ships of the country. It was not, however, intended, that the permission under this act should go further than the permission under the eighth section; and it is expresly provided, that this permission should be exercised under the regulations of that and the other two acts beforementioned. The construction has accordingly been, that where British-*built* ships are required by the eighth section, they must still be employed under this act. In like manner, the permission here given is not to be construed to take away the prohibitory clause in stat. 13. & 14. *Car.* 2. nor is the saving in stat. 6. *Geo.* 1. which takes off part of that prohibition, to be extended beyond the limitations annexed to it, which require the goods imported to belong to the king's subjects, and the importation to be in British-*built* ships(a).

(a) Vid. ant. 204. 208.

CHAPTER

## CHAPTER IV.

### THE COASTING TRADE.

THE Coasting Trade, as far as shipping were concerned, seems to have been left in the state in which it was placed by the Act of Navigation, and stat. 1. *Jac.* 2. c. 18. The late laws made to prevent smuggling do, in some measure, affect this trade, but are not properly within the limits of the present work.

## CHAPTER V.

### THE FISHERIES.

*The Newfoundland Fishery—The Greenland Fishery—The Southern Whale Fishery—The British Fisheries—The Herring Fishery—The Deep-Sea Fishery.*

PART III.
PEACE 1783,
TO A.D. 1793.
FISHERIES.

THE extending and improving of the Fisheries occupied a considerable portion of that attention which has lately been bestowed on the shipping and navigation of the country. The regulations for conducting these in a great measure, and the bounties for their encouragement altogether, depended upon certain temporary laws, which were near expiring in the twenty-sixth year of his majesty's reign. Thus, the bounties granted by stat. 15. *Geo.* 3. c. 31. for the Newfoundland Fishery were to expire on 1 January 1787. The bounties given by stat. 11. *Geo.* 3. c. 38. for the Greenland Fishery were to expire on 25 De-

25 December 1786. The bounties given by ſtat. 15. *Geo.* 3. c. 31. and ſtat. 16. *Geo.* 3. c. 47. for the Southern whale fiſhery were to expire 1 January 1787. The bounties given by ſtat. 11. *Geo.* 3. c. 31. and ſtat. 19. *Geo.* 3. c. 26. for the Britiſh white herring fiſhery, were to expire with the cloſe of the ſeſſion of parliament next after 22 October 1785. It became immediately neceſſary to conſider the policy to be obſerved reſpecting theſe objects of trade and navigation. The reſult of this conſideration was, that bills were brought into parliament and paſſed into laws, in the twenty-ſixth year of the king, for granting new bounties, and making new regulations for carrying on theſe fiſheries with every poſſible advantage to the nation. We ſhall now take a view of theſe acts, and the general ſcope of them, without entering too far into their detail. The firſt is c. 26. for the Newfoundland fiſhery; the next is c. 41. for the Greenland fiſhery; c. 50. for the Southern whale fiſhery; and c. 81. for the Britiſh fiſheries.

THE bounties granted by c. 26. are for ten years, for veſſels employed in the Britiſh fiſhery on the banks of Newfoundland. They are to be Britiſh-built, and wholly owned

owned by his majesty's subjects residing in Great-Britain, Ireland, Guernsey, Jersey, or Man, navigated with a master and three-fourths of the mariners of the same description. They are also to be qualified and subject to the regulations of stat. 10. & 11. *Will.* 3. c. 25. and they are to clear out from some port in Great Britain, Guernsey, Jersey, or Alderney, after 1 January in every year, and proceed to the banks of Newfoundland; and having catched there a cargo of not less than ten thousand fish, they are to land them at one of the ports on the north, east, or south side of the island, between Cape St. John and Cape Raye, on or before 15 July, and then make one more trip at least to the banks, and return with another cargo of fish, catched there, to the same port. The one hundred ships which shall first do this are, if navigated with not less than twelve men, to be intitled to 40l. each; if with less than twelve, but not less than seven men, 25l. each: provided, that if in either of those cases the vessel is wholly navigated by men going out upon shares, that is, receiving a certain share of the profits of the voyage in lieu of wages, such vessel shall in the first case be intitled to 50l. and in the latter case to 35l. Again, the next one hundred vessels

vessels so arriving are in the first case to have 25l. each, in the latter case 18l. each; and such of them as are wholly navigated by men going out upon shares shall in the first case be intitled to 35l. and in the latter case to 21l.

In order to prevent frauds, a certificate is to be exhibited to the collector of the customs before he pays the bounty, from the governor of Newfoundland, that all the requisites were there complied with (a). The sanction of oaths by the master and mate is required to certain facts (b). Provision is made for preventing the desertion of seamen (c), and the selling of boats, vessels, or tackle, for the fishery to foreigners (d). Powers are given to his majesty's officers on that station to seize vessels (e).

Again, by stat. 29. *Geo.* 3. c. 53. it was declared, that no fish taken or caught by any of his majesty's subjects or other persons arriving at Newfoundland, or its dependencies, or on the banks thereof, except

(a) Sect. 1. (b) Sect. 1. 4. 7. (c) Sect. 12, 13.
(d) Sect. 14, 15. (e) Sect. 20, 21.

from Great-Britain, or one of the British dominions in Europe, should be landed or dried on that island; with a saving of the rights granted by treaty to the French king (a): a provision that was occasioned by persons from the Bermuda Islands having lately aimed at possessing themselves of a share in the fishery.

*The Greenland Fishery.*

THE bounties granted by c. 41. are for five years; they are for British ships, owned by British subjects usually residing in Great Britain, Guernsey, Jersey, or Man, which proceed from those places on the whale fishery to the *Greenland Seas* or *Davis's Streights*, or to the seas adjacent, manned and navigated with a master and three-fourths at least of the mariners British subjects, usually residing in Great Britain, Ireland, or Guernsey, Jersey, or Man. Such ship, after she has been visited and admeasured by the officer of the port, and it shall appear upon inspection and examination upon oath of certain persons, and it shall be certified by such officer, that she is properly furnished with tackle and equipment for the whale fishery, according to the requisites of the

(a) By stat. 28. Geo. 3. c. 35. his majesty is empowered to make regulations for more peaceably carrying on the French Fishery.

act,

act, and means to proceed thither, and endeavour to take whales, or other creatures living in the seas, and on no other design or view of profit in the voyage, and to import the whale-fins, oil, and blubber thereof, into Great Britain, specifying the port, and shall give bond for so doing; upon these terms such ship may have a licence from the commissioners of the customs to proceed on such voyage (*a*); and upon the return of such ship, and her condition being reported by the officer of the port, and oath made by the master as to the performance of the voyage, and that all the whale-fins, oil, and blubber, imported were really and *bonâ fide* caught and taken in those seas by the crew of such ship, or with the assistance of some other ship licensed for that voyage, there is to be paid by the commissioners of the customs a bounty of thirty shillings *per* ton of such ship (*b*).

Such ship must sail on her voyage on or before 10 April, and continue in those seas diligently endeavouring to catch whales or other creatures, and not depart before 10 August, unless laden with a certain quantity of oil, blubber, or whale-fins, unless they shall be compelled, by some unavoidable accident,

(*a*) Sect. 2.    (*b*) Sect. 3.

accident, to depart (a). Ships of more than four hundred tons, already employed in the fishery, might continue to be rated as of four hundred tons, and not more. All ships coming into the fishery after 25 December 1786, and being more than three hundred tons, shall not receive a bounty for more than three hundred tons (b); and such ships respectively are not to equip and man for more than four hundred or three hundred tons (c).

If a log-book has not been constantly kept on board, no bounty will be allowed (d). The log-book must be produced to the captains of his majesty's ships of war with which they may chance to fall in, and also to the British consul at any foreign port (e).

Provision was made, that ships owned by the king's subjects residing in Ireland, and fitting out from thence, should, on complying with the conditions of this act, be intitled to these bounties (f). Permission was given to insure the bounties, in order that when ships were lost the owners might have some indemnity (g). Harpooners, line-managers, and boat-steerers, are se-

(a) Sect. 4. (b) Sect. 8. (c) Sect. 9. (d) Sect. 10.
(e) Sect. 11. (f) Sect. 12. (g) Sect. 13.

cured

cured from pressing (*a*). The extent of the fishery is defined to fifty-nine degrees thirty minutes north, and no farther (*b*). The commissioners of the customs are annually to lay before parliament an account of the ships employed (*c*).

It appearing not necessary to keep ships in the Greenland seas so long, it was enacted by stat. 29. *Geo.* 3. c. 53. that they should have the bounty although they left those seas before the 10th August, and were not laden with the quantity of whale-fins and of oil and blubber required by stat. 26. *Geo.* 3. c. 41. s. 4. provided they did not depart from thence till the expiration of sixteen weeks from the time of sailing from the port from whence they cleared out (*d*). A penalty of 50l. is by the same act imposed on masters who wilfully dismiss their apprentices before the expiration of the time for which they were indentured (*e*). By an act of the last session, these bounties were continued for one year longer; and by another of this session they are continued for six years; during the first three at twenty-five shillings; during the second three years at twenty shillings *per* ton.

(*a*) Sect. 17. (*b*) Sect. 18. (*c*) Sect. 19.
(*d*) Sect. 2. (*e*) Sect. 5, 6, 7.

THE

THE next is the *Southern Whale Fishery.* Premiums are granted by c. 50. of this session, for ten years, to twenty ships employed in that fishery; they are to appear by their register to be British-built, and they are to be fitted and cleared out from Great Britain or Ireland, Guernsey, Jersey, or Man, and wholly owned by the king's subjects usually residing there (a).

WITH regard to fifteen of these ships clearing out between the 1st May and the 1st September, and sailing to the southward of seven degrees of north latitude, and there carrying on the fishery and returning before the 1st July in the subsequent year to Great Britain, there is to be paid 500l. to the three which shall first arrive with the greatest quantity of oil, or head-matter, being not less than twenty tons in each ship, the produce of whales or other creatures living in the sea, taken and killed by the crews of such ships respectively; 400l. to the three that shall first arrive with the next greatest quantity; 300l. to the three that shall first arrive with the next greatest quantity; 200l. to the three that shall first arrive with the next greatest quantity; and 100l. in like manner to the next three (b).

(a) Sect 2.   (b) Sect. 3.

WITH

With regard to the remaining five, they are to proceed to the southward of the thirty-sixth degree south latitude, and there carry on the fishery, and return in not less than eighteen months nor more than twenty-eight months from the 1st of May in the year in which they clear out; and there is to be paid 700l. to the first which shall arrive with the greatest quantity of oil or head-matter in manner before mentioned; 600l. to the next; and 500l. 400l. and 300l. to the others in order respectively (a).

The ships are to be navigated by a master and three-fourths of the mariners being the king's subjects usually residing in Great-Britain, Ireland, Guernsey, Jersey, or Man; or if the ship clears out from Great-Britain, then it may be navigated by persons being protestants, and who, not being subjects of his majesty, have been heretofore employed in carrying on this fishery; and who shall first make oath, if it is their first voyage from Great-Britain, that they have already established, or intend to establish, themselves and families in Great-Britain, as subjects thereof; and if it is their second voy-

(a) Sect. 4.

age,

age, that they actually have so established themselves (a).

VARIOUS regulations are contained in this act for attaining the object designed and preventing frauds. Each ship is to have on board, for every fifty ton, an apprentice indentured for three years (b). A log-book is to be regularly kept and produced to the collector of the customs at the return home, and verified on oath; and is likewise to be produced to the captain of any of his majesty's ships with which they may happen to fall in (c). The master, mate, and two of the mariners, are to make oath, that the oil and head-matter are the produce of their own fishing (d). A penalty of 50cl. is incurred if the cargo is made up from the fishing of any other crew (e). If oil or head-matter is mixed with water to increase the quantity, the whole is forfeited and the premium lost (f). The quantities are to be ascertained by an officer of the customs (g).

ANY produce of the fishing in the going out or returning home, although not taken

(a) Sect. 5.  (b) Sect. 6.  (c) Sect. 7, 8.
(d) Sect. 9.  (e) Sect. 10.  (f) Sect. 21.
(g) Sect. 22.

within

### SHIPPING AND NAVIGATION.

within the prescribed latitudes, may be reckoned towards the requisite quantity (*a*). If a ship makes two voyages within any of the periods, she is to have only one premium (*b*). Harpooners, line-managers, and boat-steerers, are privileged from being impressed (*c*).

As these voyages would carry ships within the limits of the charters granted to the East-India and South-Sea Companies, some special provision was necessary to qualify them to make this incroachment. It was accordingly enacted, that they might go to the eastward of the Cape of Good Hope, and to the westward of Cape Horn, or through the Streights of Magellan, in order to carry on the Southern whale fishery, provided those sailing to the eastward of the Cape of Good Hope did not pass to the northward of thirty degrees south latitude, nor make more than fifteen degrees east longitude from the Cape of Good Hope; and those passing to the westward of Cape Horn, or through the Streights of Magellan, did not pass to the northward of the equi-

(*a*) Sect. 11.   (*b*) Sect. 20.   (*c*) Sect. 25.

noctial line, nor make more than fifteen degrees west longitude from Cape Horn *(a)*.

Such ships were also to take a licence from the East India Company; but the Company were not obliged to grant it to more than ten ships in one year, if it was for passing to the eastward of the Cape of Good Hope; and this, under certain conditions calculated to guard against illicit trade *(b)*. Those who exceeded these limits were liable to the penalty attending the infringement of the Company's trade *(c)*. When ships return from a voyage to the eastward of the Cape of Good Hope; they must bring a certificate from the officer of the port, testifying there are no goods on board the produce of those places, but only oil, head-matter, or bone of whales or fish, otherwise they will not be intitled to the premium *(d)*. Those sailing within the limits of the South-Sea Company's charter, as described by stat. 9. *Ann.* c. 21. are to have a licence from that Company *(e)*.

Lastly, temptations were held out to invite foreigners to come and settle here,

(*a*) Sect. 14, 15.    (*b*) Sect. 16.    (*c*) Sect. 17.
(*d*) Sect. 18.    (*e*) Sect. 19.

and

and carry on the Southern whale fishery from this country (a).

Some amendments were made in this act by stat. 28. *Geo.* 3. c. 20. As to the fifteen ships, they are now to sail between the 1st Jan. and 1st Nov. and to return to some port in Great Britain on or before 1st Sept. in the following year. As to the remaining five ships, they are to sail between the same periods of 1st Jan. and 1st Nov. and to return on or before 1st Dec. in the following year (b). The following additional premiums are granted for the same period as the former: they are for three ships clearing out, as in the former act, between 1st Jan. and 1st of Nov. and which shall double Cape Horn or pass through the Streights of Magellan into the South Seas, and there carry on the fishery for four months to the westward of Cape Horn; namely, to such ship which shall return to some port in Great Britain on or before the 1st Dec. in the second year after clearing out, but not in less than eighteen months, and with the greatest quantity of oil or head-matter, not being less in the whole than thirty tons,

(a) Sect. 14. 26, 27, 28.   (b) Sect. 1.

there should be paid 800l.; to the next 700l.; to the next 600l. (a).

AGAIN, ships sailing to the eastward of the Cape of Good Hope, may pass as far as the equator northward, and as far as fifty-one degrees longitude east from London, and no farther; and those passing to the west of Cape Horn, or through the Streights of Magellan, may pass as far as the equator northward, and as far as one hundred and eighty degrees longitude west from London, and no farther. Such ships are to have licences from the East-India and South-Sea Companies (b); and the East-India Company are not obliged to grant any licence to sail within the limits of their trade round the Cape of Good Hope, until the owners have given bond in the penalty of 2000l. for such ship not taking on board goods the produce or manufacture of the East Indies, or other places between the Cape of Good Hope and the Streights of Magellan, to the value of 100l. except such as are necessary for their voyage (c). Doing any thing in breach of this and the former act, shall disable a ship from being entitled to any licence in

(a) Sect. 2.   (b) Sect. 3.   (c) Sect. 4.

future.

future (*a*). Power was given to the governor of St. Helena, the commanders of the Company's ships, or agents thereto authorised by the Company, to search licensed ships for East India goods (*b*).

Ships doubling the Cape of Good Hope, or Cape Horn, or passing through the Streights of Magellan, and not being less than two hundred tons burthen, may be armed for resistance and defence, on a licence being obtained from the Admiralty; which licence is to be granted on exhibiting a certificate from the commissioners of the customs, testifying that such ship is entered out for such voyage, and that the owner has entered into bond in a penalty of 2000l. with condition that such arms shall be used only for resistance and defence in cases of involuntary hostility (*c*).

No ship is to have more than one of the additional premiums, although she make two voyages within one of the periods (*d*).

Lastly, there was held out to foreigners a similar temptation to come and settle

(*a*) Sect. 5.   (*b*) Sect. 6.   (*c*) Sect. 7, 8.
(*d*) Sect. 10.

here for the purpofe of carrying on this fifhery *(a)*.

An amendment was made in ftat. 28. *Geo.* 3, c. 20. by ftat. 29. *Geo.* 3. c. 53. it being thought fufficient, if, inftead of eighteen months, fuch three fhips were kept out only fixteen months *(b)*. Again, it was declared, that fhips need not clear out fpecially for the latitudes mentioned in ftat. 26. and ftat. 28. *(c)*. If any mafter permitted his apprentice to quit his fervice before the expiration of three years, he is to forfeit fifty pounds *(d)*. In all thefe fifhery-acts there is provifion made for importing the produce thereof duty free.

*The British Fisheries.*

THE laft act made in this feffion of parliament refpecting the fifheries, is ch. 81. for the encouragement of the Britifh fifheries. In the former feffions, by ftat. 25. *Geo.* 3. c. 65. the bounty given by the former acts of 11. *Geo.* 3. and 19. *Geo.* 3. was extended to veffels and buffes above eighty tons burthen *(e)*; and the regulations in thofe acts compelling the buffes to rendez-

*(a)* Sect. 14, 15, 16, 17, 18.     *(b)* Sect. 3.
*(c)* Sect. 4.    *(d)* Sect. 5.    *(e)* Sect. 1.

vous at certain times and places were repealed (*a*). This act extends the bounty, upon certain conditions, even to those under twenty tons (*b*). But the old bounties now expiring, it was enacted by stat. 26. *Geo.* 3. c. 81. that from 1 June 1787, for the term of seven years, and from thence to the end of the then next session of parliament, a bounty of twenty shillings *per* ton should be paid annually to the owner of every decked vessel built in Great Britain after 1 Jan. 1780, of not less than fifteen tons burthen, manned and navigated according to law, which shall be fitted and cleared out for and employed in the British white herring fishery (*c*).

PART III.
PEACE 1783, TO A.D. 1798. FISHERIES.
The Herring Fishery.

The manner in which these vessels are to be equipped and proceed in their voyage, with the manner of making up their cargo, compose a very long detail not necessary to be here repeated.

The act gives likewise several other bounties; namely, four shillings *per* barrel for herrings packed and completely cured, and landed from any buss intitled to the

(*a*) Sect. 2.    (*b*) Sect. 3.    (*c*) Sect. 1, 2.

D d 2       twenty

twenty shillings bounty *per* ton; or if a greater proportion than two barrels and a half to a ton is so landed, then one shilling *per* barrel (*a*). Also a bounty of one shilling *per* barrel for all such herrings landed from boats not intitled to the twenty shillings bounty (*b*).

**The Deep Sea Fishery.**

IT gives also additional encouragement to *the Deep Sea Fishery* on the north and north-east coasts of this kingdom; namely, for the greatest quantity of herrings caught by the crew of a buss intitled to the above bounties of twenty shillings *per* ton, and four shillings and one shilling *per* barrel, and brought in by such buss between 1 June and 31 Nov. the premium of eighty guineas; for the next greatest quantity, sixty; the next, forty; and the next, twenty guineas (*c*).

ALL duties in respect of herrings, cod, ling, hake, and salmon, or other white fish caught and cured by British subjects, and removed for home consumption, were to cease, excepting the equalizing duties paid on the importation from Scotland into En-

(*a*) Sect. 8, 9.  (*b*) Sect. 11.  (*c*) Sect. 14.

gland

gland of salmon, cod, ling, hake, tusk, and other white fish (*a*). The distinction with regard to the bounty made by stat. 5. *Geo.* 1. c. 18. between that called *haberdine* and other dried cod, was taken away, and instead of the five shillings bounty there is to be paid in all cases that of three shillings *per* hundred weight (*b*).

A BOUNTY of one shilling *per* barrel is given to the inhabitants of the Isle of Man for herrings caught and cured by them; and also on the export thereof, the bounties allowed by stat. 5. *Geo.* 1. c. 18. (*c*); and the duty on the import of herrings from the Isle of Man was from thenceforth to cease (*d*).

LASTLY, in order better to protect the British fishery, it was endeavoured to give further sanction to stat. 1. *Geo.* 1. c. 18. and stat. 9. *Geo.* 2. c. 33. for prohibiting the importation of foreign-caught fish. To facilitate the prosecution of offenders against those acts, power is given to two justices, upon the information of an officer suspecting such fish being brought into the port of

(*a*) Sect. 15.   (*b*) Sect. 16.   (*c*) Sect. 33, 34.
(*d*) Sect. 35.

London,

London, to summon the parties and proceed to hear the complaint, and convict in a summary way upon their non-appearance (*a*).

Some alterations were made in this act in the subsequent session of parliament. By stat. 27. *Geo.* 3, c. 10. the bounty, which by the former act was confined to busses built before 1 Jan. 1780, is extended to those built after that period (*b*). Some trifling alterations were also made as to the cargoes of vessels (*c*); and the bounty of twenty shillings *per* ton is not to be allowed to more than fifty vessels fitting out in one year from the same port (*d*).

Such are the regulations of this long act for promoting and protecting the fisheries on our coasts; to which we have only to add, that by stat. 25. *Geo.* 3. c. 58. an additional bounty was given on the export of pilchards for that season only, which was continued, with other additional bounties, by stat. 26. *Geo.* 3. c. 45. to 24 June 1786, which makes the whole of the parliamentary

(*a*) Sect. 43, 44, &c.  (*b*) Sect. 1, 2.  (*c*) Sect. 3, 4.
(*d*) Sect. 5.

provisions passed at this time for increasing and extending the British fisheries.

NOTHING remains to add but the following provision in the Consolidation Act, stat. 27. *Geo.* 3. c. 13. which enacts, that fresh fish of every kind or sort whatever, caught or taken in any part of the ocean by the crews of any ships or vessels built in Great Britain, Ireland, the islands of Jersey, Guernsey, or Man, or in any of the colonies, plantations, islands, or territories, which now belong, or at the time of building such vessels did belong, or which may hereafter belong to, or be in possession of his majesty, his heirs or successors, and wholly belonging to and owned by his majesty's subjects usually residing in Great Britain, Ireland, or the islands of Jersey, Guernsey, or Man, and navigated and registered according to law, may be imported into Great Britain in ships so built, owned, and navigated without payment of any duty of customs whatever (*a*).

THE sum and result of all these various laws regarding the fisheries, seem to be

(*a*) Sect. 31.

this. The following advantages are obtained by *permanent* laws: namely, By ſtat. 10. & 11. *Will.* 3. c. 24. ſtat. 1. *Geo.* 1. ſt. 2. c. 18. enforced by ſtat. 9. *Geo.* 2. c. 33. and ſtat. 26. *Geo.* 3. c. 81. ſ. 43, 44. no ſort of fiſh whatever of foreign fiſhing (except eels, ſtock-fiſh, anchovies, ſturgeon, botargo or caveare, turbots and lobſters), can be imported into *England*.

By ſtat. 27. *Geo.* 3. c. 13. ſ. 32. all freſh fiſh caught by veſſels built in the king's dominions, and owned by perſons uſually reſiding in his majeſty's European dominions, may be imported free of duty; and by ſtat. 5. *Geo.* 1. c. 18. ſ. 6. and ſtat. 26. *Geo.* 3. c. 81. ſ. 16. a bounty is paid on the export of pilchards or ſhads, codfiſh, ling, or hake, whether wet or dried, ſalmon, white herrings, red herrings, and dried red ſprats, being of Britiſh fiſhing and curing.

The following advantages are obtained by *temporary* laws: namely, By ſtat. 26. *Geo.* 3. c. 81. and ſtat. 27. *Geo.* 3. c. 10. a tonnage bounty and various other bounties are given on the fiſh caught in the Britiſh fiſheries on the coaſt. By ſtat. 26. *Geo.* 3. c. 45. a bounty on the export of pilchards.

By

By stat. 26. *Geo.* 3. c. 26. a bounty on the fish taken in the Newfoundland fishery. By stat. 26. *Geo.* 3. c. 41. a tonnage bounty on ships employed in the Greenland fishery. By stat. 26. *Geo.* 3. c. 50. premiums on the arrival of ships from the Southern whale-fishery. The seal-skins, oil, head-matter, blubber, and whale-fins, taken in the Newfoundland, Greenland, or Southern whale-fisheries, are importable without payment of any duty.

CHAP.

## CHAPTER VI.

### OF BRITISH SHIPS.

*Frauds in Registering—Smuggling—Defects in the Registering Laws—Intended Amendments therein—Points submitted to the Commissioners of the Customs—Their Report thereupon—Proposals for amending the Laws—The Opinion of the Committee of Trade thereupon—Stat. 26. Geo. 3. c. 60.—Of British-built Ships—Of Registering—The Bond—Indorsement on the Certificate—Bill of Sale—Change of Name—Certificate lost or mislaid—Prize Ships—Amendments made in Stat. 26. Geo. 3. c. 60.—Of Shipping in the Eastland Trade—Remedies proposed in Aid of British Shipping—Easement in Duties for British Ships—The Case of a Bill of Sale—Macneal's Case.*

PART III.
PEACE 1783,
TO A.D. 1792.
BRITISH
SHIPS.

IN the 26th year of the present king very considerable alteration was made in the whole concern of registering shipping, with a view of securing to ships of the built of this country a preference and superiority which they

they had not enjoyed so completely before. The plan of regulation then proposed to parliament was the result of an enquiry and deliberation of great length before the committee of privy council for the affairs of trade and plantations; and that enquiry was commenced and carried on, and the measure at length decided upon, principally by the exertion and perseverance of a noble lord, to whom I have had occasion before to allude.

A VIEW of the change which had happened in America, suggested the necessity of some regulations respecting the registering of shipping for the plantation-trade.

THE frauds which used to be committed before the war were chiefly confined to the West Indies; and they principally consisted in the Dutch inhabitants of St. Eustatia, and Curaçoa, and the Danes at St. Croix, purchasing British vessels with their plantation registers, and then employing them in the West Indies as British bottoms. Besides this practice by the Danes, and Dutch themselves, there were many British subjects who resided and were admitted burghers in those islands, and carried on their trade from thence

*Frauds in Registering.*

thence to our islands, the same as if they were resident in a British plantation.

But these abuses were far exceeded by those which had prevailed during hostilities, and since the termination of the war.

It appeared, that the custom-house officers in our plantations had granted registers to qualify several ships to trade in our plantations, which were built in some of the provinces in North America, during the time they were in actual rebellion, and of which the owners as well as the masters were now really and truly subjects of the United States, and resident there. These registers had been granted under an idea, that vessels built before the acknowledgement of the American independence, and while his majesty stiled them his rebellious *subjects*, were to be considered as plantation built, and the owners and masters as British subjects.

This was a very important consideration in the commerce of the colonies, and involved in it a point of law, upon which it was necessary to consult the law-officers; when it was held by them, that a vessel built in America during the existence of the prohibitory

hibitory acts, could not be considered as intitled to the privileges of a British-built ship; because the ships and effects belonging to the inhabitants of the revolted colonies were declared to be forfeited; and those colonies had never been restored to his majesty's peace, but had been declared Independent States.

Thus, all ships built since the prohibitory act 16. *Geo.* 3. that is, since the beginning of the year 1776, were held to be foreign ships in point of law. But the evil, in point of fact, would still in a great degree continue to prevail, and it was necessary to resort to some remedy that would have the effect of making such registers useless.

From the registering of plantation ships, it was natural to pass on to the consideration of British shipping in general; respecting which some points of great importance presented themselves.

It appeared upon enquiry among merchants and underwriters, that by the course of insurance, the shipping of this country had upon the same voyages a preference over the shipping of all the other countries in Europe,

PART III.
PEACE 1783,
TO A. D. 1791.
BRITISH
SHIPS.

Europe, and over that of America. With respect to American ships bound to and from America and the northern parts of Europe, the premium of insurance was double that on British ships; and to and from the southern parts of Europe the difference was confiderably greater. This preference was to be afcribed to British ships being better built, better fitted, and better navigated; but the difference in the latter case was to be afcribed to the war carried on against the Americans by the Barbary States; that although there was not much difference between the two in the infurance to the Weft Indies or to Africa, the preference would, for the firft of the above reasons, be given to a British ship.

It appeared alfo, that British shipping had greatly the preference of the shipping of Ruffia, and of Denmark; of Sweden, except their Chinamen, which are few in number, and of the shipping of Hamburgh, but not fo great as over the more northern nations; that it was preferred before the Dutch shipping, the Spanish, and Portuguefe; but that the premium on French and British shipping was much the fame. Upon the whole there feemed, on a general view of the commerce of of the world, to be such an advantage on the side of British shipping, that new obligations to employ them might be imposed with safety; that the time was now arrived for excluding almost entirely foreign-built ships from the European as well as the plantation trade; and that the scheme of registering should, for that purpose, be extended to ships employed in all trades whatsoever.

THE suppression of smuggling had lately occupied the attention of the Legislature, and it was thought that the intended scheme of registering might be made auxiliary to the completion of this object.

IT is the business of the master of a smuggling vessel to pass, if possible, unknown and undiscovered; it was found, therefore, that a smuggler was frequently changing not only his own name, but that of his vessel; and although informations were given against both, it was generally difficult to proceed in a course of justice against either. Another practice was to change the port or place to which the vessel was said to belong, as often as it suited the views and necessities of the smuggler.

PART III.
PEACE 1783,
TO A.D. 1792.
BRITISH
SHIPS.

Not only the masters of such vessels, but the owners, found it convenient to keep themselves concealed. Some smuggling vessels, liable to forfeiture under stat. 24. *Geo.* 3. c. 47. if they belonged to British subjects, and were found in port, or within four leagues of the coast, unless licensed by the admiralty, frequently escaped by obtaining documents certifying they were the property of foreigners residing at Ostend, Flushing, and other foreign ports; and they had often so been claimed, although known to be built in this kingdom, solely navigated by British seamen, and employed in the contraband trade.

These evils, it was thought, might be remedied, if every vessel was to be registered at the port to which it belonged; it would then be easy to ascertain the true name of the vessel, of the master, and of the port; and if the names and occupations of *all* the owners were required to be described before a certificate of registry should be granted, it might be expected that many persons would be discouraged from being concerned in building, equipping and employing, vessels of this description, from the apprehension that their names must appear: if such ships were

were made liable to forfeiture, upon being found without a register, they could not escape under the colour of such foreign documents.

THE underwriters of ships against the perils of the sea, felt an interest to promote any regulations that would tend to ascertain the name and description of ships, with the names of all the owners, and of the master. They foresaw, that this would tend to detect and prevent frauds, and would facilitate the redress to be obtained in proceedings at law, by rendering the evidence on trials more attainable, and clear: this it was believed would contribute to make persons more ready to insure British than foreign ships, which would diminish the premium of insurance on British ships, and of course give them a preference in all sorts of trade and employment.

SUCH were the leading points in the intended reform to be made in the law for registering shipping; but in looking into the existing laws, many other points suggested themselves, as deserving revision and amendment.

E e   As

PART III.
PEACE 1783,
TO A.D. 1792.
BRITISH
SHIPS.

Defects in the Registering Laws.

As the law then stood, registers were granted in pursuance of stat. 7. & 8. *Will.* 3. c. 22. and stat. 15. *Geo.* 2. c. 31. The first of these acts confines the trade to and from the British plantations in Asia, Africa, and America, to British-built ships; that is, to ships built in England (and since the Act of Union in Great-Britain) and in Ireland, Guernsey, Jersey, or the plantations, as before mentioned, and wholly owned by the people thereof; or to foreign ships taken as prize, and legally condemned in the courts of admiralty; and all such ships trading to the plantations without producing a register agreeable to the directions of that act were liable to forfeiture, as if they were foreign ships (*a*).

NOTWITHSTANDING no other sort of ships was legally intitled to a British register than those before mentioned, yet it had been a practice for many years to grant registers to *foreign* ships also, that had been wrecked or stranded upon the coasts of this kingdom,

(*a*) The form of register is not specially set down in the act: one was devised conformably to the requisites of the act. The form of oath to be taken, as a ground for obtaining the registry, is in the act. See them both in the APPENDIX.

on their being purchased and repaired here by British subjects, and after such a sum had been expended on them as might be deemed nearly equal to a re-building (a). Whatever might have been the first motive for extending this privilege to foreign ships, it had been the invariable practice of the custom-house never to permit any such ship to be registered, until the proprietor had first stated his case to the attorney-general, and laid before him all the tradesmen's bills and other vouchers for the sums expended in repairs, authenticated by affidavits, and the attorney-general had given his opinion, that under all the circumstances of the case, such ship appeared to him to be entitled to the privileges of a British ship.

It does not appear, that the commissioners of the customs in Scotland had adopted any check of this sort, nor that they confined the indulgence to such foreign ships as were stranded or wrecked on the coasts, but they extended it to all foreign ships *becoming British property, and greatly repaired at home*. And notwithstanding the precaution observed in England, there was great rea-

(a) Vid. ant. 329.

son to believe the practice of granting registers to such foreign ships had been productive of many frauds, and that oaths and alledged facts not founded in truth had been the means of extending this indulgence, to the great injury of ship-building in this kingdom.

As to the regulations observed by the custom-house in granting registers, the form of the oath being laid down in the statute, the certificate of registry was made in pursuance of it; but the description of the ship there made was so vague and indefinite, that it might be used to protect any other of nearly the same burthen with little or no risk of detection. The requisites, also, were so few and inadequate, that persons not legally intitled to the benefit of a register, nor perhaps competent to speak with certainty to the proofs required, used to comply with the law, and take the oath enjoined as a mere matter of form; and so obtained, with the greatest ease, this very material document, which had the consequence of raising the value of the ship, and entitling it to all the advantages that were meant by the Legislature to be confined to British ships solely, owned by British subjects. In instances where the commissioners

missioners of the customs had discovered registers to have been granted improperly, and called upon the officers to account for their conduct; the officers had urged, that the persons applying having performed all the requisites of law, they did not conceive themselves warranted in refusing the register. Again, the oath, when taken and subscribed by the person procuring the register, was delivered into his own custody; and if he should afterwards be discovered to have sworn falsely, he was in possession of the principal evidence upon which he could be convicted of the offence.

THE practice of granting registers *de novo* in lieu of those alledged to be either lost or mislaid, differed widely from that of granting original ones; and such second registers could not be obtained with the same facility, under the regulations of stat. 15. *Geo.* 2. c. 31. which gives directions for granting such new registers, as well when the case happened in the plantations, as in Great Britain.

IF in the plantations, and the loss had happened at a great distance from the port

PART III.
PLACE 1783,
TO A.D. 1790.
BRITISH
SHIPS.

port proper for the registering *de novo*, the master was at liberty to take the oath prescribed in the act (*a*), and give large security to perform the conditions upon which he was to be relieved; and this relief was no more than the governor and collector granting him a certificate, that such oath and such security had been given, which entitled the ship to trade for one voyage only (*b*). If in Great Britain, and the owner or owners, or any of them, should reside in Great Britain, Ireland, Guernsey or Jersey, and the master, or one or more of the owners, should make proof to the satisfaction of the commissioners of the customs of the loss of the register, and should likewise give the security required, the ship was entitled to be registered *de novo*. This was a practice that perhaps might be sufficient, with the addition of an oath (*c*).

STAT. 7. & 8. *Will.* 3. directed all prize ships to be *specially registered*, mentioning the capture and condemnation, instead of the time and place of building, on proof upon oath that the intire property was British. Besides the register, it had become the practice, in order to make all the circumstances

(*a*) See the oath in the APPENDIX.
(*b*) Sect. 2.   (*c*) Sect. 3.

of these ships appear more at large, to grant to the owners of them another document, called *a certificate of freedom (a)*; but this practice does not seem to have been obtained in Scotland: this certificate recited when and by whom the duties on such prize-ships were paid.

It had become a rule with the lords of the admiralty not to issue *a Mediterranean pass* to any ship that had not a register; a check which they had imposed, to guard against the danger of such passes being granted to ships for whose benefit they never could have been intended. In consequence it had become the practice of ships which needed the latter document only, to apply previously for the former; so that many ships not trading to the plantations became in this manner possessed of registers; which becoming of little use to the procurer after they had served the turn they were intended for, were disposed of, for money, or otherwise, and so applied to the protection of many ships, that were not entitled to them.

(*a*) No form was set down in the statute; but see in the APPENDIX a certificate of freedom made in pursuance of the directions of the statute.

The nature of a Mediterranean pafs is this: In the treaties that have from time to time been made with the different Barbary States, it has been agreed, that the fubjects of the king of Great Britain fhould pafs the feas unmolefted by the cruifers of thofe States; and for better afcertaining what fhips and veffels belong to Britifh fubjects, it is provided, that they fhall produce *a pafs*, under the hand and feal of the lord high admiral, or the lords commiffioners of the admiralty. In purfuance of thefe treaties paffes are made out at the admiralty, containing a very few words, written on parchment, with ornaments at the top, through which a fcolloped indenture is made; the *fcolloped tops* are fent to Barbary, and being put in the poffeffion of their cruifers, the commanders are inftructed to fuffer all perfons to pafs who have paffes that will fit thefe fcolloped tops. The protection afforded by thefe paffes is fuch, that no fhips, which traverfe the feas frequented by thefe rovers, ever fail to furnifh themfelves with them; whether in the trade to the Eaft-Indies, Africa, or the Levant, or in the trade to Spain, Italy, or any part of the Mediterranean; and from the more particular need of them in the latter, they, no doubt, obtained the name of

*Mediterranean*

*Mediterranean passes.* For the accommodation of merchants in distant parts, blank passes, signed by the lords of the admiralty, are lodged with the governors abroad, and with the British consuls, to be granted to those who comply with the requisites necessary for obtaining them.

As this piece of security is derived wholly from the stipulations made by the crown with a foreign power, the intire regulation and management of it has been under the direction of his majesty, who, with the advice of his privy council, has prescribed the terms and conditions upon which these passes shall be granted. Among others are the following: They are to be granted for none but British-built ships, or ships made free, navigated with a master and three-fourths of the mariners British subjects, or foreign protestants made denizens. Bond is to be given in the sum of 300 l. if the vessel is under one hundred tons, and in 500 l. if it is of that or more, for delivering up the pass within twelve months, unless in the case of ships trading from one foreign port to another; and such passes need not be returned in less than three years.

THE

PART III.
PEACE 1783,
TO A.D. 1792.
BRITISH
SHIPS.

The rules and orders under which Mediterranean passes are now granted were made by the king in council on 14 June 1722, and on 28 August 1776, upon representations made by the board of admiralty of the abuses then practised.

It has been found expedient at the conclusion of a war, and sometimes during a peace, to recall and cancel all passes that have been issued, and to issue others in a new form. This has been done for two reasons: First, That these useful instruments by various means, either accidental or fraudulent, came into the hands of foreigners, who, under cover of them, carried on in security a trade which otherwise would belong to British subjects, and which had been purchased by the crown at the expence of keeping up this sort of alliance. Secondly, That the Barbary States complained, that adhering to the rule of fitting the other part of the indenture to the passes, they were obliged to suffer ships to pass that did not belong to British subjects. For these reasons, the passes were called in in the years 1722, 1729, 1750, 1765, 1776, and for the last time in 1783, and new ones issued.

By

By stat. 4. *Geo.* 2. c. 18. it is made felony without benefit of clergy to forge, counterfeit, or alter Mediterranean passes; and such offences committed out of the kingdom may be prosecuted in any county (*a*).

To return to registers:—It was directed by stat. 7. & 8. *Will.* 3. c. 22. s. 21. that when the name of a ship was changed after registering, or the property in part, or in the whole, was transferred to *another* port, the register should be delivered up to be cancelled, and the ship be registered *de novo*; but if the property was altered in the *same* port, by the sale of any share, it should be acknowledged by an indorsement on the register before two witnesses.

The practice, however, appears to have differed somewhat from the directions of the law; for in case of a change of property, even in the *same* port, the old register was generally given up, and a new one granted in lieu thereof; because the document would not admit of many indorsements of this sort without inconvenience, the small space be-

(*a*) See in the Appendix the form of a Mediterranean pass, and of the bond entered into on granting it.

PART III.
PLACE 1783,
TO A. D. 1792.
BRITISH
SHIPS.

ing soon covered by the indorsements required by the act to be made on every change of the master.

Such being the law and practice, and such the frauds and defects in the registering of ships, it was considered what regulations could be made, which would secure to British ships the preference which it was intended they should hereafter enjoy; and it was thought, that some plan like the following would be the most likely to answer that design.

Intended Amendments therein.

THAT, in future, no ship foreign-built, though owned by British subjects, and navigated according to law, should have the privileges of a British ship, if purchased after the passing of the intended act. The reason given for this was, that it was right and wise to exclude foreign-built ships, as well from our foreign trade as from the plantation and coasting trade, as soon as we had shipping enough of our own built, and were otherwise qualified to do it; that this had now become more adviseable than before the American war, as the United States from friends had become our rivals in ship-building.

AGAIN,

AGAIN, the advantages thereby given to British-built ships above those that were foreign-built, must be considered as very little more than a compensation for the extraordinary costs of building in this kingdom. The customs were now twenty-five *per cent.* which in Charles II.'s reign were only five *per cent.* upon all the materials of which ships were built; so that the customs amounted to 300l. upon a ship of eight hundred tons; all which duties on the raw material ought to be compensated by a countervailing duty on foreign ships, if a preference was not given to ships of British-built. On this principle a duty was already payable on prize ships, and on foreign ships employed in the coasting trade.

IT seemed to be agreed, that no ship should thenceforward be allowed to be registered that was built on a foreign bottom, as well because the present practice was not founded in law, as that it was liable to great frauds; however, that all foreign-built ships, and all ships built on a foreign keel, should be allowed to be used by the owners of them, till they were worn out.

It was agreed, that every ship above fifteen tons burthen, and having a deck, whether employed in the coasting trade or the foreign trade, should be registered, the same as vessels were before registered for the plantation trade, there being no reason why they should not be all equally registered. Ships hitherto had been registered for two purposes: First, To prove that they were owned by British subjects: Secondly, To prove that they were British-built. It was intended all ships should hereafter be owned by British subjects, and for that reason alone they ought to be registered: if they were also to be British-built, that was another reason for their being registered. Indeed, already, ships employed even in the foreign trade procured registers, if they needed a Mediterranean pass; and this circumstance had given occasion to great frauds. The expence of registering was not so great as to be any reason against this plan.

It was agreed, that no ship, in future, should be registered but in the port to which she belonged, or where she was condemned as prize; nor otherwise than upon a certificate of the person who built her,

her, or of the court of admiralty which condemned her; nor without giving bond, that the regifter fhould not be lent, fold, or difpofed of, but fhould be employed for the ufe of that fhip only; and that when the fhip fhould be worn out, or fold to a foreigner, it fhould be delivered up to the collector at the port to which the fhip belonged: That the regifters fhould be returned from every part of Great Britain and the plantations to the chief officer in London, there to be entered.

It was thought proper, that there fhould be a general revifion of the fhipping of Great Britain and the plantations, in order to detect thofe then trading under falfe regifters; and with this view, every fhip not already regiftered fhould be regiftered, and every fhip already regiftered fhould be regiftered anew, on their return to the port to which they belonged; and no old regifter to be valid after a certain day. This would have the effect of fubjecting to the inconvenience of regiftering anew fuch fhips as were qualified for the plantation trade, and fuch as were foreign-built. But this inconvenience, it was thought, fhould be fubmitted to, as it was impoffible to detect the frauds then

then committed without such revision. The trouble of office would not be more than that which the admiralty went through when they called in all Mediterranean passes. The trouble to the subject would be no more than what he was already liable to when a ship changed her port. The expence of fees ought to be made small.

In this proposal for a revision of old registers, it was thought reasonable to make allowance and exemption for particular cases. Thus, ships which had been promised registers in consideration of their having assisted in removing the king's troops and subjects from New-York and other places; ships that had been registered by the governors of the plantations, before the law as to the subjects of the United States was explained to them; ships that had been promised registers in consideration of the owners and their families having removed into the king's dominions from the countries of the United States; it was thought, that power should be lodged in the crown to grant relief in all such cases, that appeared to be clear of fraud and collusion.

AFTER

After the subject of registering had been canvassed, and these conclusions drawn, it only remained to put it into a course of official enquiry. His majesty was accordingly moved to order in council, that the lords of the committee appointed for the consideration of all matters relating to trade and foreign plantations should consider and report their opinion, whether it might not be proper, that a bill should be offered to parliament for enforcing the several provisions of the laws made for the encouraging and increasing of the shipping and navigation of his majesty's dominions, and for preventing the frauds practised respecting registers, and other securities for ascertaining the built and property of British ships. This order was made 1 March 1786.

The committee of council proceeded immediately to take into consideration the question referred by his majesty, and endeavoured to obtain every information and light that could be procured, by examination of merchants, underwriters, and other persons conversant with mercantile affairs, and by consultation with the officers of the crown, in the departments to which this sort of business belonged. A letter had been previously

viously written to the commissioners of the customs, apprizing them of the intended investigation; and on the very day on which his majesty referred the question, the lords of the committee opened to the commissioners the several objects that appeared proper for their consideration, in framing the report they were to make on this subject. Their lordships called likewise upon the board of customs in Scotland, to report their opinion upon the question; and this report, when made, their lordships caused to be transmitted to the commissioners of the customs for their consideration. So much dispatch was used by the commissioners of the customs, that on 31 March they made a very elaborate report upon all the points submitted to them, with a very full opinion as to the defects of the law, and the probable amendments to be made therein. This report of itself comprizes the substance of the discussion, which this subject underwent.

*Points submitted to the Commissioners of the Customs.*

THE lords of the committee, when they opened the subject of enquiry to the commissioners of the customs, broke it into the following points. First, That there should be a general inspection and revision of all British shipping and new registers granted. Secondly, That

That some further regulation should be made to prevent frauds, when the property of a ship was transferred to other British owners. Thirdly, That there should be made a further description of British subjects; such as, *British subjects residing in his majesty's dominions,* specifying the place, *or British subjects belonging to such a factory abroad.* Fourthly, That there should be some further description of a ship by way of ascertaining it to be the same. Fifthly, That there should be some further penalty upon false swearing, and upon forging or altering certificates or registers. Sixthly, That further regulation should be made for securing a proper return of all registers from any part of his majesty's dominions to the chief office of the customhouse in London. Seventhly, To collect as many circumstances as the commissioners were able, of the frauds committed in order to intitle a foreign ship to the privilege of a British ship navigated according to law. Eighthly, To state the present defects or omissions in transmitting to the chief office in London registers and certificates granted to British ships according to the law as it then stood. Ninthly, To give an account of the shipping of England, as it appeared at the Register's Office, or from any other information the commissioners of the customs could obtain.

*Their Report thereupon.*

To these points the commissioners made distinct answers and observations. As to the first, they concluded it to be the design in future to keep a registry of *all* ships and vessels belonging to this country of every description, including those employed in the coast trade and fisheries; and they proposed, with a view of carrying this design into execution, that the shipping should be divided into the three following classes. *First*, Ships of the built of Great-Britain, Ireland, Guernsey, Jersey, or the British plantations, or those taken and condemned as prize, or such foreign ships as may be wrecked or stranded, and afterwards admitted to the privilege of British, unless, indeed, it should be thought adviseable that this indulgence should be altogether discontinued. *Secondly*, Ships foreign-built, but wholly owned by British subjects and legally navigated; without alteration, however, in any respect of the duties then payable on goods and merchandize imported and exported in such ships. *Thirdly*, Ships or vessels British-built, or those taken and condemned as prize, not employed in the foreign-trade:

in

in this class also foreign wrecked or stranded ships might be included, if permitted in future to be made free.

THE first class was considered as the only description of ships that could legally trade to and from any of the king's dominions in Asia, Africa, or America. The second included those that were then confined to the European trade, but which could not import goods of the growth, product or manufacture of Turkey (a). The third was limited to coasters, as also to such fishing-vessels the navigation of which was confined to the rivers or coasts, and which are more particularly described in the twentieth section of stat. 7. & 8. *Will.* 3. c. 22.

CONFORMABLY with this division, they proposed, that certificates of registry should in future be made out separately in this manner, and should be distinguished in their titles as follows:

FIRST, *Certificate of British Plantation Registry, &c.*

IT was proposed, that ships should by virtue of this certificate be intitled also to trade to Europe, and all other foreign parts, or, if occasion should require, to go coastwise.

(a) Vid. ant. 198.

SECONDLY,

SECONDLY, *Certificate of a Foreign Ship's Registry for the European Trade, British Property, &c.*

THIS clafs would be confined wholly to this trade, fuch fhips not being permitted to go to the plantations, nor even to carry goods coaftwife, unlefs on payment of the duty impofed by ftat. 1. *Jac.* 2. c. 18. f. 2. which has hitherto been found to operate as a prohibition.

THIRDLY, *Certificate of a Coafting or Fifhing Veffel's Regiftry.*

IT was propofed, that no certificate fhould be taken out for this clafs of veffels when under fifteen tons burthen; and that no veffel, during the time it had this certificate, fhould be allowed to take out one of the firft clafs.

IT was further propofed, with regard to all thefe certificates, that none fhould in future iffue but at the port to which the fhip belonged, without the fpecial leave of the board of cuftoms, to which all the circumftances fhould be previoufly ftated. The defign of this was, that the officers granting the certificate living on the fpot where the parties applying for the certificate refided, would have an opportunity of enquiring into to the truth of facts stated by them for obtaining it. They further thought, that no certificate should be granted on the oath of one of the owners, but that the major part of them should join therein, provided they did not reside at a greater distance than twenty miles from the port to which the ship belonged; and if the major part of them did not appear, sufficient proof on oath should be made by one or more of the owners present, that the rest did not reside within that distance.

WITH regard to " the granting of new registers," although they were fully convinced of the necessity of that measure, yet the means of effecting it appeared to them to be attended with great difficulty. For as the oath of the owner or owners was required, it might frequently happen for the ship to arrive at a port, as well in Great Britain as in the British plantations, where none of the owners resided; and to deliver a new certificate of registry on the return of the old one, merely on the oath of the master (which could only be to the best of his knowledge) would by no means tend to remedy the evil apprehended. Great inconveniences must also arise in receiving the old

old register, and in lieu thereof granting a letter of licence for one voyage only, as such voyage might not carry the ship to the port to which it belonged.

The plan that occurred the most likely to answer the end proposed, and not to interrupt the navigation of the country, was one similar to the practice of the lords of the admiralty, when they had reason to apprehend that Mediterranean passes had fallen into the hands of persons, and were used for the protection of ships, for which they were not originally intended: in such cases, they caused an advertisement to be published and continued for some time in the Gazette and other public prints, giving notice, that passes of a *new* form would be issued in a short time after the date of such publication; but that such passes of the *old* form as had been issued, would nevertheless continue in force until a certain day, usually the distance of twelve months. In like manner, it was now proposed that the commissioners of the customs should give notice, that after a certain day certificates of registry should be issued of a *new* form, and that after such a day no ship would be permitted to clear out at the port to which she belonged, either in Great Britain

Britain or the plantations, as a British ship, until the owners had made proof that such ship was British-built or British-owned, as the case might be.

But considering that British ships employed in foreign trade do not return to the ports to which they belong for a considerable time, and consequently, under the regulations now proposed, could not procure a *new* form of regiſtry, certain diſtant periods were to be allowed before the owners of such ships should be compelled to take out a certificate of the *new* form, unless such ship should arrive sooner at the port to which she belonged.

It was further proposed, that at the time of taking out the certificate of *new* regiſtry, security should be given that such certificate should not be sold, lent, or otherwise disposed of, but that it should be made use of for the ship for which it was granted, so long as all the owners and the master and three-fourths of the mariners were British subjects, and should be delivered up in case the ship was lost or taken by the enemy, or was broken up. The penalties proposed for these securities are nearly such as were then given

given for the due use of Mediterranean passes. Should the ship be sold in whole or in part to any foreigner, then the certificate was to be delivered up within seven days, if within the limits of any port; and if at sea, or in any foreign port, within fourteen days after its first arrival in any port within his majesty's dominions.

As the abuses in regard to registers had principally been in the plantations, it was recommended, that the officers there should not have power to make out any certificate but only for ships taken as prize, and condemned there, and bought and equipped for sea by the inhabitants there; and as the duty on prize-ships registered in Guernsey and Jersey had in many instances been evaded, it was proposed that no ships should be registered in those islands, but, instead thereof, in some ports of this kingdom; which, it was thought, would be no great inconvenience, considering the nearness of those islands.

It seems, that where ships and their cargoes had been seized for having registers illegally granted, the lords of the treasury had often directed, if the register appeared not to have been obtained by any sinister finister means, that the cargo should be entered on condition of delivering up the register to be cancelled.

Upon the second point they observed, that the difficulty of identifying a ship was much increased by a frequent change of name, and they recommended that the name of a ship should not in future be altered, after it had been once registered. From this regulation it was thought no material inconvenience would follow, but that on the contrary an expence, which was then too frequently incurred through the mere caprice of the owners, would be saved, as the law then required the ship to be registered *de novo* on every change of name.

They further recommended, in addition to the directions of stat. 7. & 8. *Will*. 3. c. 22. s. 21. that upon the transfer of any share in a ship, even in the same port, before any indorsement thereof was permitted, an oath should be taken by the person or persons to whom it was transferred; and that upon every change of the master of a ship, an indorsement thereof should be made on the register; and as the parchment for registers in future was intended to be

much

much larger, it was thought there would be sufficient room for both indorsements.

Upon the third point they recommended, that the form of the oath upon which the certificate was to issue, should contain the occupation and place of residence of each owner; if they resided in large towns in England, the name of the parish likewise; and if in any factory abroad, the name thereof. The owners attending to take out the certificate should also swear, that they were truly and *bona fide* subjects of Great Britain, and that none of them, nor, to the best of their knowledge or belief, any of the other persons having any share or property in such ship, had taken the oath of allegiance to any foreign state, except involuntarily, under the terms of some capitulation to be noticed in the oath; and that no foreigner directly or indirectly, or any other person than those described, had any share or interest in the ship. And they submitted, whether it would not also be expedient, that the deponents should make oath, not to sell or transfer any share of the ship to the subject of any foreign state, without giving immediate notice to the commissioners of the customs in London and Edinburgh; and the

the same if any other person having a share should so transfer it, as soon as it came to their knowledge, in order that the register might be called in and cancelled.

UPON the fourth point it was judged, that such a circumstantial description of the ship might be made in the form of certificate, as would enable any officer of the water-guard of the customs to ascertain the identity of it; and they proposed, that, before registry, all ships should be surveyed by an officer of the customs, assisted by a skilful person if necessary, and in the presence of the master or some other person on behalf of the owners; and that a certificate should be delivered to the officer who was to grant the certificate, containing a description of all the particulars required to be contained in it.

BECAUSE it might sometimes be dangerous to lay a ship on shore for the purpose of ascertaining its tonnage according to the rule laid down in stat. 13. Geo. 3. c. 74. f. 1. they proposed a certain rule for measuring ships while afloat, by which the tonnage might be ascertained with nearly the same precision as when the ship was on ground.

UPON

Upon the fifth point they proposed, that a similar penalty to that contained in stat. 7. & 8. *Will.* 3. c. 22. f. 10. should be annexed to the counterfeiting of the certificate of registry now proposed; and that taking a false oath should be punished with the pains of perjury.

Upon the sixth point they observed, that by stat. 7. & 8. *Will.* 3. c. 22. f. 18. duplicates of all registers are required to be transmitted to the custom-house, to be entered in a general register; but no penalty is annexed to a failure in such duty. This being a regulation that ought to be punctually observed, they recommended, that an officer granting a certificate and delaying for three days transmitting a duplicate thereof, should forfeit a year's salary; if he was out of Great Britain, he should do it by the earliest conveyance.

As to the seventh, eighth, and ninth points they observed, that the neglect in transmitting duplicates was principally in the plantations. They subjoined an account made out by the register-general of shipping of the number of ships belonging to the several ports in England; and also a list of various frauds that had been practised with regard to

SHIPPING AND NAVIGATION. 447

to regifters; from which it appears, that regifters were frequently and without concealment granted in the Weft Indies to American fubjects of the United States, who, under cover thereof, carried on trade with our plantations.

THE commiffioners conclude their report with fubmitting the following outline of a propofal for an alteration in the laws relative to fhipping.

FIRST, That no fhip or veffel fhould be intitled to any privilege as a Britifh-*owned* fhip that was not Britifh-built, or condemned as prize the property of Britifh fubjects, legally navigated by Britifh mariners, and regiftered according to law; except fuch foreign-built fhips as being the *entire* property of Britifh fubjects, and legally navigated, were, at the time of or before the paffing of the act, employed by the prefent owners in any trade whatever in which fuch fhip enjoyed any privilege of navigation not allowed to fhips in general; but on this condition, that an account fhould be delivered to the proper officer of the cuftoms within fix months, by the owner or mafter of every fhip claiming the continuance of fuch privilege, defcribing the built, burthen, owners, and other neceffary particulars,

lars, who should prove the facts by affidavit; in which case he might receive, at the custom-house of the port to which the vessel belonged, a document for the security of her navigation, somewhat similar in its nature to, but different in form from, the certificate of registry in general, which should secure to such ship the continuance of those advantages of which she was *then* in possession; the merchandize, however, therein imported to be subject to the same duty as before. But if the owners did not, within six months after proper notice given, render the account, and procure such document, all such ships should be considered, in every respect, as foreign ships, and subject to penalties as such.

SECONDLY, That every person applying for a certificate of registry for a British ship built after the passing of the act, should produce to the proper officer of the customs a certificate, under the hands of the builder, expressing the time when, and the place where, it was built; the exact tonnage, and the name of the first purchaser; describing also the vessel, under its proper denomination, in the most explicit manner: the owner should also make oath, that the vessel

he

res to be regiſtered is the identical ſoned in the builder's certificate. every ſhip or veſſel built in any of plantations for which regiſtry ſhould be required after 1 January 1787, the like certificate ſhould be produced from the builder, with an affidavit as to the identity.

THIRDLY, That for every ſhip built in any of the colonies or plantations for which a certificate ſhould be *firſt* granted after 1 January 1787, there ſhould be paid, on its arrival in any port of Great-Britain, a duty of 5l. for every 100l. of the real value thereof (the value to be aſcertained on oath); the payment of which duty ſhould be certified by the collector and comptroller, by indorſement on the regiſter.

THEY obſerved on theſe propoſals, that the firſt would, within a few years, occaſion the excluſive employment of Britiſh-built ſhips in every trade where any privilege was at that time allowed to foreign-built ſhips *owned* by Britiſh ſubjects. The ſecond would, by means of the builder's certificate, prevent a fraudulent uſe of regiſters. The third propoſal, as to the duty, would not more than compenſate the revenue for what it would receive on the *foreign* materials subject to duty necessarily used in ships built in this kingdom; and might encourage the building of ships in Great Britain, by putting the builders here, and those in the plantations, on a more equal footing.

*The Opinion of the Committee of Trade thereupon.*

THE committee of privy council were of opinion, these regulations should, without delay, be proposed to parliament; but that, instead of the oaths recommended for the performance of acts to be done, the compliance therewith should rather be enforced by bonds and penalties; and that the duty of 5l. on plantation-built ships should be postponed for further consideration: and as in many of the cases where registers might have been obtained contrary to the laws then in force, there might have been no fraudulent intention, the committee were of opinion, that a power should be vested by parliament in his majesty for a limited time to grant relief to such owners. Their lordships accordingly on 7 April made a report to his majesty to that effect; and at the same time laid before his majesty the report of the commissioners of the customs.

THE

The committee for trade and plantations then proceeded to the framing of a bill to be brought into parliament. This was two months in paſſing through both Houſes; and during that progreſs, it was very minutely examined, both within and without doors, and underwent many alterations.

Some ſtruggle was made againſt the intended clauſe for preventing owners from changing the names of ſhips; but at a numerous meeting of merchants, aſſurers, and owners of ſhips, where this clauſe was taken into conſideration, it was reſolved, that this regulation would anſwer a very good and ſalutary purpoſe, and would prevent many frauds being committed on the merchants, aſſurers, and fair traders, who had been continually expoſed to impoſitions and great loſſes, for want of ſuch a regulation; and this reſolution was communicated to the lords of the committee for trade and plantations.

At length the bill paſſed into a law, making ſtat. 26. *Geo.* 3. c. 60. intituled, *An Act for the further Increaſe and Encouragement of Shipping and Navigation*; and the proviſions of it are as follows:

PART III.
_____
PEACE 1783,
TO A.D. 1791.
BRITISH
SHIPS.
Stat. 26. Geo. 3.
c. 60.

THE act begins by ordaining, that no ship or vessel foreign-built (except ships condemned as prize), nor any ship or vessel built or rebuilt upon a foreign keel or bottom, in the manner before that time practised and allowed—that none of these ships, although owned by British subjects, and navigated according to law, should any longer be intitled to the privileges or advantages of a British-built ship, or of a ship owned by British subjects. But to this three exceptions of a temporary nature were made: First, Any foreign-built ship that before 1 May 1786 belonged wholly to any of the people of Great-Britain or Ireland, Guernsey, Jersey, or the isle of Man, or of any of the beforementioned colonies, islands, plantations, or territories, navigated according to law, and registered in the manner directed by the act, were to continue to possess the privileges of foreign-built ships. Secondly, Any ship built or rebuilt on a foreign-made keel or bottom, and registered before 1 May 1786 as a British ship. Thirdly, Any such ship begun to be repaired or rebuilt before 1 May 1786 may be registered under this act, on an order from the commissioners of the customs in England or Scotland, if it is made appear to them

upon

upon oath, that such ship was stranded by act of Providence, and not with a fraudulent intent, and was at the time of such stranding the property of some foreigner; or that such ship was a *droit* of admiralty, and was rendered unfit to proceed to sea without undergoing a thorough repair in this kingdom, and was necessarily sold for the benefit of the foreign owner; or being a *droit* of admiralty, was sold under an order or commission from the court of admiralty, and fairly and openly purchased by a British subject, and has been so much repaired since it was his property, that two-thirds of her at least are British-built.

Such were the descriptions of ships to be excluded henceforward from the privileges of British shipping, and such the peculiar circumstances that were suffered to exempt from exclusion some which came under those descriptions.

The privileges of a British-built ship were, generally speaking, to be confined to such ships only as have been taken and condemned as lawful prize, and such as are wholly of the built of Great Britain or Ireland, Guernsey, Jersey, or the isle of Man,

Man, or of some of the colonies, plantations, islands, or territories, in Asia, Africa, or America, which at the time of passing the act, or at the time of building the ship, belonged to, or were in the possession of, his majesty (a).

Such, and such only, was in future to be the qualification of a British-built ship. To this also were subjoined the following exceptions: First, No ship is to be deemed British-built which shall be rebuilt or repaired in any foreign port or place, if such repairs exceed fifteen shillings *per* ton, unless they are necessary by reason of extraordinary damage sustained during her absence from the king's dominions, and to enable her to perform the voyage in which she is then engaged, and to return in safety to some place in the king's dominions.

Before such repairs in a foreign port are made, the master is to report on oath the condition of the ship to the British consul or chief British officer, and cause it to be surveyed by two persons approved by him, to deliver in writing an account of the damage,

(a) Sect. 1.

and

and verify before him upon oath the particulars and amount of the repairs; that they were neceſſary to enable the ſhip to perform her voyage, and return to ſome place in the king's dominions; which the conſul is to certify under his hand and ſeal. If there is no conſul or Britiſh officer, then theſe particulars are to be verified before two known Britiſh merchants, whoſe certificate is to be of the ſame force. The maſter, at the firſt port where he arrives in the king's dominions, is to make oath before the collector and comptroller, if required by them ſo to do, of the nature and amount of the charge or expence of ſuch repairs: and if the repairs appear to exceed fifteen ſhillings *per* ton, or the maſter neglects to deliver the certificate, the ſhip is to be deemed foreign-built (*a*).

Thus far the act is employed upon the *built* of ſhips: the whole of the remainder of the act is taken up with the various regulations about *regiſtering*, which we ſhall now conſider, ſtating them as briefly as the nature of them will allow. It was deſigned to make ſome alterations and amendments in

(*a*) Sect. 2.

stat. 7. & 8. *Will.* 3. and to extend that act to other ships than those particularly described therein.

EVERY ship or vessel having a deck, or being of the burthen of fifteen tons, and belonging to a subject in Great Britain, or Guernsey, Jersey, or the isle of Man, or any colony, plantation, island, or territory, belonging to the king, is to be registered by the person claiming property therein, who is to obtain a certificate of such registry, in the form given in the act, from the collector and comptroller, if in Great Britain or the isle of Man; or from the governor, lieutenant-governor, or commander in chief, and the principal officer of the customs, if in Guernsey, Jersey, or any colony or plantation (*a*).

SUCH certificate is not to be granted but in the port to which the ship properly belongs, except prize-ships condemned in Guernsey, Jersey, or Man, which are to be registered in a particular manner; and except cases where the officers are specially authorized by the commissioners of the customs.

(*a*) Sect. 3.

customs *(a)*. The port to which a ship shall be deemed to belong, is the port from and to which she usually trades, or, being a new ship, shall intend to trade, and at or near which the husband, or acting and managing owner, usually resides *(b)*. No ship the property of the king or royal family, nor any lighters, barges, boats, or vessels, of any built or description whatever, used solely in rivers or inland navigation *(c)* need be registered; and no ship built in the United States, or owned by the people thereof, during the time the prohibitory acts were in force, and not before registered, is intitled to be registered, unless it has been condemned as prize, or having been stranded shall have been built or rebuilt, and registered in the manner before practised and allowed *(d)*. No subject whose usual residence is out of the king's dominions shall, during such residence, be intitled to be owner in whole or in part of a British ship to be registered under this act, unless he is a member of some British factory, or agent for, or partner in, any house or copartnership actually carrying on trade in Great Britain or Ireland *(e)*.

*(a)* Sect. 4.    *(b)* Sect. 5.    *(c)* Sect. 6.
*(d)* Sect. 7.    *(e)* Sect. 8.

THE

THE oath prescribed in the stat. 7. & 8. *Will.* 3. is repealed, and another oath, the form of which is given in the act, is required to be taken and subscribed before the person making the registry and granting the certificate. This oath is to be taken by the owner; and, if there are two joint owners, by both, if they both live within twenty miles of the port, otherwise by one: if more than two, then by the greater part, not exceeding three, if such greater number of them are resident within twenty miles of the port; or by one, if all shall be resident at a greater distance (*a*); and where one of three joint owners takes the oath, he is also to swear, that those who are absent are not resident within twenty miles of London, and have not wilfully absented in order to avoid the oath, or are prevented by illness (*b*).

THAT the proper officers may be ascertained of the ship to be registered, one or more persons are to be appointed by the commissioners of the customs in England and Scotland, and by the governors in the plantations, for examining and admeasuring

(*a*) Sect. 10.
(*b*) Sect. 11. See in the APPENDIX the form of the oath.

ships, as to the particulars contained in the certificate; and he is to deliver an account thereof to the person who is to make the registry and grant the certificate; some person attending on the part of the owners is also to sign his name to the certificate of such surveying officer, if he agrees to the contents of the account (*a*). If such officer give false descriptions of any of the particulars so required in the certificate, or any person makes a false register, or grants a false certificate, he is to forfeit 100l (*b*). Because ships cannot always be brought on shore to be measured, a rule is laid down in the act, to be observed in measuring them afloat (*c*).

A BOND is to be entered into by the master, and such of the owners as personally attend, at the time of obtaining the certificate of registry, conditioned, that the certificate shall not be sold, lent, or otherwise disposed of, and shall be solely made use of for the service of that ship; and that in case the ship shall be lost or taken, burnt or broken up, or otherwise prevented from returning to the port to which she belongs,

(*a*) Sect. 11.   (*b*) Sect. 13.   (*c*) Sect. 14.

the certificate, if preserved, shall be delivered up, within one month after the arrival of the master in the king's dominions, to the collector and comptroller of some port in Great Britain or the isle of Man, or of the British plantations, or to the governor or lieutenant-governor of Guernsey or Jersey; and that if any foreigner shall become intitled to the whole or any share or interest in the ship, the certificate shall be delivered up, within seven days after such transfer of property, to the person authorized to make registry and grant certificates, if such transfer shall be within the limits of any port in Great Britain, Guernsey, Jersey, Man, or the British colonies; and if in any foreign port, then to the consul or other chief British officer resident there; and if at sea, then to the consul or other British officer at the first port where the ship shall arrive, immediately after arrival; or if the port at which he first arrives is in Great Britain, Guernsey, Jersey, Man, or the colonies, then within fourteen days after arrival; and if there is any Mediterranean pass, it is to be delivered up, together with the certificate of registry. The certificates are to be transmitted to the commissioners of the customs, and the Mediterranean passes to the admiralty (*a*).

(*a*) Sect. 15.

SHIPPING AND NAVIGATION. 461

PART III.
PEACE 1783,
TO A.D. 1792.
BRITISH
SHIPS.
Indorsement on the Certificate.

THE next alteration regards the indorsement directed to be made on the certificate of registry by stat. 7. & 8. *Will.* 3. Besides that indorsement, there is also to be indorsed, before two witnesses, the town, place, or parish, where the person resides to whom the transfer is made; or, if he lives in some British factory, the name thereof; if in some foreign town, and he is not member of some British factory, the name of the town, and also the name of the house or copartnership in Great Britain or Ireland whose agent or partner he is; and the person to whom the transfer is made, is to deliver a copy of such indorsement to the person authorized to make registry and grant certificates, who is to cause an entry thereof to be indorsed on the oath upon which the original certificate of registry was obtained, to make a memorandum of it in the Book of Registers, and give notice thereof to the commissioners of customs in England or Scotland under whom they act (*a*).

Bill of Sale.

As often as the property of a ship is transferred from one British subject to another, in whole or in part, the certificate of the

(*a*) Sect. 16.

registry

registry is to be truly and accurately recited in words at length in the bill or other instrument of sale, otherwise the bill of sale is to be void (*a*). As often as the master is changed, the certificate of registry is to be delivered by the master or owner at the port where the change is made to the person authorised there to grant certificates, who is to indorse and subscribe a memorandum of such change, and give notice thereof to the officer at the port where the ship was last registered, who is to make a memorandum of it in the Book of Registers, and give notice of the transaction to the commissioners of the customs (*b*).

*Change of Name.*

It has been before noticed, that the changing of the names of ships had been a mode long practised for defeating the effect of the register-laws. To prevent this in future, owners are not to change the name by which a ship was first registered; and they are, within a month after the first registering, to paint in some conspicuous part of the stern, in letters of four inches length,

(*a*) Sect. 17.  (*b*) Sect. 18.

the name of the ship; and any owner or master obliterating or concealing the name so painted (unless in square-rigged vessels in time of war), or in any written or printed paper describing a ship by any other name than that by which she was registered, or verbally describing her by any other name to an officer of the customs, is to forfeit 100l. *(a)*.

PERSONS applying for registry for any ship built after 1 Aug. 1786, are to produce a true account, under the hands of the builder, of the time and place of building, the tonnage, and the name of the first purchaser, and make oath that the ship in question is the same *(b)*.

IF a certificate of registry obtained under this act is lost or mislaid, a registry or certificate *de novo* may be granted according to the regulations of stat. 15. Geo. 2. c. 31. provided the security above required be given, and the oath prescribed by this act be taken instead of that prescribed by stat. 15. Geo. 2. c. 31. *(c)*.

(*a*) Sect. 19.   (*b*) Sect. 20, 21.   (*c*) Sect 22, 23.

If a ship shall, after registering, be altered in form or burthen, or be converted from a sloop into a brigantine, or from any one denomination of vessel to another by the mode of rigging or fitting, she must be registered *de novo*, as soon as she returns to the port to which she belongs, or to any other port where she may be legally registered, otherwise she will be deemed a foreign ship (*a*).

*Prize-Ships.*

The owners of prize-ships, before registering, are to produce a certificate of the condemnation under the hand and seal of the judge, and also an account of the particulars contained in the before-mentioned certificate, to be made and subscribed by skilful persons appointed by the court to survey the ship; and they are to make oath that the ship in question is the same mentioned in the judge's certificate (*b*). Prizes condemned in Guernsey, Jersey, or the Isle of Man, are to be registered at Southampton, Weymouth, Exeter, Plymouth, Falmouth, Liverpool, or Whitehaven (*t*). This was to secure the duties payable on such ships; and, for the same purpose,

(*a*) Sect. 24.   (*b*) Sect. 25.   (*c*) Sect. 26.

when such prizes are regiſtered in the plantations, an exact and particular account is to be joined to the certificate of regiſtry of the ſum the ſhip ſold for, verified by the oath of the perſon applying for the regiſter (a).

In order to make the affair of regiſtering more clear, a diſtinction was to be made between Britiſh-built ſhips, which are alone qualified for the plantation-trade, and ſuch foreign ſhips, as are owned by Britiſh ſubjects, and can only be employed in the European trade, in which they are allowed to continue till they are worn-out, it was ordained, that the certificates ſhould diſtinguiſh the ſhips in theſe two ways, either by being intituled, *Certificate of Britiſh Plantation Regiſtry*; or, *Certificate of Foreign Ship's Regiſtry for the European Trade, British Property* (b).

To carry this part of the act into complete execution, and to put an end to the fraudulent practice of foreign ſhips trading to the plantations under certificates, that had been illegally granted, it was reſolved to

(a) Sect. 27.    (b) Sect. 28.

call in all former registers; and the commissioners of the customs were to give public notice that certificates of registry would be granted, at a certain reasonable time, to all ships legally entitled to them; and all owners of ships, not before required to be registered, were, at the expiration of that notice, to cause their ships to be registered, and obtain a certificate according to this act. With respect to those before registered, they were to cause them to be again registered, and obtain a certificate according to this act, and deliver up the register before granted; or if it had been lost or mislaid, make oath thereof, and give security in the same manner as is required by stat. 15. *Geo.* 2. in the case of registers and certificates *de novo* (a). Certain periods after the expiration of that notice were allowed for ships to come in, according as they belonged to the British dominions in Europe, or those in the more distant parts of the world.

At the end of those periods no register or certificate was to be in force but such as was granted by virtue of this act (b); unless

(a) Sect. 29.   (b) Sect. 30.

where

where some unavoidable necessity or reasonable cause should have prevented any ship from returning to the port to which she belongs; and then the commissioners of the customs, on proof thereof made to their satisfaction, might cause the ship to be registered (*a*).

No such ship after her first arrival at the port to which she belonged, at the expiration of the above notice, was to be permitted to clear out as a British ship, or was to be entitled in any wise to the privileges of a British ship, unless the owner had obtained a certificate according to the directions of this act; and any ship departing from port, without being so registered, and having obtained a certificate, is to be forfeited (*b*). If, after the expiration of the above notice, any ship, being square-rigged, should be found in any port within the distance of twenty leagues by water from that to which she belongs, or not being square-rigged, be found in any port but that to which she belongs, without having obtained a certificate of registry, the principal officer of the port is to detain such ship until the master give

(*a*) Sect. 31.   (*b*) Sect. 32.

bond in a penal sum (which is proportioned to the different tonnage of ships), with condition that he will forthwith (or, being employed in the Newfoundland-fishery, at the end of the fishing-season) repair with her to the port to which she belongs, and there cause her to be registered, and obtain a certificate, and produce the same to the officer at a certain time to be limited in the bond, according to the distance of the port and the nature of her voyage.

In the case of square-rigged ships so circumstanced, or if the water of the port to which a square-rigged ship belongs is so shallow as not to admit her without danger, in either of those two cases, the master is, within forty-eight hours, to make known his arrival to the collector and comptroller, and require him to cause his ship to be surveyed; and such survey shall be certified, as before directed, and the certificate shall be transmitted by the officer to the officer at the port to which the ship belongs; who, upon that and other requisites being complied with, is to register the ship and grant a certificate; and the officer of the first port may detain such ship till the survey is made (*a*).

(*a*) Sect. 33.

THE masters of ships are, on demand, to produce their certificates to the principal officer in any port in his majesty's dominions, or to the British consul or chief officer in any foreign port, in order to satisfy them that she has been properly registered; under the penalty of 100l. (*a*).

THE officers are to number progressively the certificates as they are granted, beginning afresh at the commencement of every year. They are to enter an exact copy of each certificate in a book, and within one month transmit to the commissioners of the customs a true and exact copy, together with the number thereof, under the penalty of 100l. for the first offence, and for the second offence 200l. and under pain of dismissal from office (*b*).

THE commissioners of the customs in Scotland are to transmit copies of certificates granted by them or their officers to the commissioners of the customs in England (*c*). The fees of registry are specially limited by the act (*d*).

LASTLY, it was declared, that all former acts made for the registry of ships should be

(*a*) Sect. 34.  (*b*) Sect. 35.  (*c*) Sect. 36.
(*d*) Sect. 37.

taken

taken to extend to ships required by this act to be registered (a).

Such is the detail of regulations contained in this act. To these are subjoined two provisions of a special nature; the one regarding ships whose owners were supposed to have a claim of merit, and were to be indulged with a register, although by the terms of this law they were not entitled to it; the other respects ships belonging to the kingdom of Ireland.

At the time of evacuating the countries held by his majesty's forces in America, many families who had property in ships, removed into the British colonies. To such persons, and also to others who had the same sort of property, and had rendered services to the cause of Great Britain, the king's governors and officers of the customs had granted or promised registers. Again, registers had been granted or promised to other ships by governors, under a misconception of the law, and the property of those ships had been, *bond fide*, transferred to others of the king's subjects, who under

(a) Sect. 43.

protection

protection thereof continued to employ them. It was now thought proper, in consideration of the merit belonging to the first description of owners, and wherever in the latter case no fraud or collusion appeared, that these ships should be admitted to a registry. Accordingly power was given to his majesty in council to order any ship of the above descriptions to be registered, and have a certificate, and to direct all proceedings to be stayed in suits commenced for condemnation of such ships, upon such terms and conditions as he in his wisdom should think fit (*a*). Governors in the plantations were in like manner empowered to cause all proceedings in suits of the same kind to be stayed, if they saw just cause for so doing, until his majesty's pleasure was known; they were to transmit hither copies of the proceedings, together with their reasons for causing them to be stayed (*b*).

The provision respecting Ireland was, for continuing to ships belonging to persons residing in Ireland, the privileges they were entitled to before the passing of this act, until the end of four months after the com-

(*a*) Sect. 38.   (*b*) Sect. 39.

mencement

mencement of the next session of the Irish parliament; in which session it was expected an act would be passed similar to this, for registering the ships of that kingdom; and therefore the act further goes on to provide, that from the end of those four months every ship registered in any port of Ireland, under regulations similar to those in the present act, should continue to enjoy the privileges of a British-built ship, or foreign-built ship owned by the king's subjects, as the case might be, according to the provisions of this act *(a)*.

In the following session of the Irish parliament an act was passed containing similar regulations about shipping and navigation; and the English parliament in stat. 27. *Geo.* 3. c. 19. confirmed expresly to Irish ships registered under that act, the privileges of British-built or foreign-built ships, as the case might be; those registered under the former laws were to enjoy the same privileges, as the case might be, till the expiration of the time appointed by the commissioners of the revenue in Ireland for registering under the new act *(b)*. But if any

*(a)* Sect. 44.     *(b)* Sect. 1, 2.

Irish

Irish ship should have been prevented by unavoidable necessity or reasonable cause from returning to port in Ireland, and the same was proved to the satisfaction of the commissioners of the customs in England and Scotland, they might permit such ship to enjoy the privilege for that time only, and to clear out to her port in Ireland, and to no other port, for the purpose of being registered (a).

THE plan of regulations made by stat. 26. Geo. 3. were not so well considered, but that the experience of a few months pointed out something to amend in a piece of machinery so extensive and complicated as this. Some of these defects were corrected in stat. 27. Geo. 3. just quoted.

THUS, in the oath to be taken by owners for the purpose of obtaining the registry, the person taking the oath is to swear, amongst other things, that he has not, nor has any of the other owners to the best of his knowledge and belief, taken an oath of allegiance to any foreign state whatever, except under the terms of some capitulation. This,

(a) Sect. 3.

though

though aimed chiefly at Americans, was found so largely worded as to comprehend persons residing abroad in factories and in foreign towns, who were objects rather of praise than of blame; it was therefore provided, that an oath taken for the sole purpose of acquiring the rights of a citizen or burgher in any foreign city or town in *Europe*, to be enjoyed only during residence there, and for a limited time after such residence, should not be deemed an oath of allegiance within the meaning of this act (*a*).

AGAIN, the oath, as far as it regarded the property in the ship, could not strictly be taken by any one where the ship belonged to the East India Company, or any other body corporate; a new oath therefore was devised to be taken by the secretary or any other officer authorised by the Company (*b*).

DOUBTS had arisen whether the bond to be given on registering could be entered into at any other port than that where the ship was required to be registered: it was now

(*a*) Sect. 4.    (*b*) Sect. 5.

ordained,

ordained, that the commissioners of the customs and the governors abroad might, where it seemed to them expedient, permit such bond to be taken before any person whatever, and in such manner, and at such port, as they should judge fit (*a*). It was also ordained, that every new master of the ship shall give a fresh bond; and an indorsement being made *toties quoties* of such new bonds on the original bond, shall from thenceforward be a discharge of it, as far as regards the former master (*b*).

It was thought that in the island of *Newfoundland*, and in the provinces of *Quebec*, *Nova Scotia*, and *New Brunswick*, there was not a sufficient number of officers to carry the act into execution, and that difficulties would, on that account, be occasioned to small vessels carrying on the fishery and trading coastwise in those parts; it was therefore ordained, that no vessel not exceeding thirty tons, and not having a whole or fixed deck, and being employed in the fishery on the banks of the shore of Newfoundland and the parts adjacent, or on the banks or shores of the provinces of *Quebec*, *Nova Scotia*,

(*a*) Sect. 6.　　(*b*) Sect. 7.

or *New Brunswick*, adjacent to the gulph of *St. Lawrence*, and to the north of Cape *Canfo*, or of the iflands within the fame, or trading coaftwife within thofe limits, fhall be fubject to be regiftered under ftat. 26. Geo. 3 *(a)*.

AGAIN, many fhips were built in thofe places on account of owners refiding in the king's European dominions, which could not for that reafon be regiftered in thofe places; it was now provided, that fuch fhips might be regiftered there on the hufband or principal agent of them taking the oath; and the certificate fo granted is to be of force till they arrive at fome port in the king's European dominions, where they may be regiftered on the oath of the owners, and no longer; upon their arrival fuch certificate is to be given up to be cancelled *(b)*.

LASTLY, in explanation of the fenfe of that act in general, it was declared, that all fhips pronounced by that act not to be entitled to the privileges of a Britifh built fhip, or of a fhip owned by Britifh fubjects, and all fhips not regiftered according to

(*a*) Sect. 8.    (*b*) Sect. 9.

that

that act, shall, although they may be owned by his majesty's subjects, be deemed, to all intents and purposes, as alien ships *(a)*.

WHILE the subject of British shipping was under consideration, it was observed, that the quantity of foreign ships employed in the importation of goods from Denmark, Norway, Sweden, and the East Country, was much greater in proportion to the British, than the foreign tonnage employed in other trades; and that it was increasing in general, and the British shipping employed in some of these trades was at the same time decreasing. The lords of the committee for trade were desirous, that some measures should be taken to prevent this increase of foreign shipping, and to promote that of British; and they proposed for the consideration of the board of customs, whether it might not be proper to augment the duty called the aliens' duty, or petty custom, on such of the goods enumerated and described in the eighth and ninth sections of the Act of Navigation as were now subject to it, and were imported from the beforementioned countries; and whether such increase would

(*a*) Sect. 13.

materially

materially operate to increase the burthens on, and consequently the prices of, those articles, if such duty were increased gradually; that is, by making it double from 1 January 1787, and treble from 1 January 1788: and if they thought this inconvenience would happen, then they were called upon to consider, whether some advantage might not be given to British-built ships employed in those trades, by lowering the duties on those articles when imported in such ships; or whether both these methods might not be pursued in such proportions as might best attain the end proposed, and not materially affect the revenue.

This enquiry brought before the board of customs the measures which had been pursued in former times, for encouraging British shipping; and from the effect of those measures they collected what appeared the most probable remedy on the present occasion. They observed, that the high duty imposed by the Act of Navigation, and other acts, on wines imported in foreign ships, had given a decided preference to British ships; insomuch that little or no wine was ever imported in a foreign ship, not even from Portugal, in Portuguese shipping.

shipping, except in time of war: that the alien duty upon the other articles was at the period when impofed confiderable, being no lefs than 25l. *per cent.* on the duty then payable on thofe articles; and no part of this was drawn back on exportation, except in the cafe of *currants.* But, on the other hand, it was obferved, this high duty did not operate as an inducement with *foreign* merchants to employ Englifh fhips, becaufe foreign merchants were at that time *perfonally* liable to the payment of aliens' duty on their merchandize, without regard to any diftinction of fhipping; from which duty, indeed, they had been relieved by ftat. 24. *Geo.* 3. c. 10. and in that refpect they were now put on an equal footing with the Britifh merchant.

It was lamented, that in the tract of time which had elapfed fince the Act of Navigation, when this aliens' duty was impofed, upon all the occafions of impofing additional duties, as had been done from time to time, to fupply the exigencies of the State, there had not been fhewn fo much attention, as fhould have been, to the encouragement of Britifh fhipping The articles enumerated and defcribed in the eighth and

PART III.
PEACE 1783,
TO A.D. 1792.
BRITISH
SHIPS.

and ninth sections of that act, when imported in a foreign ship, now became subject to a very inconsiderable additional duty. The preference given to British shipping, in the act of tonnage and poundage, by easement in duties, was confined to very few instances; the instances in which such preference had been given in the imposition of duties since that act were few; so that, upon the whole, it did not seem, that British shipping had received so much favour as might have been conferred on it, by properly imposing and proportioning the duties of customs.

WHEN they saw so many occasions let pass without doing any thing to encourage British shipping, they were sorry to notice an act lately passed, namely, stat. 22. *Geo.* 3. c. 78. which had a tendency, very materially, to injure the British navigation. By this act the articles enumerated and described in the eighth and ninth sections might be brought from any foreign port in Europe, in any ship the property of subjects under the same sovereign as the country of which the goods were the produce. This law, which was supposed to have been made in order to

permit

permit his Prussian majesty's subjects to import Pomeranian merchandize in East Friesland ships, was so worded, as to extend this indulgence beyond what was originally intended. This act, they submitted, not only deserved to be reconsidered, but should be materially corrected; as, in its present form, it would be productive of the most serious consequences to the navigation of this country. As an instance of it, they said, the same indulgence had been already claimed by a Danish-*owned*, though not Danish-*built*, ship; which was clearly within the words of the act; and the same privilege might equally well be claimed in many other instances.

AFTER these representations, the board submit their opinion on the points proposed for their consideration. As to the first point, they thought, that as the aliens' duty had not been increased, from time to time, as additional subsidies and impositions were laid on the enumerated and described articles in question, the increasing them generally, and at once, might operate on the trade between this kingdom and Denmark, Norway, Sweden, and the East Country, and also on that of other countries from whence some of those articles come. But these objections would not equally lie to a gradual increase of those duties, in the manner suggested.

As to the second point, it was doubted, whether lowering the duty on the enumerated articles imported in British-built ships could be recommended by a board of revenue. But they thought, if the above reasons were not sufficient to dissuade the imposing any additional aliens' duty, such an addition might be laid on the enumerated goods imported in ships belonging to Denmark, Norway, Sweden, and the East Country, as was adequate to the difference of duties and other charges payable by British subjects in those countries beyond what is payable by their own subjects; and out of such additional aliens' duty a fund might be raised for encouraging, by bounties, the subjects of this kingdom to engage more extensively in the trade to those countries, and to build ships properly adapted to the nature of that commerce; the neglect of which had operated in a great degree to give a preference to foreign ships. Besides, it had been represented by those skilled in ship-building, that English ships might be built

built with more advantage, better adapted to those trades, and more commodious for conveyance of bulky goods, in proportion to their measure, than any other ships whatever.

Other remedies were suggested that might be applied in aid of British shipping and navigation. It was observed, that lately great quantities of *rock salt* had been exported from Liverpool and Chester, in foreign ships, to Denmark, Russia, and the East Country, Flanders, and Germany; and this being a native raw commodity, it was proposed to lay such a duty on it when exported in any other than British shipping, as would give a decided preference to them. Again, the export of refined sugars, in foreign ships to the countries in question, exceeded very considerably the export in British ships. There being a great bounty on this article, and much of it being relanded after it had served the purpose of obtaining the bounty, it was proposed, that less bounty should be allowed, where the export was in any other than a British-built ship. This would obtain a preference for British-built ships; and if there should be an attempt to smuggle, these

these could not so easily escape as foreign ships, which after relanding were gone, and out of the reach of penalties and forfeitures.

This principle here meant to be applied to sugars might fairly be applied to every article of merchandize where a bounty or drawback was payable; and a small difference made in bounties and drawbacks on these terms might contribute very much to favour British-built shipping, and promote the navigation of the country.

It was likewise thought, that some small difference might be made in favour of British-built ships, in the case of goods now admitted free of duty in *any* ships. This was seen in the instance of *raw linen yarn*, which on importation was subject to one penny *per* pound, if brought in a foreign ship, and was free if brought in a British ship; and this distinction has given a decided preference to the latter. It was said to be chiefly owing to this circumstance, as to raw linen yarn, and to the duty imposed on logwood when exported in foreign ships, that we have any shipping employed in the Hamburgh Trade.

We

We have before noticed the prejudicial effects of stat. 22. *Geo.* 3. and the remedy applied thereto by stat. 27. *Geo.* 3. which latter statute probably owed its origin to the suggestion made upon this occasion. It is probable also, that some alterations afterwards made in duties upon articles imported from the Baltic sea, and the East Country, were made in consequence of what was here thrown out.

The interest of British shipping had, in various instances, been assisted by this policy of giving an easement in duties to goods imported in British ships; as will appear from the following view of the provisions made for this purpose, at different times, by parliament.

In the Act of Tonnage and Poundage an easement was given in point of duty, where drugs, spicery, estridge wool, and wrought silks from the East Indies and Italy, were imported in English-built shipping, and where whale-fins were imported in English shipping. The duty outwards was also lessened on coals and beer, if exported in English-built shipping. In the Navigation Act passed the same sessions, a distinction

distinction was made, as we have before seen, in favour of English shipping, by imposing an alien's duty on French and German wines imported in any other than shipping *belonging* to England or Ireland, and also upon all the articles enumerated and described in the eighth section (except currants and Turkey commodities), and on currants and Turkey commodities imported in any other than English-*built* shipping (a).

This distinction in duty made in respect of the ship was followed up by the Legislature in other instances; as on the importation of iron, and beaver wool, by stat. 2. *Will. & Mary*, c. 4. raw linen yarn, cotton wool, and goat skins raw and undressed, by stat. 24. *Geo.* 2. c. 46. stat. 6. *Geo.* 3. c. 52. and stat. 5. *Geo.* 3. c. 35. and for a certain period, and under certain circumstances, flax, tallow, *succus liquoritiæ*, corn, pot-ashes, German pearl-ashes, and brandy (b). Again, on the exportation of corn, the bounty was confined to such as was exported in British

(a) Sect. 9.
(b) Vid. stat. 4. Geo. 2. c. 27. stat. 7. Geo. 3. c. 12. stat. 7. Geo. 3. c. 47. stat. 13. Geo. 3. c. 43. stat. 20. Geo. 3. c. 25. stat. 22. Geo. 3. c. 28.

ships by ſtat. 1. *Will. & Mary*, c. 12. Other articles of export favoured in the duty were theſe ; *coals* by ſtat. 9. *Ann*. c. 6. and ſtat. 12. *Ann*. ſt. 2. c. 9. ; *logwood* by ſtat. 7. *Geo*. 3. c. 47. and *cotton wool*, by ſtat. 19. *Geo*. 3. c. 53.

WHEN the old duties were repealed, and new ones formed in their ſtead by the Conſolidation Act, ſtat. 27. *Geo*. 3. c. 13. attention was paid to all theſe caſes, and ſome new inſtances were added. It appears, on examining the tables of import and export in ſtat. 27. *Geo*. 3. c. 13. that a difference was made where the importation was in Britiſh-built ſhips, and where in foreign ſhips, in the following articles ; namely, briſtles, down, and feathers of Muſcovy or Ruſſia; flax, currants, figs, raiſins, iron, Ruſſia linens, ſallad-oil, and ordinary oil of olives; roſin; crapes or tiffanies of the manufactory of Italy; undreſſed goat ſkins; ſeal ſkins; emery ſtones of Turkey; tar; tow of Muſcovy or Ruſſia; wine; unmanufactured wood of various denominations (*a*); beaver wool combed in Ruſſia;

(*a*) What an important article that of wood is, will appear from the following ſpecifications in the table of imports; namely, anchor ſtocks, balk, battens, batten ends, beech plank, beech quarters, beech boards, clap boards, linn boards, or white boards of ſhoemakers; oak

Russia; estridge wool; to which may be added, oil and fins the produce of whales and other creatures; but these must also be of British catching, and under special regulations that are spoken of under the head of *The Fishery*.

In the duties laid on the articles which are the subject of the Commercial Treaty with France, three of them are distinguished in respect of the ship; namely, wine, sallad oil, and ordinary oil (*b*). Among the few articles that are liable to a duty on exportation, that of coals is one; and a difference of duty is made in the case of coals, and also of culm,

oak boards; paleing boards; paste boards, or mill boards; pipe boards; scale boards; wainscot boards; boxwood; deals; deal ends; ebony; fire woods; fir quarters; fir timber; handspikes; knees of oak; lath wood; masts; oak plank; oak timber; oars; olive wood; round wood; spars; spokes for wheels; staves; timber of all sorts; ufers; wainscot logs; bever wood; all of them bulky articles, and employing much shipping.

(*b*) The other articles included in this Treaty are subject to the same duty, if imported in ships of the built of either country, owned and navigated according to law; namely, vinegar, brandy, iron or steel work; cotton manufactures, cambrics, lawns, linens, sadlery, gauzes, millinery, porcelain, plate glass, and glass ware.

culm, when exported in a British-built ship, and when in a foreign ship.

Besides this express distinction in favour of British-built ships, there are other distinctions in duty, which also operate in favour of British-built shipping; as where articles imported from the plantations, or by the East India Company, have a preference in point of duty beyond the same articles not so imported.

Conformably with the plan that has hitherto been followed, there should now be laid before the reader such information as can be collected from the judgments of courts, the opinions of lawyers, or other sources, respecting the sense and consequences of this law for registering ships. After the disappointment the reader has already experienced in the search for judgments of courts, he will not expect much assistance of this sort upon a law which has passed so recently. But it has so happened, that I am able to furnish two judicial opinions which have already been delivered on this act, one in the court of king's bench, the other in the privy council.

The

The effect of a bill of sale not containing a recital of the certificate of registry, was fully considered in the court of king's bench, in the case of *Rolleston v. Hibbert* (a). A bill of sale of a ship then at sea was executed by way of security, and at the same time for the same purpose was deposited the grand bill of sale. The bill of sale was *absolute* on the face of it, and in the usual form, but it did not contain a recital of the certificate of the registry of the ship, as required by the seventeenth section of the act. These securities were all to be returned on payment of a note of hand, for which they were collateral securities. The person giving the bill of sale became a bankrupt; the person to whom the security was given seized the ship on her arrival, and the assignees brought trover to recover her.

It was contended, that the ship could not be detained by the defendants, either on the ground of a *purchase* or *lien*.

First, It could not be supported as a contract of sale, because the bill of sale, not being conformable to the statute, is declared null and void to all intents and purposes. They

(a) 3. Term Rep. 406.

said, since the act ships can only be transferred by bill of sale, otherwise the clause requiring a recital of the certificate in the bill of sale would be nugatory. All the checks provided in the act (*a*) might be defeated, if any other instrument should be permitted to have the same operation as a bill of sale under the statute.

SECONDLY, It could not be supported as a lien; for, being void by the statute, it is a mere nullity: and then this is a mere naked bailment, the ship not having been delivered for any specific purpose; in which case the plantiffs may recover it in an action of trover, or a court of equity would decree restitution. This could not be binding in a court of law, because that would be to create *an interest* in the ship, which is expressly guarded against and forbid in the statute. For foreigners might say, although bills of sale, under which they might claim, are void, still the lien is valid. Therefore, unless this construction was put upon the statute, foreigners may have *shares and interests* in British ships, by advancing money on them and taking the grand bill of sale, and an assignment

(*a*) Sect. 3. 10. 15. 16. 17.

of the ship, and thus totally disregarding the provisions of this act.

On the other side it was contended on two grounds, First, That this was not such a transfer of property to the defendants, as the act was intended to attach upon at all; Secondly, That if it were, yet, as between these parties, the defendant had a right to retain possession of the ship till the lien was discharged.

Upon the first point, they said, the objects intended were, to prevent any but British-built ships being navigated in the trade of Great Britain; and to prevent foreigners from navigating even British-built ships with the privileges of British subjects; so that the *right of navigation* was the great object of the act; and unless the right acquired by the defendant was such in its nature as would enable him to *navigate* the ship, the act was never intended to attach upon it. Now the whole of the right intended to be conferred or acquired was, that of a mortgage on the ship to a certain amount; for though the bill of sale was absolute upon the face of it, yet the defendant gave an accountable receipt, whereby he promised to restore that, and the

the other muniments, on payment of the note. The contract therefore was merely executory; the only right acquired was that of *possession*, which was to remain as a security; he had no right to the intermediate profits of the voyage, nor could, independently of the omission in the bill of sale, have been enabled to navigate the vessel; for he not only could not have taken the oath prescribed by the tenth section, namely, that he was the *sole* owner, and that no other person had any " right, interest, share, or property therein," but while the ship was at sea it was absolutely impossible to get at the certificate (which by the thirty-fourth section must always be kept on board), either for the purpose of inserting it in the bill of sale, or of having it indorsed according to the sixteenth section. And this argument bears much stronger, when it appears that this difficulty is provided for in the case of a sale to a foreigner; for unless the Court can go so far as to say, that the Legislature did not intend a ship at sea should, in future, be capable of being transferred to a British subject, this will at least appear to be a *casus omissus* in the act, because of the impossibility of complying with some of the requisites.

FURTHER

FURTHER it appears, by reference to stat. 7. & 8. *Will.* 3. which is referred to as the basis of the sixteenth section, that a mortgage was not the sort of transfer intended by the latter; for the statute of William requires the indorsement on the certificate in the case of *a sale of one or more shares*; and the latter act only requires the addition of another circumstance to that indorsement: it confines therefore the indorsement to the case of an *absolute sale* of specific shares, which a mortgage can never be said to be. The act cannot extend to *all* transfers; if it did, it would include those by operation of law.

IF then this were not such a sale as comes within the sixteenth section, requiring the indorsement of it on the certificate, it follows, that the certificate need not be set out in the bill of sale under the seventeenth section. But supposing it were requisite, the utmost penalty on such omission was, that the bill of sale was void, but it by no means avoided the *contract*: nor was it necessary it should; for as the right of navigation was the only object in view, and that was specifically provided for by other clauses, the only reason for avoiding such an imperfect bill of sale was, to prevent that being made use

use of, towards acquiring a *right of navigation*, unless the main object of the act appeared on the face of it to have been complied with. In this case, even if the defendant had had a more formal bill of sale, the ship could not have cleared out, unless the defendant had been guilty of perjury in swearing to the *absolute* property, when he had only a *conditional* one. As the only claim, therefore, which the defendant had on the ship was a mortgage, or lien, and as he never could, independently of the clause in question, under such a title have navigated the ship, it was not necessary for him to have had any written instrument whatever, but the lien might have attached by the mere delivery of the thing. Having now taken this bill of sale among other collateral securities, it never can be said, that if one among several securities is void, the rest are thereby avoided.

THEN, SECONDLY, whatever might have been the question as between the defendant and third parties, at any rate the plaintiffs cannot make this sort of objection, standing exactly in the situation of the bankrupt himself, subject to all his equities, and bound to make good all his *bona fide* engagements. The utmost they can alledge is, that the defendant has

has not the legal title; but admitting that to be the case, the assignees are bound in equity, and so cannot recover in trover.

Such were the arguments on the two sides of this question. The Court gave judgment for the plaintiffs, and stated the following as their reasons.

Lord Kenyon observed, that this clause was couched in the most positive terms which the language affords, and renders such a bill of sale an absolute nullity. The statute, he said, was framed by an able statesman, who is peculiarly conversant in the commercial interests of this country; and from the experience which has already been had of it, it is acknowledged to be founded in wisdom, and to have produced all those beneficial consequences to the commerce and shipping of the country that were expected from it; and therefore, if Judges could have any leaning in their minds on such occasions, they should not have an inclination to put such a construction on the words of this act as would tend to evade the wholesome provisions of it.

He said, it was not necessary that the property in a ship should pass by a written instrument,

instrument; but certainly, if the parties chuse to convey by a written instrument, that shews what their intention and the rights of the parties were, and they shall not be permitted afterwards to refer to any other agreement. For if a person execute a bill of sale of goods without stamp, such an instrument cannot be received in evidence; yet the vendee cannot resort to any parole evidence of the agreement: so here, the title of the defendant being reduced to writing, he cannot refer to any other agreement, although the written instrument is void by the act. The words of the seventeenth section are *general*, and make no exception of cases where ships are at sea; and with respect to the impossibility of complying with the requisitions of the act while the ship was at sea, the parties might have extracted from the registry at the custom-house all that was necessary for this purpose. It was wholly unfounded to insist, that if the bill of sale did not take effect, there was a lien for the amount; for the bill of sale professes to transfer the absolute property; and though the property would be devested by the payment of the money, yet the intermediate property in the vendees under the bill of sale would not be devested. He likened this to the case of conditional surrenders by tenants for life before stat. 14. *Geo.* 2. c. 20. in which cases the whole property actually passed in the mean time, although it was devested on performance of the condition.

As to the assertion, that a court of equity would not compel the defendant to deliver up the ship till his demand was satisfied, he said he did not know that a court of equity would put a different construction on the act; but, at any rate, in a court of law they were to put on it a legal construction. Where the parties have relied on an invalid security, he did not know that a court of equity would decree a performance of the contract. As the instrument is not valid in point of law, the contract cannot be supported here on grounds on which they did not think a court of equity would act. The other Judges agreed in the same opinion in favour of the plaintiff.

Mr. Justice Buller considered the other clauses of the act as decisively against the first ground taken by the counsel for the defendant; namely, that the statute did not apply to the case of a ship sold at sea, because the case of a sale of a ship, either at sea or in a foreign port, *to a foreigner*, is expressly provided for by the fifteenth section: then if we see that in one part of this statute the Legislature had in view the sale of a ship at sea, or in a foreign port, and made special provisions for such a purchase by a foreigner, it cannot be argued that the selling of a ship at sea in other cases was not in the contemplation of the Legislature; but it shews that they only intended to make one exception, leaving all other cases within the general words of the seventeenth section: besides, before such an argument is adopted, it ought to appear, beyond all controversy, that the parties could not comply with the requisites of the statute, and that this was a *casus omissus*; which is by no means to be collected from the statute.

As to the second ground, he said, the bill of sale purports to be an absolute transfer of the property; and the defendant having possession of the grand bill of sale, and also of this bill of sale, nothing could have prevented him navigating the ship but the provisions of the act. As to the difficulty of the defendant's taking the oath, all that the act requires was, that he should state fairly and truly what his interest was. In the present case, the defendant had such a property as would have justified him taking the oath; for the bill of sale being *absolute* on the face of it, if the certificate of registry had been inserted, it could not have been disputed; and if there was any right of redemption in the bankrupt, that also might have been stated. As to what was said upon transfers *by operation of law*, these he held to be always excepted; but this is a *transfer by the party*; in which case the requisites of the act must be complied with. As to the arguments upon the equity of the case, they did not apply; and it must be remembered, that he who asks equity must first do equity; and if a bill was filed in this case, and was dismissed, it would be because the plaintiff's demand was *unconscientious:* but that would not decide *the property* of the ship; the argument, to be of force, should go further, and shew that a court of equity would have decreed a legal conveyance of the ship. But he knew of no case where that court had gone so far; if he did, it would have great weight with him; for in mercantile transactions especially, he thought where a defendant had a clear, indisputable, equitable title, they ought

ought not, sitting even in a court of law, to permit the possession to be taken from him.

ANOTHER judicial opinion on this act is contained in a judgment of the privy council delivered by the present lord president on an appeal from the vice-admiralty court at *Nassau* in the *Bahamas*. It was in *Macneal's* case, where a ship had been navigated without being registered, and no sufficient excuse could be shewn for such omission.

THE ship in question had originally been registered, and was said to be bought by *Macneal* at *Savannah* in *South Carolina*. Having taken in a cargo there, he sailed for *Nassau*, where he applied to the governor for a register. The officer whose duty it was to make out the certificate of registry, alledged that he had no printed forms left, but that he was ready to make an indorsement upon the old certificate, on *Macneal's* taking the oath prescribed by stat. 26. *Geo*. 3. *Macneal* afterwards sailed to *Savannah*, and returned again to *Nassau* with a cargo, where the ship was seized; but on a hearing in the court of admiralty, she was released as not forfeited.

PART III.
PEACE 1783,
TO A.D. 1792.
BRITISH
SHIPS.

ON the part of *Macneal* it was now contended, that the sale of a British ship in a foreign port was not an act forbid by any law; that he did all in his power to obtain a fair and legal registry; that it was a blunder in the collector not to give him a certificate, alledging he had no printed forms; that on his return to *Nassau* he meant to renew his endeavours to obtain a registry, his intention being to trade between *Nassau* and *Savannah*; and that in the case of a change of property in a foreign port, he was left at large as to the *proper* port for the registry of the ship; and having declared his intention to trade thereafter from *Nassau*, that, and that only, became the *proper* port where the ship should be registered.

UPON which it was observed by the lord president, how material it was to ascertain, in cases where a ship was sold, whether in a foreign or British port, what shall be the port to which such ship shall be said *to belong*, and within what space of time she shall repair to such port? For if it should once be laid down that such a ship might register in any other port than that where she was first registered, he was satisfied the act of the 26th of the king, which, he said,

is

is founded upon the best principles, and is wisely and sagaciously contrived by the noble person who was the author of it to prevent the many frauds committed under the act of king *William*, would be wholly disappointed of its effect.

He then considered the defects in stat. 7. & 8. *Will*. 3. the frauds that were committed under it, and to what those frauds were owing. It directs, that in all cases of change, whether of the name or the property of the ship, if in another port, it should be registered *de novo*; but in neither case does the act give any direction to point out the particular port where such ship should be registered. The consequence of this want of provision in the act had been the multitude of frauds that were continually practised in the registry of ships; for in any port whatsoever, if a person presented himself and took the oath required by that act, he was intitled to have the ship registered. For it was remarkable, that that act required no other security than the transient oath, as he called it, of any man whatsoever who chose to offer himself, and who the next minute might slip away and never be heard of afterwards. He said, he did not wonder

wonder that the noble person who framed the statute of the 26th of the king considered these frauds, and the preventing of them, as particularly deserving his attention; and he was very happy to say, that if they were right in the judgment they were then going to give, he believed they should so fully second the design of this act, that he would defy any man finding a loop-hole to evade it.

He thought that stat. 26. *Geo.* 3. was an act which in every view of it should be considered as a remedial act; it was for preventing a public mischief, to amend and alter stat. 7. & 8. *Will.* 3. It had appeared that frauds without number were committed under that act; and that was, and was stated to be, the reason of making this act.

The rule, therefore, of construction in applying and explaining the act, should be such as will most aid in advancing the means of relief and in suppression of fraud. And should it be considered in any light as a penal act, he was clearly of opinion, that every thing arising from such a consideration

tion should be controlled by the other character of it as a remedial act.

He observed, that by sect. 5. of the act, the port where the registry ought to be made, was expressly defined *the port from and to which she has usually traded*; and if a new ship, *the port to and from which she intends to trade*. It is essentially necessary, and expressly required, that the husband's or acting owner's residence should be near such port. This circumstance of residence seems to be made the most indispensable requisite in the section. Besides this there are added securities, controls, surveys of the ship; all which if complied with, especially that of residence near the port, it should seem that fraud would be almost impossible.

He forbore making more observations on the act, except only as to one point; that is, *how long time should be allowed after the change of property in the ship for arriving at the proper port where the ship ought to be registered:* for if the time allowed were indefinite, so that a ship might be trading from port to port without registering, the design and object of the act would be at an end.

It

PART III.
PEACE 1783,
TO A.D. 1798.
BRITISH
SHIPS.

It is remarkable, that stat. 7. & 8. *Will.* 3. specifies no time for new registering; no more does stat. 26. *Geo.* 3.; but the latter act does in one clause (*a*) decide what is to be done in a particular case; and he thought the direction there given might, by analogy, be applied to all cases of a new registry—" or to any other port in which she " can be legally registered by this act."— Now there is no case under this act but that of a change of property in a foreign port. Every court before which a case of this sort comes, is to consider *the time*. Common sense and common reason must say, a ship shall be at liberty to navigate without a register, and shall be protected by law, if in the mean time she is using due diligence to reach a port where a register may be obtained. As for instance, suppose a ship is sold at sea, and she is then making a voyage under a charter-party, and the port at which she first arrives after such sale is not a proper port for her registering, he held she would be justified in going to such port; but that no further delay would be excused, as she ought in convenient time

(*a*) Sect. 14.

to proceed to the port where she can be registered.

Upon the whole the rule is this: Where the property of a ship is transferred in a foreign port, she must with all due diligence proceed to the proper port where she may be registered: this port must be that of which she is, as it were, an inhabitant. This circumstance is a part of the certificate, is a part of the oath, and is essentially necessary to the registry.

Compare *Macneal's* situation with these requisites. He was said to be the purchaser of this ship at *Savannah*; nothing more appears of him: it might fairly be asked, Who is he? Whence comes he? What property has he? what relations? what friends? By his own account he paid only a part of the purchase-money, for the remainder he was to draw on merchants in *Jamaica*: whether those bills were paid or not, does not appear. These merchants, by his account, were to become part owners of the ship; which alone makes his oath incorrect, and brings great suspicion on the whole transaction. He comes to *Savannah* with a cargo belonging to some American merchants,

merchants, but which in the bill of lading, is made to belong to *Macneal*; all which was probably a mere colour to give him the credit of the property, in order to enable him to obtain a regiſtry.

He confidered it as a fundamental objection to this ſhip, that *Macneal* had no known refidence. He looked upon him as a ſea-vagabond; and obferved, that he felt he was under the neceſſity of ſwearing with care; for in his oath he did not go farther than to fay, "he had not been a refident in any country not under the dominion of his majeſty."

On this ſingle objection, without taking into confideration any other, the court might decide againſt this ſhip. But he had thought it proper to give more at large the fenfe of the court upon the policy of the act, becauſe it is extremely material that its principle ſhould be thoroughly underſtood; and as to the point in queſtion, if the act was not fcrupulouſly adhered to, he was perfuaded the whole of its regulations would be futile and uſeleſs. It became the more neceſſary to be thus explicit, as the Judge below had ſeemed greatly to have

misunder-

misunderstood the act; declaring, that *Macneal* had offended only against the letter of the act, and not against its spirit. Indeed, said his lordship, it is in general beyond sea, in our plantations, that the laws of navigation are broke through and evaded; added to which, the application of them is left for a time with governors, collectors of the customs, and other persons not sufficiently conversant with legal matters, who contribute to aggravate such mischiefs by misconstruction and false interpretations of the law *(a)*.

THIS is all the information of a judicial nature that is to be found on this act. To this I can only add some queries and doubts that have arisen upon parts of the act, and which may become subjects of future discussion.

FIRST, as to the description of British-built ships; the act excludes from that privilege all ships *built or rebuilt on a foreign-made keel or bottom in the manner heretofore practised and allowed.* This gave rise to the following case: An American-built ship was sold at Whitehaven: she was then taken to pieces; and this operation of separating all the parts of

*(a)* 25 March 1790.

her

her was carried so far, that the keel, which was composed of two pieces of timber riveted in the middle, was unriveted, and separated. After this, the materials were shewn to the custom-house officers. The workmen then scarfed and new-modelled the two pieces of timber composing the former keel, and laid them down in a very different manner from that in which they had been for the keel of the former vessel, and proceeded to build another vessel with the other timbers. Could this be said to be a rebuilding on a foreign-made keel, or was the keel made of the timber so separated an entire new keel?

AGAIN, a British-built ship is no longer to enjoy her privilege, if she is repaired in a foreign port to an amount exceeding fifteen shillings for every ton of her burthen, unless such repairs are necessary. A ship had undergone repairs to that amount, and they were reported by the custom-house officer, not to be necessary. This ship therefore, by the terms of the act, ceased to be deemed a British-built ship.

WITH regard to both of these ships, it may be asked, If they are not British-built ships, in what class or denomination of ships can they be reckoned? They cannot come under the

the consideration of foreign-built ships British property, because they were not foreign-built, but actually built here, and because they come under none of the circumstances of the act which are to belong to ships of that sort.

BEING excluded from both classes of registry, is such a ship, owned and used in trade by a British subject, to pass as an alien ship under the last clause of stat. 27. *Geo.* 3. c. 19. or is she to be forfeited under sect. 32. of stat. 26. *Geo.* 3. c. 60. or can she be registered generally, without reference to the two classes of registry specified in the act? In short, can a British subject legally own and use in trade a ship which does not come within one or other of those two classes of registry, and is neither British-built, nor foreign-built British-owned, according to the circumstances and requisites specified in the 26. *Geo.* 3. c. 60. and stat. 27. *Geo.* c. 3. 19.

AGAIN, an American ship built or owned in the United States during the continuance of the prohibitory acts may not be *registered*, nor have any of the privileges of a British-*built* ship. If this is construed in the full extent of these words, these ships are put into a worse situation than French or Spanish

Spanish ships, which, though built or owned in France or Spain during the war, may be registered as foreign-built British property, if they come under the special circumstances required by the act. Is the meaning of this merely to deprive those ships of the privilege that would otherwise belong to them as built in British colonies? or to proscribe and stigmatize the property of rebellious subjects, by putting it in a worse situation than that of foreigners?

THESE are little difficulties that may arise in the detail of any great regulation like the present, but vanish from the mind when the advantages resulting from the policy of this act are considered. Many of these have been already noticed; such as the prevention of frauds either to the underwriters or to the revenue, and the securing in future to this country the building and equipping of all the ships that are to carry on its foreign and domestic trade. Besides these, a very considerable utility arises from the documents that are formed in the execution of this plan of regulation. The registry of shipping, which is made up to the 30 Sept. in every year, contains facts of importance that may be made a ground for reflections both of a political and commercial nature.

nature. In this register is seen, how many ships and vessels belong to every distinct port, their tonnage and size, and the number of men employed in navigating them. It is now accurately known, whereto look for the most abundant supply of seamen, when the public service demands them; it is known, at what ports to look for ships of a particular tonnage, whether they are wanted by the government for transports, or by the merchant for freight.

THE sum and result of these particulars present us with a fact, which will give a better idea than any reasoning of the importance as well as magnitude of the trade and shipping of Great Britain. It appears by the last register, that England and Scotland possessed 1,365,000 tons of mercantile shipping; which estimated at eight guineas *per* ton, including the rigging and stores, may be valued at 11,466,000l.; and that 80,000 seamen are employed in navigating these ships. The keeping up of this stock of shipping, reckoning the wear and tear at 12l. *per cent.* causes the annual sum of 1,375,920l. to be expended among ship-builders, sail-makers, and the numerous artificers employed about ships; after which a clear profit of 687,960l. remains in the pockets of the owners of those ships

every

every year, reckoning such profit at 6l. *per cent.* of the sum employed; the whole profit upon mercantile shipping being reckoned at 18l. *per cent.*

It further appears, that this great capital has been increasing every year since these registers have been kept.

These are facts of great importance to be known, but were never brought forward and authenticated before the general register of shipping was made under this act.

# CONCLUSION.

HAVING thus traced the history of the changes in laws and opinions that took place in different periods, we will now look back; and separating such matter as is repealed, or become obsolete, we will endeavour to extract as much as constitutes the law of the present day; not indeed the whole of it, for that would be an unwarrantable repetition, but the outline and leading features, which may easily be filled up by reference to what has been before delivered. To assist in bringing the reader's mind home to the present state of the Law of Shipping and Navigation, I will condense its governing principles into certain *Rules*, and the *Exceptions* to them, following the distribution that has all along been made of the subject; and to each *Rule* and *Exception* shall be subjoined the grounds and reasons on which it is founded. To begin with the *Plantation Trade*.

RULE

## RULE I.

*Plantation Trade.*

"No goods or commodities may be imported into, or exported out of, any colony or plantation to his majesty, in Asia, Africa, or America, belonging, or in his possession, but in British-built ships, owned by British subjects, and navigated by a master and three-fourths at least of the mariners British subjects."

This Rule is founded on stat. 7. & 8. *Will.* 3. c. 22. (a).

Except *such goods and commodities as may be imported into, and exported from, the Free Ports in the Islands of Jamaica, Grenada, Dominica, and New Providence, by foreign ships, owned and navigated by the subjects of some foreign European sovereign or state, or by persons inhabiting any country under the dominion of some foreign European sovereign or state on the continent of America; and except salt which may be exported from Turk's Islands in ships belonging to any of the United States.*

(a) Vid. ant. 82.

CONCLUSION.

These Exceptions are made by stat. 27. *Geo.* 3. c. 27. stat. 30. *Geo.* 3. c. 29. and stat. 31. *Geo.* 3. c. 39. for establishing Free Ports (a); and stat. 28. *Geo.* 3. c. 6. s. 9. respecting Turk's Islands (b).

### RULE II.

"No sugar, tobacco, cotton-wool, indigo,
"ginger, fustic, or other dyeing woods,
"rice, molasses, copper-ore, coffee, pi-
"mento, cocoa-nuts, whale-fins, raw-silk,
"hides or skins, pot or pearl ashes, iron
"or lumber, of the growth, production, or
"manufacture, of any British plantation in
"Asia, Africa, or America, may be trans-
"ported to any place whatsoever, other
"than to some British plantation, or to Great
"Britain, or to Ireland.

This prohibition was begun by the eighteenth section of the Act of Navigation; several of these goods are there enumerated, the rest were added by other statutes (c). Ireland was excepted by force of stat. 20. *Geo.* 3. c. 29. (d).

(a) Vid. ant. 373.  
(b) Vid. ant. 355.  
(c) Vid. ant. 61. 91. 92. 101.  
(d) Vid. ant. 112.

EXCEPT *sugars, which may be carried from the sugar colonies to any port in Europe, in a ship clearing out from Great Britain, and having a licence from the commissioners of the customs for that purpose; and lumber, which may be carried from any British colony or plantation to the Madeiras, or the Western Islands called Azores, or to any part of Europe to the southward of Cape Finisterre.*

THIS depends on ſtat. 12. *Geo.* 2. c. 30. and ſtat. 5. *Geo.* 3. c. 45. (*a*). By an act of this ſeſſion, the liberty to carry ſugar is ſuſpended during the time that ſugars are at a certain price in London.

### RULE III.

" ALL other goods and commodities, not
" ſo enumerated, being the growth, pro-
" duction, or manufacture, of any Britiſh
" colony or plantation in Aſia, Africa, or
" America, may be tranſported to any place
" whatſoever."

BECAUSE what is not prohibited or reſtricted by any ſtatute is open and free.

(*a*) Vid. ant. 95. 103.

EXCEPT

CONCLUSION.

EXCEPT *hops to Ireland, rum, and other spirits, to the Isle of Man, rum to Guernsey and Jersey, and East India goods, which must be brought to the port of London.*

By ſtat. 5. *Geo.* 2. c. 9. for Ireland (*a*); ſtat. 5. *Geo.* 3. c. 39. for the Iſle of Man (*b*); ſtat. 9. *Geo.* 3. c. 28. for Guernſey and Jerſey (*c*); and ſtat. 7. *Geo.* 1. ſt. 1. c. 21. for the Eaſt India Company's goods (*d*).

RULE IV.

" No goods or commodities of the growth,
" production, or manufacture, of Europe,
" may be imported into any land, iſland,
" plantation, colony, territory, or place, to
" his majeſty belonging, or in his poſſeſſion,
" in Aſia, Africa, or America, but ſuch as
" ſhall be ſhipped in Great Britain or Ire-
" land."

THIS prohibition is founded upon ſtat. 15. *Car.* 2. c. 7. ſ. 6. and ſtat. 20. *Geo.* 3. c. 10. (*e*).

(*a*) Vid. ant. 95.   (*d*) Vid. ant. 152.
(*b*) Vid. ant. 104.   (*e*) Vid. ant. 63. 113.
(*c*) Vid. ant. 108, 109.

CONCLUSION.

EXCEPT *salt for the fisheries of Newfoundland, and wines from the Madeiras, and from the Western Islands of Azores; and craft, clothing, or other goods, the growth, production, or manufacture, of Great Britain, Guernsey, or Jersey, or food or victuals the growth, production, or manufacture, of Great Britain, Ireland, Guernsey, or Jersey, from Guernsey or Jersey to Newfoundland, or any other British colony where the fishery is carried on, for the use of the fishery.*

THESE Exceptions are derived from the seventh section of stat. 15. Car. 2. c. 7. as to salt and Madeira wines (*a*); and stat. 9. Geo. 3. c. 28. as to Guernsey and Jersey (*b*).

### RULE V.

" LANDS, islands, territories, or places,
" to his majesty belonging, in Asia,
" Africa, or America, not being colo-
" nies or plantations, are not included in
" any of the foregoing prohibitions or re-
" strictions, other than the prohibition con-
" tained in the Fourth Rule, and the re-
" striction that all goods and commodities

(*a*) Vid. ant. 64.    (*b*) Vid. ant. 108.

" must

CONCLUSION. 521

" must be imported into and exported out
" of them in British-built ships, or in
" British ships owned by his majesty's sub-
" jects, and navigated by a master and
" three-fourths at least of the mariners
" British subjects."

IF the beforementioned prohibitions and restrictions are confined, by the statutes enacting them, to *colonies* and *plantations*, then all *lands, islands, territories*, or *places*, that are judged not to be colonies or plantations (if there are any such) are not within the meaning of them; and such lands, islands, territories, and places, are only included in the first section of the Act of Navigation, and the sixth section of stat. 15. *Car.* 2. c. 7. where they are so named, and not in the second section of the Act of Navigation concerning the enumerated goods, where colonies and plantations only are named; nor in stat. 7. & 8. *Will.* 3. c. 22. which confines the import and export of the colonies and plantations to British-built ships (*a*).

THUS far we have considered the general trade with the foreign dominions of his ma-

(*a*) Vid. ant. 134, 135, 136, 137.

jesty

jesty in Asia, Africa, or America. We come now to state the law respecting the trade of the colonies in the West Indies and on the continent of America with the territories of the *United States*. First, of the West Indies.

### RULE VI.

" SUGAR, molasses, coffee, cocoa-nuts,
" ginger, and pimento, and all goods and
" commodities which were not prohibited
" in the year 1788 to be exported to any
" foreign country in Europe, may be ex-
" ported from the West India Islands to the
" United States."

Such is the provision of stat. 28. *Geo.* 3. c. 6. f. 3. *(a)*.

### RULE VII.

" No goods or commodities may be im-
" ported from the United States into the
" West India Islands, except tobacco, pitch,
" tar, turpentine, hemp, flax, masts, yards,
" bowsprits, staves, heading-boards, tim-
" ber, shingles, and lumber of any sort;

(a) Vid. ant. 354.

" horses,

" horses, neat-cattle, sheep, hogs, poultry,
" and live-stock of any sort; bread, biscuit,
" flour, peas, beans, potatoes, wheat, rice,
" oats, barley, and grain of any sort, being
" the growth or production of any of the
" territories of the United States."

THIS is under the first section of the same act (a).

RULE VIII.

" No goods or commodities may be im-
" ported from the United States by sea or
" coastwise into the province of Quebec,
" or the countries or islands within that
" government, or up the river St. Lawrence,
" nor at all into the provinces of Nova
" Scotia or New Brunswick, the Islands of
" Cape Breton, St. John's, or Newfoundland,
" or any country or island within their re-
" spective governments,"

THIS is under the fourteenth and twelfth sections of the same act (b).

EXCEPT *that the governors of Nova Scotia, New Brunswick, the Islands of Cape Breton and*

(a) Vid. ant. 353.   (b) Vid. ant. 358.

Ss.

CONCLUSION.

St. *John's, may, in cases of public emergency and distress, authorize the importation of scantling, planks, staves, heading-boards, shingles, hoops, or squared timber of any sort; horses, neat-cattle, sheep, hogs, poultry, or live-stock of any sort; bread, biscuit, flour, peas, beans, potatoes, wheat, rice, oats, barley, or grain of any sort, for a limited time; and the governor of New-foundland, being impowered by order of his majesty in council, may authorise, in case of necessity, the importation of bread, flour, Indian-corn, and live-stock, for the then ensuing season only.*

This is under the thirteenth section of the same act *(a)*: and these make the leading points of the law respecting the trade of the British plantations, We come next to the *intercourse* between this kingdom and the *United States*, which in the body of this work has been considered as a branch of the plantation-trade.

### RULE IX.

" Goods and merchandize being the
" growth or production of any of the terri-
" tories of the United States of America,

(*a*) Vid. ant. 357.

" may

"may be imported directly from thence in British-built ships, owned by British subjects, and navigated according to law, or in ships built in the countries belonging to the United States, owned by such subjects, and navigated with a master and three-fourths of the mariners of those countries; namely, unmanufactured goods and merchandize (except fish-oil, blubber, whale-fins, and spermaceti); and also tobacco, pig-iron, bar-iron, pitch, tar, turpentine, rosin, pot-ash, pearl-ash, indigo, masts, yards, and bowsprits, upon the same duties as if they came from any British island or plantation in America. Secondly, Fish-oil, blubber, whale-fins, spermaceti, and all other goods and merchandize (except snuff), upon the lowest of the duties imposed by law upon those articles, if they came from countries not under the British dominion. Thirdly, Snuff upon the same duties as if it was the product and manufacture of Europe."

This stands upon the order of council of 1 April 1792, made by virtue of stat. 23. Geo. 3. c. 39. continued by an act of the present session. The duties to be taken on the second class of goods and merchandize
are

are those contained in the tables and schedules A. D. and F. of the Consolidation Act, 27. Geo. 3. c. 13. and those enacted by any law passed subsequent touching the duties in those schedules. Snuff is further to be subject to the regulations of stat. 29. Geo. 3. c. 68. (a). We now come to the *Trade with Asia, Africa, and America.*

## RULE X.

*Trade with Asia, Africa, and America.*

"No goods or commodities of the growth, "production, or manufacture, of Asia, "Africa, or America, may be imported into "Great Britain, in any other than in British- "built ships, or in British ships owned by "his majesty's subjects, and navigated by a "master and three-fourths at least of the "mariners British subjects."

This prohibition is grounded on the third section of the Act of Navigation (b).

Except *such goods and commodities of the growth or production of the United States, as are permitted by the beforementioned order in council to be imported in ships belonging to the United States, as is stated in the Ninth Rule.*

(a) Vid. ant. 371.   (b) Vid. ant. 139.

This

THIS is the only direct Exception; but some of the instances which are given as Exceptions to the subsequent Rule are Exceptions also to this, as far as they relate to ships.

## RULE XI.

"No goods or commodities of the growth,
"production, or manufacture, of Asia,
"Africa, or America, may be shipped or
"brought from any other place or country
"but only from those of their growth, pro-
"duction, or manufacture, or from those
"ports where they can only, or are, or
"usually have been, first shipped for trans-
"portation."

THIS restriction applies as well to the trade with the plantations as the general trade with Asia, Africa, and America; and is founded on the construction of the fourth section of the Act of Navigation (a).

EXCEPT *the commodities of the Streights or Levant Seas, from the usual ports for lading them within the Streights or Levant Seas; East*

(a) Vid. ant. 140.

## CONCLUSION.

*India commodities, from the usual ports for lading them to the southward and eastward of the Cape of Good Hope; the goods of the Spanish or Portuguese plantations or dominions, from the ports of Spain or Portugal, or the Western Isles commonly called Azores, or the Madeira or Canary Islands; all bullion and prize-goods, from any port, in any sort of ships; jesuits bark, sarsaparilla, balsam of Peru and Tolu, and all drugs the produce of America, from the British plantations; raw silks, or other goods of Persia, from any place belonging to the emperor of Russia, in British-built ships; cochineal and indigo, from any port, in British ships, or ships of a State in amity; gum senega, coarse printed callicoes, cowries, arangoes, and other East-India goods, prohibited to be worn here, from any port in Europe, in British ships; cotton-wool, and goat-skins, raw or undressed, from any place, in British-built ships; and goods the merchandize of the dominions of the emperor of Morocco, from Gibraltar, in British ships.*

These Exceptions are founded on the following acts: The goods of the Streights and Levant on the twelfth section, those of the East Indies on the thirteenth section, those of the Spanish and Portuguese colonies on the fourteenth section, and bullion and prize-goods

CONCLUSION. 529

goods on the fifteenth section, of the Act of Navigation (*a*); jesuit's bark, &c. stat. 7. *Ann.* c. 8. (*b*); Persian silks, stat. 14. *Geo.* 2. c. 36. (*c*); cochineal, stat. 13. *Geo.* 1. c. 15. (*d*); indigo, stat. 7. *Geo.* 2. c. 18. (*e*); gum senega, stat. 25. *Geo.* 2. c. 32. (*f*); coarse printed callicoes, &c. stat. 5. *Geo.* 3. c. 30. (*g*); cotton-wool, stat. 16. *Geo.* 3. c. 52. (*h*); goat-skins, stat. 15. *Geo.* 3. c. 35. (*i*); goods of Morocco, stat. 27. *Geo.* 3. c. 19. (*k*).

We come now to the *European Trade*.

### RULE XII.

"No goods or commodities of the growth, *The European* "production, or manufacture, of Europe, *Trade.* "hereinafter enumerated and described, "namely, no goods or commodities the "growth, production, or manufacture, of "Muscovy, or of any territories belonging "to the emperor of Russia; nor any sort of

(*a*) Vid. ant. 142, 143.    (*b*) Vid. ant. 145.
(*c*) Vid. ant. 148.    (*d*) Vid. ant. 147.
(*e*) Vid. ant. 147.    (*f*) Vid. ant. 149.
(*g*) Vid. ant. 149.    (*h*) Vid. ant. 149.
(*i*) Vid. ant. 149.    (*k*) Vid. ant. 378.

M m      "masts,

"masts, timber, or boards; no foreign salt, pitch, tar, rosin, hemp, or flax; raisins, figs, pruens, olive-oils; no sorts of corn or grain, sugar, pot-ashes, wines, vinegar, or spirits called aqua-vitæ, or brandy wine; may be imported but in British-built ships, or in British ships owned by his majesty's subjects, and navigated by a master and three-fourths at least of the mariners British subjects; nor any currants, or commodities of the growth, production, or manufacture, of any country belonging to the Turkish empire, may be imported but in British-built ships, owned by British subjects; and navigated by a master and three-fourths at least of the mariners British subjects; or in ships of the built of any country or place in Europe under the dominion of the sovereign or state in Europe of which such goods are the growth, production, or manufacture; or of the built of such port where the said goods can only be, or most usually are, first shipped for transportation; and navigated by a master and three-fourths at least of the mariners of that country, place, or port."

THIS

CONCLUSION.

This Rule is founded on the eighth section of the Act of Navigation, amended by stat. 27. *Geo.* 3. c. 19. f. 10. (*a*).

## RULE XIII.

" No fort of wines (other than Rhenish), no fort of spicery, grocery, tobacco, pot-ashes, pitch, tar, falt, rosin, deal boards, fir-timber, or olive-oil, may be imported from the Netherlands or Germany, upon any pretence, in any fort of ships or vessels whatfoever."

This prohibition is made by the twenty-third section of stat. 13. & 14. *Car.* 2. c. 11. (*b*). Afterwards the following Exception was made to this prohibition:

Except *timber, fir-planks, masts, and deal-boards, the production of Germany, from any port or place in Germany, by British subjects, in British-built ships; and wines, the growth or production of Hungary, the Austrian dominions, or any part of Germany, from the Austrian Netherlands, or any port or place belonging to the emperor of Germany, or the house of Austria,*

(*a*) Vid. ant. 197. 382, 383. (*b*) Vid. ant. 204.

*in any such ships as are described in the Twelfth Rule.*

This is founded on stat. 6. *Geo.* 1. c. 16. s. 2. as to the first-mentioned articles (*a*); and as to wines, on stat. 22. *Geo.* 3. c. 78. s. 2. amended by stat. 27. *Geo.* 3. c. 19. s. 10. (*b*).

## RULE XIV.

" Bullion and prize-goods, and all
" other goods and commodities, of the
" growth, production, or manufacture, of
" Europe (not prohibited absolutely to be
" imported), may be imported from any
" country, place, or port, in any sort of
" ships, owned and navigated in any sort of
" manner."

Because bullion and prize-goods are excepted, by the fifteenth section, out of all the provisions of the Act of Navigation; and because, as was before said with regard to plantation goods, what is not prohibited or restricted by any statute is open and free. We now proceed to *the Coasting Trade.*

*(a)* Vid. ant. 208.   *(b)* Vid. ant. 218. 382, 383.

RULE

## RULE XV.

"No perſon may lade or carry on board any ſhip or veſſel, other than a Britiſh-built ſhip, or a Britiſh ſhip owned by Britiſh ſubjects, and navigated by a maſter and three-fourths at leaſt of the mariners Britiſh ſubjects, any commodities or things, of what kind ſoever, from one port or creek of Great Britain or Ireland, or of the iſlands of Guernſey or Jerſey, to another port or creek of the ſame, or any of them."

*The Coaſting Trade.*

This is grounded on the ſixth ſection of the Act of Navigation.

## RULE XVI.

"Every foreign-built ſhip or veſſel bought and brought into Great Britain, to be employed in carrying goods and merchandize from port to port, is to pay at the port of delivery, for every voyage, five ſhillings *per* ton, over and above all other duties."

CONCLUSION.

This is under stat. 1. *Jac.* 2. c. 18.— We come next to the last employment for ships, *The Fisheries*.

## RULE XVII.

*The Fisheries.*

" FRESH fish of every kind, caught by
" the crew of any British-built ship or vessel,
" owned by British subjects usually residing
" in Great Britain, Ireland, Guernsey, Jersey,
" or Man, and navigated by a master and
" three-fourths at least of the mariners
" British subjects, may be imported in such
" ships free of duty."

This is by the thirty-second section of 27. *Geo.* 3. c. 13.

## RULE XVIII.

" No sort of fish whatever of foreign
" fishing (except eels, stock-fish, anchovies,
" sturgeon, botargo or caveare, turbots,
" lobsters, and oysters) may be imported
" into Great Britain."

This depends on stat. 10. & 11. *Will.* 3. c. 24. (*a*); stat. 1. *Geo.* 1. st. 2. c. 18. en-

(*a*) Vid. ant. 285.

forced

forced by ſtat. 9. *Geo.* 2. c. 33. *(a)*; and ſtat. 26. *Geo.* 3. c. 81. ſ. 43, 44. *(b).* Oyſters are not ſpecially excepted in any ſtatute, but there is a duty on them in the Conſolidation Act, which not being leviable on Britiſh-caught fiſh, muſt be conſtrued as a permiſſion to import foreign-caught oyſters.

### RULE XIX.

" PERPETUAL BOUNTIES are payable on
" the export of pilchards or ſhads, cod-fiſh,
" ling, or hake, whether wet or dried,
" ſalmon, white-herrings, red-herrings, and
" dried red-ſprats, being of Britiſh fiſhing
" and curing."

THIS depends on ſtat. 5. *Geo.* 1. c. 18. ſ. 6, and ſtat. 26. *Geo.* 3. c. 81. ſ. 16. *(c).*

### RULE XX.

" TEMPORARY BOUNTIES are payable on
" the tonnage of ſhips carrying on the
" Britiſh and the Greenland fiſheries; on
" the quantity of fiſh taken in the Britiſh

*(a)* Vid. ant. 287, 288.   *(b)* Vid. ant. 405.
*(c)* Vid. ant. 456. 465.

" and

"and the Newfoundland fisheries; on the quantity of oil, head-matter, blubber, and whale-fins, taken in the Southern whale-fishery; and on the export of pilchards. Seal-skins, head-matter, blubber, and whale-fins, taken in the Newfoundland, Greenland, and Southern whale-fisheries, may be imported free of duty, provided British-built ships are employed, owned by British subjects usually residing in the king's European dominions, and navigated by a master and three-fourths at least of the mariners usually residing in the king's European dominions."

THESE temporary bounties all depend on statutes passed in 26. *Geo.* 3. *viz.* c. 81. *(a)*; c. 26. *(b)*, c. 41. *(c)*, c. 50. *(d)*; and such statutes as were made afterwards for amending or continuing them.

LASTLY, we shall see what is the present state of the law as to the requisites which constitute a British-*built* ship, or a *British* ship, and what regards the registry and certificate of such ships. These points depend on stat. 26. *Geo.* 3. c. 60. and may be

*(a)* Vid. ant. 402.   *(b)* Vid. ant. 387.
*(c)* Vid. ant. 390.   *(d)* Vid. ant. 394.

stated

CONCLUSION. 537

stated in Rules, without need of qualifying them by Exceptions, or recurring to other acts for explanation or amendment of them.

## RULE XXI.

"A BRITISH-BUILT ship is such as has  *British Ships.*
"been built in Great Britain or Ireland,
"Guernsey, Jersey, or the Isle of Man, or
"in some of the colonies, plantations,
"islands, or territories, in Asia, Africa, or
"America, which at the time of building
"the ship belonged to, or were in the pos-
"session of, his majesty; or any ship what-
"soever which has been taken and con-
"demned as lawful prize."

EXCEPT *such British-built ships as shall be rebuilt or repaired in any foreign port or place, to an amount exceeding fifteen shillings per ton, unless such repairs shall be proved to have been necessary to enable the ship to perform her voyage.*

THIS Rule and Exception are contained in the first and second sections of the act (a).

(a) Vid. ant. 453, 454.

RULE

### RULE XXII.

"A British ship is, First, Such as is foreign-built, and which before 1 May 1786 belonged wholly to any of the people of Great Britain or Ireland, Guernsey, Jersey, or the Isle of Man, or of any colony, plantation, island, or territory, in Asia, Africa, or America, in possession of his majesty.

"Secondly, Such as has been built or rebuilt on a foreign-made keel or bottom, and registered before 1 May 1786 as a British ship.

"Thirdly, Such as had begun to be repaired or rebuilt on a foreign-made keel or bottom before 1 May 1786, and has been since registered by order of the commissioners of the customs in England or in Scotland."

### RULE XXIII.

"Every ship or vessel having a deck, or being of the burthen of fifteen tons, and belonging to a subject in Great Britain

" or

CONCLUSION.

"or Ireland, Guernsey, Jersey, or the Isle
"of Man, or any colony, plantation, island, or
"territory, to his majesty belonging, must be
"registered by the person claiming property
"therein, who is to obtain a certificate of
"such registry in the port to which the ship
"or vessel properly belongs; and the cer-
"tificate is to distinguish the ship or vessel
"under one of these two classes: CERTI-
"FICATES OF BRITISH PLANTATION
"REGISTRY; or, CERTIFICATES OF
"FOREIGN SHIPS REGISTRY FOR THE
"EUROPEAN TRADE, BRITISH PROPERTY."

This is by the third and twenty-eighth sections (*a*).

### RULE XXIV.

"No ship is to be permitted to clear out
"as a British-built ship, or a British ship,
"nor to be intitled to the privileges of a
"British-built ship, or a British ship, unless
"the owner has obtained a certificate of
"registry; and any ship departing from
"port without being so registered, and ob-
"taining such a certificate, shall be for-
"feited (*b*)."

(*a*) Vid. ant. 456. 465.   (*b*) Sect. 32.

RULE

## RULE XXV.

"ALL ships not intitled to the privileges of a British-built ship, or a British ship, and all ships not registered as aforesaid, are deemed, although they may belong to British subjects, to all intents and purposes, alien or foreign ships (a)."

## RULE XXVI.

"As often as the master of a ship is changed, a memorandum thereof is to be indorsed on the certificate by the proper officer of the customs."

## RULE XXVII.

"THE owner is to cause the name by which a ship is registered to be painted in a conspicuous part of the stern; and such name is not to be changed (b).

## RULE XXVIII.

"IF a certificate of registry is lost or mislaid, or if a ship shall be altered in

(a) Stat. 27. Geo. 3. c. 29. s. 13. vid. ant. 511.
(b) Sect. 19. vid. ant. 462.

" form

"form or burthen, or from any denomination of veſſel to another, by rigging or
fitting, ſhe muſt be regiſtered *de novo*,
and a new certificate granted (c)."

## RULE XXIX.

"Masters of ſhips are, on demand, to
produce their certificates to the principal
officer in any port within the king's dominions, or to the Britiſh conſul or chief
officer in any foreign port (b)."

Such is the preſent ſtate of the laws which
the Legiſlature has ſeen fit to provide for
the encouragement and increaſe of Britiſh
ſhipping and navigation. It is a ſeries of
reſtrictions and prohibitions, and it tends
to the eſtabliſhing of monopoly; but it is a
plan of regulation which our anceſtors, who
were more verſed in the practical philoſophy
of life than the ſpeculative one of the cloſet,
thought neceſſary for the welfare and ſafety
of the kingdom. Reaſoning from the ſelf-
preſervation of an individual to the ſelf-pre-
ſervation of a people, they conſidered the
defence of this iſland from foreign invaſion

(c) Sect: 22, 23. vid. ant. 465.
(b) Sect. 34. vid. ant. 469.

as the first law in the national policy; and judging that the dominion of the land could not be preserved without possessing that of the sea, they made every effort to procure to the nation a maritime power of its own. They wished that the merchants should own as many ships, and employ as many native mariners, as possible. To induce, and sometimes to force, them to this application of their capital, restrictions and prohibitions were devised. These affected not only foreigners but natives; the interests of commerce were often sacrificed to this object. Trade was considered principally as the means for promoting the employment of ships, and was encouraged chiefly as it conduced to the one great national object, the naval strength of the country.

This policy was pursued by those who came after them in directing the public councils; and in the last century, when many institutions of our ancestors fell a sacrifice to the rage of reformation, the wisdom of the navigation-system was respected: measures were even taken for rendering it more narrow and restrictive. The foreign war which those measures then brought upon us, and the odium which they have

never

never ceased to cause, to the present day, among neighbouring nations, have not induced the Legislature to give up any one of its main principles.

EXPERIENCE has shewn the advantage of adhering to this maritime policy. The inducement and obligation to employ British ships had the effect of increasing their number. The increase of their number became a spur to seek out employment for them. Foreign trade and the fisheries were, by various expedients, made subservient to advance the interests of shipping. Trade and shipping thus reciprocally contributed to advance each other; and thus combined they constituted very considerable sources of national wealth. Having been at first encouraged for the sake of the navy, they were afterwards encouraged for their own. From being subordinate and auxiliary to another object, they are now become principal objects themselves in the national policy; and, in the mean time, the naval power of the country is sure of supply and support, without being directly in contemplation.

THIS action and re-action between shipping and trade has even been promoted by the

the effects of naval armaments. It has been found, that after the conclusion of a war there has constantly been a great increase of mercantile shipping. This has been caused, first, by the government having employed, during the war, a number of transports, which has induced the merchants to invest their money in the building of ships for that service. Secondly, The privateers which were fitted out during hostilities have no employment at the peace but the merchants' service. Transports and privateers fall into foreign trades or the fisheries; and in this manner does the service of the navy pay back to trade and navigation the obligations it had before received.

If the wisdom of any scheme of policy is to be measured by its effects and consequences, our navigation-system is intitled to the praise of having attained the end for which it was designed. Whether we regard the primary or inferior objects in this system; whether it is the increase of shipping, the extension of our foreign trade, or the strength of our navy, they have all advanced to a degree of consideration unexampled; and they owe that advancement to this system.

With

## CONCLUSION.

WITH regard to our shipping, it is well known, that we enjoy a greater share in what may be properly called our own navigation, that is, in the navigation by which our own trade is carried on, than any other nation in Europe; and that after we have furnished these demands of our own commerce, we are able to supply with ships the trade of foreign nations. This extensive employment has gradually increased the mercantile shipping of Great Britain to upwards of 1,365,000 tons, which is valued at the sum of 11,466,000l.

THAT this increase in our shipping is to be ascribed to our navigation-system may be made appear from recent experience, in the application of it to the trade of the United States. When those countries were part of our plantations, a great portion of their produce was transported to Great Britain and our West-India Islands in American bottoms; they had a share in the freight of sugars from those islands to Great Britain; they built annually more than one hundred ships, which were employed in the carrying-trade of Great Britain. But since the Independence of those States, since their ships

CONCLUSION.

have been excluded from our plantations, and that trade is wholly confined to British-built ships, we have gained that share of our carrying-trade from which they are now excluded; and we moreover enjoy a confiderable proportion in the carriage of the produce of the United States.

The increafe of our trade and naval ftrength has kept pace with that of our shipping and navigation. We can reflect with pride, that our foreign trade, combined with our manufactures and domeftic induftry, enables us to raife annually fixteen millions of money with more eafe, than four millions were raifed during the reign of king William; and this upon a people, who, in their different ranks, enjoy more riches, more competency, and more comfort, than any people in Europe; and who are more induftrious, becaufe they are better protected by a conftitution, which has been progreffively improving, both in the theory and practice of it, to the prefent time.

It was chiefly owing to the effects of this wife fyftem of navigation, that during the late war we were enabled, notwithftanding the defection of our colonies, to maintain an arduous

arduous conteſt againſt France, Spain, and Holland, till in the end the fleets of this country might be ſaid to have triumphed over the naval powers of Europe.

After this experience, no one can doubt but that it is the policy of Great Britain to give her principal attention to maritime affairs; to carry on her own trade, in her own ſhips, directly to all parts of the world; and to encourage her fiſheries in every ſea: and from theſe ſources ſhe may always hope to obtain a naval force adequate to guard her ſhores from hoſtile invaſion, and to ſecure her domeſtic felicity, both public and private, firm and unſhaken as the foundations of the iſland.

Σοὶ δὲ μέλοι, Ἐνηπ'ἔυχε Διοτρεφὶς, ἔργα θαλάσσης:
Σοὶ δ' αἰεὶ νῆες μὲν ἀπήμονες ἰθύνοιντο,
Πεμπόμεναι λιαροῖσι καὶ ἰθυπόροισιν αὔταις,
Αἰεὶ δ' ἰχθυόεσσα τεραπληθοιτο θάλασσα·
Γαίης δ' ἀςυφέλικία Ποσειδάων ἰρύοιτο
Ἀσφάλιος ῥιζῦχα θεμείλια νέρθε φυλάσσων.

Oppiani Halieut. in Fin.

## APPENDIX.

# APPENDIX.

I. AMERICAN ORDER OF COUNCIL.
II. FORM OF OATH IN STAT. 7 & 8. WILL. 3.
III. CERTIFICATE OF REGISTER UNDER STAT. 7. & 8. WILL. 3.
IV. CERTIFICATE OF FREEDOM UNDER STAT. 7. & 8. WILL. 3.
V. FORM OF OATH IN STAT. 13. GEO. 1.
VI. FORM OF OATH IN STAT. 16. GEO. 3.
VII. FORM OF CERTIFICATE OF REGISTRY IN STAT. 16. GEO. 3.
VIII. FORM OF A MEDITERRANEAN PASS.
IX. FORM OF THE BOND ON GRANTING A MEDITERRANEAN PASS.

## No. I.

THE ANNUAL ORDER OF COUNCIL for the INTERCOURSE with the UNITED STATES, dated 1 APRIL 1792.

WHEREAS by an act made in the 23d year of the reign of his present majesty, intituled, *An Act for preventing certain instruments from being required from ships belonging to the United States of America; and to give to his majesty, for a limited time, certain powers for the better carrying on trade and commerce between the subjects of his majesty's dominions and the inhabitants of the said United States*; which said act has been continued by several subsequent acts until the 5th day of April 1792: AND WHEREAS by an act made in the 24th year of his present majesty's reign, intituled, *An Act to extend the Powers of an act made in the 23d year of the reign of his present majesty, for giving his majesty certain powers for the better carrying on trade and commerce between the subjects of his majesty's dominions and the inhabitants of the United States of America, to the trade and commerce of this kingdom with the British colonies and plantations in America, with respect to certain articles therein mentioned*, the powers given by the said recited act were extended to the trade and intercourse between this kingdom and the British colonies and plantations in America, so far as the same might relate to iron, hemp, and sail-cloth, and other articles of the produce of any place bordering on the Baltic, which might be exported from this kingdom; which last mentioned act has also, by several subsequent acts, been continued until the said 5th day of April 1792.

AND WHEREAS, by another act passed in this present session of parliament, intituled, *An Act to continue the laws now in force for regulating the trade between the subjects of his majesty's dominions and the inhabitants of the territories belonging to the United States of America, so far as the same relate to the trade and commerce carried on between this kingdom and the inhabitants of the countries belonging to the said United States*—it is declared to be expedient, that the said act of the 23d year of his present majesty's

# APPENDIX.

majesty's reign, so far only as the same extends to the trade and commerce carried on between this kingdom and the people and territories belonging to the United States of America, and also, that the said act of the 24th year of his present majesty's reign, should be further continued and be in force; and it is thereby enacted, that the said acts shall continue and be in force until the 5th day of April 1793: His majesty doth thereupon, by and with the advice of his privy council, hereby order and declare, that any unmanufactured goods and merchandizes, the importation of which into this kingdom is not prohibited by law (except tobacco, for which provision is herein after made, and except oil made from fish or creatures living in the sea, and blubber, whalefins and spermaceti), and any pig-iron, bar-iron, pitch, tar, turpentine, rosin, pot-ash, pearl-ash, indigo, masts, yards and bowsprits, being the growth or production of any of the territories of the United States of America, may be imported directly from thence into any of the ports of this kingdom, either in British-built ships owned by his majesty's subjects, and navigated according to law, or in ships built in the countries belonging to the United States of America, or any of them, and owned by the subjects of the said United States, or any of them, and whereof the master and three-fourths of the mariners at least are subjects of the said United States, or any of them; and may be entered and landed in any port of this kingdom, upon payment of such duties as the like sorts of goods or merchandize are or may be subject and liable to, if imported in British-built ships owned by his majesty's subjects, and navigated according to law, from any British island or plantation in America, notwithstanding such goods or merchandize, or the ships in which the same may be brought, may not be accompanied with the certificates or other documents heretofore required by law.

And it is further ordered, that all other goods and merchandize not herein before enumerated or described, the importation of which into this kingdom is not prohibited by law (except snuff, for which provision is herein-

# APPENDIX.

after made) and also oil made from fish, or creatures living in the sea, and blubber, whale-fins and spermaceti, being the growth, production, or manufacture of any of the territories of the said United States of America, may be imported from thence into this kingdom, in British or American ships, owned and navigated as herein before required, upon payment of such duties of customs and excise as are payable on the like goods or merchandize, upon their importation into this kingdom from countries not under the dominion of his majesty, according to the schedule and tables marked A. D. and F. annexed to an act passed in the 27th year of his present majesty's reign, intituled, *An Act for repealing the several duties of customs and excise, and granting other duties in lieu thereof, and for applying the said duties, together with the other duties composing the public revenue; for permitting the importation of certain goods, wares, and merchandize, the produce or manufacture of the European dominions of the French king, into this kingdom; and for applying certain unclaimed monies remaining in the exchequer for the payment of annuities on lives to the reduction of the National debt*; or by any other laws in force, passed subsequent to the said act, touching the duties contained in the said schedule and tables marked A. D. and F; and in cases where different duties are imposed upon the like goods imported from different countries not under the dominion of his majesty, then that such goods shall be imported upon the lowest duties which by the said schedule and tables marked A. D. and F. are required to be paid on the importation of any such goods from any European country not under the dominion of his majesty.

AND his majesty is hereby further pleased to order, that all such goods and merchandize shall be entitled to the same drawbacks as are allowed upon the exportation of the like goods and merchandize when exported from this kingdom, according to the said schedule and tables marked A. D. and F. annexed to the beforementioned act, passed in the 27th year of his present majesty's reign; or according to any other law in force, passed subsequent to the said act, touching drawbacks. And it is hereby further ordered, that there shall be allowed and paid

## APPENDIX.

paid the same drawbacks and bounties on goods and merchandize exported from this kingdom to the territories of the said United States, or any of them, as are, or may hereafter be allowed by law, upon the exportation of the like goods or merchandize to any of the islands, plantations, or colonies, belonging to the crown of Great Britain in America. And it is hereby further ordered, that there shall be allowed and paid the same drawbacks upon the exportation of any sort of foreign hemp, or foreign iron, exported from this kingdom into any British colony or plantation in America, or into the territories of the United States of America, or any of them, as are, or may hereafter be allowed by law, upon the exportation of the like sort of hemp or iron to other foreign parts; and all such drawbacks and bounties respectively shall be allowed and paid in the same manner, and under the same rules, regulations, restrictions, and forfeitures, in all respects, as such drawbacks and bounties are allowed and paid, or are subject and liable to by law.

And his majesty is hereby further pleased to order, that any tobacco, being the growth or production of any of the territories of the said United States of America, may be imported in British or American ships, owned and navigated as herein before required, upon payment of the same duties as tobacco imported by British subjects from any British colony or plantation, is, or may hereafter be subject to; and that any snuff, being the production or manufacture of any of the said territories, may be imported in manner beforementioned, upon payment of such duties as snuff, being the production or manufacture of Europe, imported from Europe, is, or hereafter may be, subject to, and may be warehoused and again exported; subject respectively, nevertheless, to all and singular the regulations of an act made and passed in the 29th year of the reign of his present majesty, intituled, *An Act for repealing the duties on tobacco and snuff, and for granting new duties in lieu thereof* (a); and another act, passed in the 30th year of his present majesty's reign, intituled, *An Act to explain and amend an Act made in the last session of parliament*, intituled,

(a) Chap. 68.

# APPENDIX.

*An Act for repealing the duties on tobacco and snuff, and for granting new duties in lieu thereof* (a).

And his majesty is hereby further pleased to order, that any rice, being the growth or production of any of the territories of the United States of America, which shall be imported directly from thence into any of the ports of this kingdom, in manner abovementioned, may, upon the importer paying down, in ready money, the duty of eightpence the hundred weight, being part of the duties now payable upon the importation of rice, be landed and warehoused (except as herein after excepted) under his majesty's locks, in such warehouses as shall be approved of for that purpose by the commissioners of his majesty's customs, or any four or more of them, upon the importer's own bond for payment of the remainder of the duties due and payable for such rice, within eighteen months, according to the nett weight and quantity of such rice at the time it shall be so landed; but it is his majesty's pleasure, nevertheless, that upon the importation of any such rice into the ports of London, Bristol, Portsmouth, Cowes, Liverpool, Lancaster, Falmouth, Poole, Whitehaven, Hull, Greenock, and Port Glasgow, or either of them, in the manner herein before expressed, the importer shall be at liberty to enter and land the same without payment of any duty whatever; in which case such rice shall be warehoused under the joint locks of his majesty and the proprietors, in such warehouse or warehouses as shall be approved of for that purpose by the commissioners of his majesty's customs, or any four or more of them, in that part of Great-Britain called England; and any three or more of them in that part of Great-Britain called Scotland; every expence attending which warehousing shall be borne by the said proprietors; and that such proprietor or proprietors, or his or their known agent, shall from time to time, at all seasonable hours, as occasion may require, have free access to such warehouses, in the presence of some proper officer of the customs, for the purpose of screening and shifting the rice, to prevent its receiving damage. And that if any rice which shall be so imported from the territories of the said United States

(a) Chap. 40.

## APPENDIX.

into any of the ports above mentioned respectively, and warehoused as aforesaid, shall be taken out of the warehouses wherein the same shall be secured under the joint locks of his majesty and the proprietors, as aforesaid, for home consumption, the full duties due and payable by law upon the importation of such rice into this kingdom for home consumption shall, previously to its being taken out of such warehouses, be paid to the collector of his majesty's customs at the ports where such rice shall be so warehoused; but that such proprietor, if he intends to export such rice, shall have liberty to export the same from such warehouses respectively, under the usual regulations, without payment of any duty whatever: and that if any rice which shall have been imported into any port of this kingdom not hereinbefore specially named, and shall have been warehoused upon the importer's bond, in manner aforesaid, shall, within the time hereinbeforementioned, be taken out of the warehouse wherein it shall have been so secured, to be exported directly from thence, the bond entered into for the payment of the said duties thereon, shall be discharged and cancelled by debenture or debentures made out and passed in the usual manner, for the quantity or quantities of rice duly exported. And if any rice imported into any port of this kingdom not hereinbefore specially named, and warehoused in manner aforesaid, shall be taken out of any such warehouse for home consumption, the remainder of the duties due and payable by law, shall, previously to its being taken out of such warehouse, be paid to the collector of his majesty's customs at the port where such rice shall be so warehoused.

AND the right honourable the lords commissioners of his majesty's treasury, and the lords commissioners of the admiralty, are to give the necessary directions herein, as to them may respectively appertain.

# APPENDIX.

## No. II.

FORM of OATH which was directed by Stat. 7. & 8. *Will.* 3. to be taken before a REGISTER was granted.

JURAT' A. B. That the ship [*name*] of [*port*] whereof [*master's name*] is at present master, being a [*kind of built*] of [*burthen*] tons, was built at [*place where*] in the year [*time when*] and that [*owner's name*] of and of, &c. are at present owners thereof; and that no foreigner, directly or indirectly, hath any share or part or interest therein.

---

## No. III.

A CERTIFICATE of the REGISTER for a BRITISH SHIP, which used to be made in Pursuance of Stat. 7. & 8. *Will.* 3.

IN pursuance of an act made in the seventh and eighth years of the reign of king William the Third, intituled, *An Act for preventing Frauds, and regulating Abuses in the Plantation Trade*, William Strong, of London, merchant, maketh oath, That the ship the Mary of London, whereof James Smith is at present master, being a square-sterned brigantine of one hundred and twenty-five tons or thereabouts, was built at Bristol in the year one thousand seven hundred and eighty-five; and that James Green, of Bristol, James Smith, and William Strong, abovementioned, of London, in Great Britain, are at present owners thereof; and that no foreigner,

(L. S.)
Wm. Bates,
Deputy Collector.

(L. S.)
J. Heard,
Deputy Comptroller.

# APPENDIX.

reigner, directly or indirectly, hath any share, or part, or interest therein. Dated at the Custom-house, London, the third day of October 1785.

WILLIAM STRONG.

Sworn before me,
E. *Meller*, D. Coll<sup>r</sup>.

---

## No. IV.

A CERTIFICATE OF FREEDOM, which used to be made in Pursuance of Stat. 7. & 8. *Will.* 3. and other Statutes.

TO ALL TO WHOM this present writing shall come, Edward Louisa Mann, Esq. collector of his majesty's customs inwards in the port of London, sendeth greeting: WHEREAS by an act of parliament, intituled, "*An Act for preventing Frauds, and regulating Abuses in his Majesty's Customs,*" it is, among other things, therein enacted, that no foreign-built ship should enjoy the privilege of a ship belonging to England or Ireland, although owned and manned by English (except such ships only as should be taken at sea by letters of mart or reprisal, and condemnation made in a court of admiralty as lawful prize); but all such ships should be deemed as aliens ships, and be liable to all duties that aliens ships are liable unto by virtue of another act of parliament, intituled, *An Act for increasing and encouraging of Shipping and Navigation:* And by two several acts passed in the 20th and 29th years of his majesty king George the Second, it is further enacted, That all prize ships or vessels which shall be legally condemned, shall to all intents and purposes whatsoever be considered as British-built ships or vessels, and be deemed and taken as such: Now KNOW YE, That the ship or vessel formerly called Le Marquis de Sordiz, and now called The Scattergood, whereof John Marsham is at present master, French-built, of the burthen of 160 tons or thereabouts,

# APPENDIX.

abouts, square-sterned, having two decks and two masts, was a prize taken from the French king's subjects, and legally condemned in a court of vice-admiralty held at the town of St. Jago della Vega, 23d November 1756, as by sentence of condemnation doth appear: AND John Marsham, of London, mariner, hath made oath, That the said ship or vessel is still in being, and the same which was taken and condemned, as aforesaid, by the name of Le Marquis de Sordiz, and is now called The Scattergood, and the same for which this certificate is granted; That no foreigner or alien directly or indirectly hath any part, share, or interest therein; but that he the said deponent, together with Isaac Kemp, Anth. Facer Kemp, Charles Childs, John Grant, and Thos. Gill, all his majesty's native subjects, are now the only owners; as also, that no former certificate hath been taken out for making free the said ship or vessel, by this or any other name or names whatsoever: And John Marsham did on the 18th January 1758 pay his majesty's customs for the said ship; her tackle, apparel, and furniture, being valued on oath at 310l.——Certified 20th January 1758.

IN WITNESS whereof, Benjamin Scott, Esq. deputy to Edward Louisa Mann, Esq. collector of his majesty's Collector. customs inwards in the port of London, hath hereunto set his hand, and caused the seal of the office to be affixed, dated the 4th day of October 1759, in the 33d year of the reign of our sovereign lord George the Second, by the grace of God of Great Britain, France, and Ireland, king, defender of the faith, and so forth.

Certified and entered fo. 497.
in the General Register for
Prize Ships.

C. R. p. Coll'.

(A Copy)

No.

APPENDIX.

## No. V.

FORM of OATH which is directed by Stat. 15. Geo. 2. c. 31. to be taken of a CERTIFICATE of REGISTER being lost or mislaid, in order to have the SHIP registered *de novo*.

A. B. being master (or having the charge) of the ship or vessel called the        , does swear (or solemnly affirm), That the said ship or vessel has been, as he verily believes, registered according to law, to qualify her to trade to, from, and in his majesty's plantations in *America*, and that he had a certificate thereof granted at the port of        , but that the same is lost or mislaid, and that he cannot find the same, and does not know where the same is, or what is become thereof; and that the same hath not been, nor shall be, with his privity or knowledge, sold or disposed of to any person or persons whatsoever; and that he this deponent (or affirmant) and three-fourths of the mariners navigating the said ship or vessel are his majesty's *British* subjects, and the said ship or vessel does now, as he believes, belong wholly to his majesty's *British* subjects, and that no foreigner has, to his knowledge or belief, any share, property, or interest therein.

## No. VI.

FORM of OATH directed by Stat. 26. Geo. 3. c. 60. to be taken, in order to making a REGISTRY, and granting a CERTIFICATE thereof.

I A. B. of [*place of residence and occupation*] do make oath, That the ship or vessel [*name*] of [*port or place*] whereof [*master's name*] is at present master, being [*kind*

# APPENDIX.

[*kind of built, burthen, etcetera, as described in the certificate of the surveying officer*] was [*when and where built; or if prize, capture and condemnation*]; and that I the said *A. B.* [*and the other owners names and occupations, if any, and where they respectively reside,* videlicet, *town, place or parish, and county, or if member of, and resident in any factory in foreign parts, or in any foreign town or city, being an agent for, or partner in any house or co-partnership actually carrying on trade in* Great Britain, *or* Ireland, *the name of such factory, foreign town or city, and the names of such house or copartnership*] am [*or are*] sole owner [*or owners*] of the said vessel, and that no other person or persons whatever hath or have any right, title, interest, share, or property, therein or thereto; and that I the said *A. B.* [*and the said other owners, if any*] am [*or are*] truly and *bona fide* a subject [*or subjects*] of *Great Britain*; and that I the said *A. B.* have not [*nor have any of the other owners, to the best of my knowledge and belief*] taken the oath of allegiance to any foreign state whatever [*except under the terms of some capitulation, describing the particulars thereof*], or that since my taking [*or his or their taking*] the oath of allegiance to [*naming the foreign states respectively to which he or any of the said owners shall have taken the same*] and prior to the passing of an Act in the twenty-sixth year of the reign of king *George* the Third (intituled, *An Act for the further Increase and Encouragement of Shipping and Navigation*), I have [*or he or they hath or have*] become a subject [*or subjects*] of *Great Britain* [*either by his Majesty's letters patent, as a denizen or denizens, or naturalized by act of parliament, as the case may be, naming the dates of the letters of denization, or the act or acts of parliament for naturalization respectively*], or [*as the case may be*] I have [*or he or they hath or have*] become a denizen [*or denizens, or naturalized subject or subjects, as the case may be*] of *Great Britain*, by his Majesty's letters patent, or by an act of parliament passed since the first day of January one thousand seven hundred and eighty-six [*naming the times when such letters of denization have been granted respectively, or the year or years in which such act or acts for naturalization have passed, respectively*], and that no foreigner, directly or indirectly, hath any share or part or interest in the said ship or vessel.

# APPENDIX.

## No. VII.

**FORM of a CERTIFICATE OF REGISTRY** directed to be granted by Stat. 26. Geo. 3. c. 60.

IN pursuance of an act passed in the twenty-fifth year of the reign of king *George* the Third, intituled, *An Act* [*here insert the title of the act, the names, occupation, and residence, of the subscribing owners*], having taken and subscribed the oath required by this Act, and having sworn that he, [*or* they] together with [*names, occupation, and residence of non-subscribing owners*], is [*or* are] sole owner [*or* owners] of the ship or vessel called The [*ship's name*] of [*place to which the vessel belongs*], whereof [*master's name*] is at present master, and that the said ship or vessel was [*when and where built, or captured, and date of condemnation*]; and [*name and employment of the surveying officer*] having certified to us that the said ship or vessel is [*whether British, foreign, or British-plantation built*], has [*number of decks*] decks, and [*number of masts*] masts, that her length, from the fore part of the main stem to the after part of the stern post aloft, is [*number of feet and inches*], her breadth at the broadest part, whether above or below the main wales [*number of feet and inches*], her height between decks [*number of feet and inches, if more than one deck, and if not, then*] the depth of the hold [*number of feet and inches*], and admeasures [*burthen*] tons, that she is a [*kind of vessel, and how built*], has [*whether any or no gallery*] gallery, and [*kind of head, if any*] head; and the said subscribing owners having consented and agreed to the above description and admeasurement, and having caused sufficient security to be given, as is required by the said Act, the said [*kind and name of the vessel*] has been duly registered at the port of [*name of the port*].

Given under our hands and seals of office, at the Custom-house in the said port of [*name of the port*], this [*date*] day of [*name of the month*], in the year [*words at length*].

No.

# APPENDIX.

## No. VIII.

FORM of a MEDITERRANEAN PASS, as prescribed by an ORDER of COUNCIL dated 28th AUGUST 1776.

BY the commissioners for executing the office of lord high admiral of Great Britain and of Ireland, and of all his majesty's plantations

Suffer the ship

to pass with her company, passengers, goods, and merchandize, without any let, hindrance, seizure, or molestation, the said ship appearing to us by good testimony to belong to the subjects of his majesty, and to no foreigner. Given under our hands and seals at the office of admiralty.

| | |
|---|---|
| To all persons | (L. S.) |
| whom these may concern. | (L. S.) |
| By command of their Lordships. | (L. S.) |

---

## No. IX.

FORM of a BOND to be given at any of the PORTS of GREAT BRITAIN or IRELAND before a MEDITERRANEAN PASS be delivered for any SHIP or VESSEL built in those Kingdoms, or in any of HIS MAJESTY's Foreign GOVERNMENTS or PLANTATIONS, or for any Foreign SHIP or VESSEL made free, and qualified to have such PASS granted, as the same is prescribed by an ORDER of COUNCIL dated 28th AUGUST 1776.

KNOW ALL MEN by these presents, That we are holden and firmly bound to our sovereign lord George the Third, by the grace of God, of Great Britain, France, and Ireland, king, defender of the faith, &c.

# APPENDIX.

in                    pounds of good and lawful money of Great Britain, to be paid to our said lord the king, his heirs, and successors: to which certain payment well and truly to be made we bind ourselves, and each of us for the whole, our and each of our heirs, executors, and administrators, firmly by these presents. SEALED with our seals, DATED the         day of         , in the         year of the reign of our said lord the king, and in the year of Our Lord 17   .

THE CONDITION of this obligation is such, That WHEREAS the above bounden                 hath received a pass, purporting to be a Mediterranean pass, signed by the right honourable the commissioners for executing the office of lord high admiral of Great Britain and so forth, for the                        called the         of         , whereof he the said         is actually master, bearing date the                        . Now if the said         , or, in case of his death or inability, the person who shall succeed him as master of the said         shall deliver, or cause the said pass to be delivered, into the admiralty office upon her return from her present intended voyage into the port of London, or to the proper officers of the customs at any other port of Great Britain or Ireland, where she shall come in order to her unloading; Or in case the said         shall not return to Great Britain or Ireland, within the term of three years from the date hereof, and during all that term shall remain, and be the property of his majesty's subjects; then if the master of the said         for the time being, do at the expiration of the said term of three years deliver, or cause the said pass to be delivered, unto the governor or commander in chief of one of his majesty's foreign governments or plantations, or unto one of his majesty's consuls in the Mediterranean or elsewhere, in order to its being by such governor or commander in chief, or consul, returned and transmitted to the commissioners for executing the office of lord high admiral of Great Britain: AND ALSO, if the said master for the time being do and shall, when and as often as the said         shall go into any foreign port or place within the reach or district of any of his majesty's consuls, deliver or cause the said

pass

# APPENDIX.

pass to be delivered unto such respective consul or consuls, or his or their deputy or deputies, upon his or their demanding the same in writing, in order to the said pass's being retained in the possession of such respective consul or consuls, or his or their deputy or deputies, until the said            shall have received the usual clearances, and be ready to depart from such port or place, at which time the said pass is to be returned for the use of the said ship: Or in case the said            shall happen to be taken by an enemy or pirates, or to be cast away and shipwrecked, by means whereof the said pass shall be inevitably lost or destroyed; THEN the above obligation to be void and of none effect. BUT if the said master for the time being shall neglect to deliver, or cause the said pass to be delivered into the admiralty office upon her return from her present intended voyage into the port of London, or to the proper officers of the customs at any other port of Great Britain or Ireland, where she shall come within the said term of three years, in order to her unloading; or in case the said ship shall not return to England within the said term, then unto the governor or commander in chief of one of his majesty's foreign governments or plantations, or unto one of his majesty's consuls in the Mediterranean or elsewhere before the expiration of that term: Or if the said master for the time being shall neglect or refuse to deliver the said pass to any of his majesty's consuls or their deputies abroad, upon demand in writing being made thereof in manner above-mentioned (to prove which demand and refusal or neglect a certificate thereof in writing under the hand of the respective consul or his deputy is to be deemed a sufficient evidence): Or if the said pass shall be sold, lent, or otherwise disposed of, to any person whatsoever, so as that the same shall not be actually and constantly made use of for the service of the said            called the            for which it is granted, so long as the master thereof for the time being shall be a British subject; THEN the above obligation shall be and remain in full force, virtue, and effect.

THERE is some difference in the time for delivering up passes in different trades.

Thus,

## APPENDIX.

Thus, for ships trading to the ports of France, Portugal, and Spain, on this side the Streights' mouth, the condition is for delivering up the pass within twelve months, either to the admiralty, or the custom-house officer at the port of unloading in Great-Britain or Ireland.

In bonds given in the Plantations, the condition is for delivering up the pass within twelve months to the governor of that plantation.

For ships in the East India trade, the condition is for delivering it up at the return from the voyage, without any limitation of time.

Passes for ships belonging to Gibraltar are different from all others in the wording, and in the ornament at the top; and they are granted by the commissioners for executing the office of lord-high-admiral at that place. The condition of the bond given on obtaining such passes, is for delivering them up to such commissioners within twelve months, or at the end of the voyage, if the ship return sooner.

INDEX.

# INDEX.

### A.

AFRICAN Company, 155. 379
Asia, Africa, and America, Trade with, regulated, 119. 159. 378
Allowance on salted fish, 189
Attorney Generals, their opinions, 9
Azores, Isles of, 64

### B.

Baltic, Goods from, exported to the Plantations, 748
Berkeley, Sir William, his letter, 75
Bill of Sale of a Ship, 461. 490
Bounties in the Fishery, 282. 291. 195
Breda, Treaty of, 206

### C.

Callicoes, coarse, 149
Canaries, Produce of the, 143
Carrying Trade, 15. 46. 141. 202. 203
Case of Lille v. Vanneck, 262
———— Macneal, 502
———— Mitchell v. Torup, 265
———— Rolleston v. Hibbert, 490
———— Scott v. D'Achez, 229. 234. 246

Case of Scott v. Schwartz, 226
Certificate of Registry, 416
————— Indorsement on, 461
————— Lost, or mislaid, 328. 411. 463
Coasting Trade, 27. 33. 178. 181
Colony, or Plantation, what, 68. 123. 124
Committee of Council for Trade and Plantations, 341. 430.
Contraband Trade in the Plantations, 69. 80. 99. 106. 203
Cotton Wool, 149
Country, or place, where foreign ships built, 138. 144
————— of foreign mariners, 145
Customs, Commissioners of, 434
————— Report of, on Registering, 436
————— Ships in the Eastland Trade, 478

### D.

Decisions of Courts, 4
Direct Importation, 140. 146. 171
Drugs from America, 145
————— Hungary, or Germany, 378
Dunkirk, whether part of the Netherlands, 213
Dutch Carrying Trade, 46. 143. 203
Duty, easement in, for goods in British ships, 10. 85

Duty,

# INDEX.

Duty, Aliens, for goods in foreign ships, 25. 459
—— on coasting vessels foreign-built, 279
—— on exports from the Plantations, 70. 85

## E.

East Friezeland ships, 248
East India Company, 249. 250
Eastland Company, 209
—— Trade, ships in, 422
Enumerated goods from the Plantations, 60. 82. 91. 94. 95. 101. 103
—————— in the European Trade, 197
European Trade regulated, 159. 197. 360
————, ships employed in, 214. 218. 344. 361
———, how navigated, 345

## F.

Fir-timber from Germany, 208
Fisheries encouraged, 27. 282. 285. 287. 366. 407
Fishery, Deep Sea, 404
—— Herring, 282. 199. 402
—— Greenland, 284. 289. 397. 390
—— Newfoundland, 30. 285. 293. 367
—————— Americans prohibited from, 300
—— Pilchard, 406
—— Southern Whale, 191. 314
—— Whale, 291. 293
—— British, 403
—— The Society of the Free British, 289
Fish foreign-caught prohibited, 184. 263
Foreign ships British-manned, 226
—— Mariners, their country, 245
—————— in British ships, 274
Forts to colour it, 265
France, Commercial Treaty with, 360

Free Ports established, 126. 123
Freight of ships regulated, 20

## G.

Gascony wines, 11. 17. 85
Germany. Vide Netherlands.
Gibraltar, Morocco goods from, 138
Governors of Plantations, 60 65. 83. 88. 90. 471
—————— Circular letter to, 82
Guadaloupe, whether a British Colony, 130
Guernsey and Jersey, European goods from, to the Fisheries, 108
Gum Senega, 148

## H.

Hamburgh Company, 214
————, sugars sent to, 96
————, Hungary wines from, 207
Holland, whether a part of Germany, 131
Honduras, whether a Colony, 136
Hovering, 192. 260
Hudson's Bay Company, 155
Hungary Wines, 207. 218
—— Drugs, 218

## I.

Importation, what, 255. 256
Intercourse with America restrained and prohibited, 119
—————————— permitted, 145
—————————— regulated, 352
—————————— annual orders in Council for, 249. 370
Iron to the Madeiras, 103
Ireland deprived of the Plantation Trade, 66
—— Plantation Trade from and to enlarged, 92. 94. 109. 110. 112. 115
Isle of Man, 394. 405. 423
Italian Merchants, 16

Jesuits

# INDEX.

## J.

Jesuit's Bark from America, 145

## L.

Labrador, Fishery on the coast of, 291
Lubec, city of, 301
Lumber to the Madeiras, 103

## M.

Manufacture, what, 144. 162
Mediterranean duty, 381
——— Pass, 413
Morocco, goods of, 328

## N.

Names of ships, 455. 461
Naturalization, 445. 116
Navigation encouraged, 10. 11. 32.
16
——— Act of, A. D. 1651, 45
——— 52, Cur. 2. 54. 58.
139. 196. 278. 280. 302
——— enforced, 73
——— complained of,
57. 100
——— dispensed with,
77. 100. 122
——— Act passed in Scotland,
57
Netherlands and Germany, goods
from prohibited, 202. 215
——— Germany, goods from
permitted, 207
——— Austrian, goods from permitted, 18
——— French, goods from permitted, 380
New Englanders evade the Acts of
Navigation, 71
Newfoundland, whether a Colony, 113
——— Supply Bill, 350
——— Vide Fishery.

## O.

Opinions of Law-Officers 9
Orders in Council respecting the
American Intercourse, 359. 370

## P.

Pass, Mediterranean, 413
Persian Goods, 148
Plantation, what, 62. 123. 134
——— Trade regulated, 36. 40.
42. 44. 78. 82. 89. 101. 344.
——— European Goods sent
to, 63. 94. 108.
——— Goods to Foreign Europe forbid, 68
——— Goods to Foreign Europe permitted, 93
——— Bonds, 41. 61. 67. 78.
86. 104
——— Intercourse with forbid,
43. 119
——— with permitted, 345
——— with and
the United States, 358
——— Spanish and Portuguese,
produce of, 80. 106.
141. 146
Portuguese. Vide Plantations.
Ports. Vide Usual Ports.
Prize Goods, 458
——— Ships, 230. 338
——— S. trade free, 421. 464
Prohibition of Goods from the Netherlands and Germany, 202. 209.
215. 380

## R.

Registering of British Ships, 307
313. 411. 455. 465. 501
——— de novo,
318. 431. 463
——— Frauds in,
431
——— Defects in,
418
——— intended
Amendments in, 428
——— considered by the Committee of Council
for Trade, 433
——— Report of
the

# INDEX.

the Commissioners of the Customs, - 416
Registering of British Ships, Proposals of the Commissioners for amending the Law of, - 447
——— Prize Ships, 422. 464
Returned Goods, - 188
Rice to Europe, 91-95
Russia Trade, - 197
Russia Company, - 233
Rum to the Isle of Man, - 204

## S.

Salt from Europe, - 64. 94
Scotland, Union of, - 316
Seamen, foreign, employed, - 323
Shipping, British, encouraged, 11 308. 477. 483
——— for the Trade with Asia, Africa, and America, 186
——— for the European Trade, 223. 244. 382
Ships, British, what, 106. 109. 231, 233, 123. 453. 472.
——— to be British built, 209
——— how navigated, 310. 323-326
——— to be registered, 107. 223. 422. 455
——— built, sold to Foreigners, 211
———, building large, - 111
———, Prize, - 121. 114
———, foreign, made free by Patent, 315
——————— by Parliament, 316
——————— by Commissioners of the Customs, 319
——— British, foreign-owned, 273. 322
——— foreign, British manned, 226
——— foreign, British-owned, 307
——— foreign, country or place where built, 238. 244
——— foreign, wrecked or stranded, 418
Silk, organzine, - 225
——— Persian, - 147

Silk, raw, - 146
——— thrown, - 144
Smuggling, - 413. 415
South-Sea Company, - 153
Spanish Plantations, - 80. 104

## STATUTES.

27. *Edw.* 3. c. 19.
Forfeitures, 263. 265
31. *Edw.* 3. st. 3. c. 2.
Fisheries, - 28
31. *Edw.* 3. st. 3.
Ditto, ibid.
31. *Edw.* 3. st. 1.
Ditto, ibid.
38. *Edw.* 3. c. 8.
Forfeitures, 263. 267
42. *Edw.* 3. c. 8.
Ships of Gascony, - 11
5. *Rich.* 2. st. 1. c. 3.
English Ships, - 12
6. *Rich.* 2. c. 8.
Ditto, - 13
6. *Rich.* 2. c. 10, 11.
Fisheries, - 28
14. *Rich.* 2. c. 6.
English Ships, - 13
3. *Edw.* 4. c. 1.
Foreign Ships, - 14
1. *Hen.* 7. c. 8.
Gascony Wine, - 17
4. *Hen.* 7. c. 10.
Thoulouse Woad, - 18
7. *Hen.* 8. c. 2.
Licences declared void, - 19
23. *Hen.* 8. c. 7.
To continue 5. *Rich.* 2. 20
25. *Hen.* 8. c. 4.
Fisheries, - 28
32. *Hen.* 8. c. 14.
Price of Freight, - 20
33. *Hen.* 8. c. 2.
Fisheries, - 28
2. & 3. *Edw.* 6. c. 6.
Ditto, - 29
5. & 6. *Edw.* 6. c. 18.
Wines of France, - 22
1. *Eliz.* c. 11.
Repeals 5. *Rich.* 2. and 4. *Hen.* 7. 24
5. *Eliz.* c. 13.
Export of Corn, - 35
5. *Eliz.*

# INDEX.

| | |
|---|---|
| 5. *Eliz.* c. 5. | |
| Conſtitutions for the Navy, | 16. 33 |
| 13. *Eliz.* c. 11. | |
| Fiſheries, | 31 |
| 13. *Eliz.* c. 15. | |
| Engliſh Hops, | 27 |
| 23. *Eliz.* c. 7. | |
| Engroſſing Fiſh, | 31 |
| 27. *Eliz.* c. 11. | |
| Ditto, | 32 |
| 39. *Eliz.* c. 10. | |
| Ditto, | ibid. |
| 1. *Jac.* 1. c. 23. | |
| Pilchard Fiſhery, | 31 |
| 3. *Jac.* 1. c. 12. | |
| Ditto, | ibid. |
| 12. *Car.* 2. c. 18. | |
| Act of Navigation, | 54. 58. 86. 130 |
| 13. *Car.* 2. c. 14. | |
| Planting Tobacco, | 70 |
| 13. & 14. *Car.* 2. c. 11. | |
| Act of Frauds, | 85. 102. 281 |
| 15. *Car.* 2. c. 7. | |
| Act of Trade, | 61. 282 |
| 18. *Car.* 2. c. 2. | |
| Herring, Cod, &c. | 283 |
| 22. & 23. *Car.* 2. c. 26. | |
| Ireland, Tobacco, | 66. 71. 86 |
| 25. *Car.* 2. c. 6. | |
| Export of Fiſh, | 283 |
| 25. *Car.* 2. c. 7. | |
| Plantation Goods, &c. | 69. 209. 384 |
| 22. *Car.* 2. c. 2. | |
| Stock-Fiſh and Eels, | 283 |
| 1. *Jac.* 2. c. 18. | |
| Coaſting-Veſſels, | 279. 312 |
| 2. *Will. & Mary*, ſt. 2. c. 9. | |
| Thrown Silk, | 144 |
| 7. & 8. *Will.* 3. c. 22. | |
| Plantation Trade and Regiſtering, | 81. 313 |
| 9. & 10. *Will.* 3. c. 26. | |
| African Trade, | 156 |
| 9. & 10. *Will.* 3. c. 44. | |
| Eaſt India Company, | 150 |
| 10. & 11. *Will.* 3. c. 6. | |
| Ruſſia Company, | 112 |
| 10. & 11. *Will.* 3. c. 24. | |
| Fiſh in foreign Ships, | 285 |
| 10. & 11. *Will.* 3. c. 25. | |
| Newfoundland, | 285 |
| 1. *Ann.* ſt. 2. c. 12. | |
| Hungary Wines, | 207 |

| | |
|---|---|
| 3. & 4. *Ann.* c. 5. | |
| Rice and Molaſſes, | 91 |
| 3. & 4. *Ann.* c. 8. | |
| Iriſh Linens, | 92 |
| 5. *Ann.* c. 8. | |
| Act of Union, | 91. 116 |
| 6. *Ann* c. 37. | |
| Manning of Britiſh Ships, | 113 |
| 7. *Ann.* c. 8. | |
| Jeſuit's Bark, | 145 |
| 9. *Ann.* c. 22. | |
| South-Sea Company, | 152 |
| 1. *Geo.* 1. ſt. 2. c. 18. | |
| Fiſh bought of Foreigners, | 287 |
| 5. *Geo* 1. c. 18. | |
| Salt Fiſh exported, | 289 |
| 5. *Geo.* 1. c. 21. | |
| Eaſt India Company, | 151 |
| 6. *Geo.* 1. c. 14. | |
| Raw Silk and Mohair, | 146 |
| 6. *Geo.* 1. c. 15. | |
| Timber from Germany, | 208 |
| 7. *Geo.* 1. ſt. 1. c. 21. | |
| Eaſt India Company, | 158 |
| 8. *Geo.* 1. c. 12. | |
| Coffee and other Enumerated Goods, | 101 |
| 8. *Geo.* 1. c. 18. | |
| Copper Ore, | 92 |
| 11. *Geo.* 1. c. 30. | |
| Tea from Holland, | 194 |
| 12. *Geo.* 1. c. 5. | |
| Salt to Pennſylvania, | 94 |
| 12. *Geo.* 1. c. 15. | |
| Cochineal, | 147 |
| 2. *Geo.* 2. c. 12. | |
| Salt to New York, | 94 |
| 3. *Geo.* 2. c. 12. | |
| Rice, | 91 |
| 4. *Geo.* 2. c. 15. | |
| Non-enumerated Goods to Ireland, | 94 |
| 4. *Geo.* 2. c. 18. | |
| Mediterranean Paſſes, | 417 |
| 5. *Geo.* 2. c. 9. | |
| Hops from Plantations to Ireland, | 95 |
| 6. *Geo.* 2. c. 13. | |
| Greenland, | 290 |
| 7. *Geo.* 2. c. 18. | |
| Indigo, | 147 |
| 8. *Geo.* 2. c. 19. | |
| Rice, | 95 |
| 9. *Geo.* | |

# INDEX.

| | |
|---|---|
| 9. Geo. 2. c. 31. | |
| Mediterranean Duty, | 282 |
| 9. Geo. 2. c. 35. | |
| Hovering, | 103 |
| 11. Geo. 2. c. 10. | |
| Sugars to Europe, | 96 |
| 13. Geo. 2. c. 1. | |
| Foreign Seamen, | 114 |
| 14. Geo. 2. c. 36. | |
| Persian Silk, | 148 |
| 15. Geo. 2. c. 31. | |
| Registering of Ships, | 117 |
| 15. Geo. 2. c. 31. | |
| Plantation Bonds, | 99 |
| 15. Geo. 2. c. 31. | |
| Sugars to Europe, | 98 |
| 17. Geo. 2. c. 36. | |
| Foreign owned Ships, | 273 |
| 19. Geo. 2. c. 45. | |
| Prize Ships, | 321 |
| 21. Geo. 2. c. 45. | |
| Greenland, | 290 |
| 23. Geo. 2. c. 14. | |
| British Fisheries, | 289 |
| 23. Geo. 2. c. 31. | |
| African Trade, | 156 |
| 25. Geo. 2. c. 32. | |
| Gum Senega, | 149 |
| 25. Geo. 2. c. 40. | |
| African Trade, | 159 |
| 26. Geo. 2. c. 18. | |
| Turkey Company, | 213 |
| 28. Geo. 2. c. 14. | |
| British Fishery, | 299 |
| 29. Geo. 2. c. 10. | |
| Ditto, | ibid. |
| 2. Geo. 3. c. 14. | |
| Salt to Nova Scotia, | 94 |
| 4. Geo. 3. c. 15. | |
| American Act, | 99 |
| 4. Geo. 3. c. 20. | |
| African Trade, | 157 |
| 4. Geo. 3. c. 27. | |
| Rice, | 95 |
| 5. Geo. 3. c. 10. | |
| Coarse Calicoes, | 149 |
| 5. Geo. 3. c. 35. | |
| Cotton-Wool, | 149 |
| 5. Geo. 3. c. 39. | |
| Isle of Man, | 104 |
| 5. Geo. 3. c. 44. | |
| African Trade, | 157 |
| 5. Geo. 3. c. 45. | |
| American Act, | 95. 103 |
| 6. Geo. 3. c. 49. | |
| Free Ports, | 106 |
| 6. Geo. 3. c. 52. | |
| Plantation Bonds, | 104. 109 |
| 7. Geo. 3. c. 2. | |
| Plantations, Ireland, | 106 |
| 7. Geo. 3. c. 45. | |
| Isle of Man, | 323 |
| 9. Geo. 3. c. 26. | |
| European Goods to the Plantations, | 108 |
| 10. Geo. 3. c. 31. | |
| British Fishery, | 299 |
| 11. Geo. 3. c. 38. | |
| Whale Fishery, | 291 |
| 11. Geo. 3. c. 26. | |
| British Ships, | 121 |
| 11. Geo. 3. c. 31. | |
| Salt Fish, | 292 |
| 14. Geo. 3. c. 19. | |
| Boston Harbour, | 119 |
| 15. Geo. 3. c. 10. | |
| Restraining Act, | 119. 300 |
| 15. Geo. 3. c. 18. | |
| Ditto, | 121 |
| 15. Geo. 3. c. 31. | |
| Newfoundland, | 193 |
| 16. Geo. 3. c. 5. | |
| Prohibitory Act, | 121 |
| 16. Geo. 3. c. 47. | |
| Southern Whale Fishery, | 295 |
| 17. Geo. 3. c. 7. | |
| Letters of Marque, | 123 |
| 18. Geo. 3. c. 55. | |
| Ireland, Plantations, | 109. 107 |
| 18. Geo. 3. c. 16. | |
| Irish Shipping, | 133 |
| 19. Geo. 3. c. 9. | |
| Organzined Silk, | 174 |
| 19. Geo. 3. c. 48. | |
| Oil Manufactures, | 170 |
| 20. Geo. 3. c. 10. | |
| Ireland, Plantations, | 118 |
| 20. Geo. 3. c. 45. | |
| Foreign-owned Ships, | 274 |
| 20. Geo. 3. c. 60. | |
| Greenland, | 296 |
| 21. Geo. 3. c. 19. | |
| Flax Seed, | 216 |
| 22. Geo. 3. c. 27. | |
| Jesuit's Bark, | 276 |

# INDEX.

| | |
|---|---|
| 21. Geo. 3. c. 61. | 27. Geo. 3. c. 19. |
| Orchilla weed, — 276 | Morocco Goods, Registering, &c. |
| 21. Geo. 3. c. 15. | — 118. 381. 422. 473 |
| Greenland, — 297 | 27. Geo. 3. c. 27. |
| 21. Geo. 3. c. 18. | Free Port Act, — 273 |
| Austrian Netherlands, — 218 | 28. Geo. 3. c. 20. |
| 21. Geo. 3. c. 1. | Southern Whale Fishery, — 395 |
| Corn and Grain, — 276 | 28. Geo. 3. c. 5. |
| 21. Geo. 3. c. 9. | Intercourse with America, — 149 |
| Indian-Corn, — 276 | 28. Geo. 3. c. 6. |
| 21. Geo. 3. c. 28. | Intercourse between the Colonies |
| Repeal of the Prohibitory Acts, 145 | and America, — 152 |
| 21. Geo. 3. c. 39. | 28. Geo. 3. c. 35. |
| Intercourse with America, — 146 | Newfoundland Fishery, — 390 |
| 21. Geo. 3. c. 65. | 29. Geo. 3. c. 53. |
| African Company, — 272 | Newfoundland, Greenland, and |
| 24. Geo. 3. c. 10. | Southern Whale Fishery, 389. |
| Assiens' Duty, — 479 | 393. 428 |
| 24. Geo. 3. c. 45. | Stettin, City of, — 242 |
| Intercourse with America, — 148 | Stranded Goods, — 219 |
| 25. Geo. 3. c. L | Sugars to Europe, — 95 |
| Newfoundland Supply, — 350 | Surat, whether a Colony, — 247 |
| 25. Geo. 3. c. 58. | |
| Pilchard Fishery, — 406 | T. |
| 25. Geo. 3. c. 65. | |
| Herring Fisheries, — 403 | Tangier not a Plantation, — 48 |
| 26. Geo. 3. c. 26. | Toulouse Woad, — 18 |
| Newfoundland Fishery, — 387 | Tobacco, Disputes concerning, 17 |
| 26. Geo. 3. c. 41. | ——— forbid to be planted, 70 |
| Greenland Fishery, — 390 | Turkey Trade, — 198 |
| 26. Geo. 3. c. 45. | ——— Company, — 213 |
| Pilchard Fishery, — 406 | Turks Islands, Trade of Salt at, 258 |
| 26. Geo. 3. c. 50. | |
| Southern Whale Fishery, — 394 | U. |
| 26. Geo. 3. c. 62. | |
| Registering Act, — 451. 490. 501 | Underwriters Opinion on Ships and |
| 26. Geo. 3. c. 81. | Registering, — 417. 451 |
| Herring Fishery, — 403 | Usual Ports, 141, 142, 145, 146, 147, |
| 27. Geo. 3. c. 7. | 148, 149, 171. 222 |
| Intercourse with America, — 149 | |
| 27. Geo. 3. c. 10. | W. |
| Herring Fishery, — 404 | |
| 27. Geo. 3. c. 13. | Westmony Fishery, — 282 |
| Consolidation Act, — 180. 487 | |

THE END.

www.ingramcontent.com/pod-product-compliance
Lightning Source LLC
Chambersburg PA
CBHW031934290426
44108CB00011B/556